FACULTY DEVELOPMENT IN PROFESSIONAL EDUCATION

PROBLEMS OF, AND PROPOSALS FOR
RECRUITMENT, PRE-SERVICE, INDUCTION
AND CONTINUING DEVELOPMENT IN
SOCIAL WORK EDUCATION

JOSEPH SOFFEN

COUNCIL ON SOCIAL WORK EDUCATION
345 East 46th Street • New York, N. Y. 10017

Grateful acknowledgment is made to the National Institute of Health, Public Health Service, U.S. Department of Health, Education, and Welfare, for a grant that supported the CSWE Faculty Development Project upon which this book is based.

PRINTED IN THE UNITED STATES OF AMERICA

#67-63-08

Foreword

The Council on Social Work Education provides leadership and assistance in the enhancement and expansion of social work education at the undergraduate, master's, and doctoral level.

An adequate supply of well qualified faculty is essential if expansion of social work education is to be accomplished without endangering the quality, and if change and improvement in social work education are to continue even while major quantitative growth is taking place.

A unique and important beginning in dealing with the shortage of faculty has been made by the Council on Social Work Education. The project described in this volume was initiated by the Council on Social Work Education, to study issues and problems in the recruitment and development of faculty, to explore measures to overcome the critical and rapidly growing shortage of faculty, to consider a variety of alternative approaches, and to make recommendations for action. As the reader of this book will quickly discover, these aims have been achieved to a large degree.

This volume includes an interesting review of the literature of social work education and higher education on faculty development, and a careful analysis of the persistent issues. Many new and valuable insights are provided and a number of action proposals are presented for consideration by the field, the universities, and the Council on Social Work Education. The findings of the project have already been shared with new and experienced faculty and deans and directors of schools of social work, and the recommendations were approved by the CSWE Board of Directors in the spring of 1967. A special program to recruit and develop new faculty, based on the analyses and recommendations outlined in this book, was initiated by the Council on Social Work Education in the fall of 1967.

It is our hope and expectation that this book can and will be used by social work and other related professions to design and test new approaches to attract and prepare faculty able to educate effectively the manpower needed to provide both current and future social and rehabilitation services.

Special recognition is due to Dr. Joseph Soffen who, as project director and author of this volume, made a unique, creative, scholarly and valuable contribution to solving a complex and critical problem. The Council on Social Work Education is most appreciative for the help of the Advisory Committee and its able chairman, Dr. William Schwartz, and for the cooperation of all the schools of social work.

We gratefully acknowledge the support of the National Institute of Mental Health, U.S. Public Health Service, Department of Health, Education, and Welfare, whose grants to the CSWE made possible the exploratory work described in this volume and the action program which has been initiated to implement the recommendations of this project.

We trust that the book will be of interest, stimulus, and value to those concerned with professional education not only for social work but for the human service professions generally.

ARNULF M. PINS
Executive Director

November, 1967

Preface

The CSWE Faculty Development Project was an absorbing experience for those who participated in the work. We of the Advisory Committee spent considerably more time in learning our subject than we did in advising; much of our effort was devoted to improving our knowledge of the issues, refining our perception of the problems, and developing a healthy respect for the complexity of the tasks involved in facing these problems.

A close involvement brings with it a growing sense of urgency, and this makes it more difficult to limit one's aspirations for what can be achieved in a single project. Trying to keep our own goals realistic, we hoped that the Faculty Development Project might yield some modest and fairly specific returns.

First, we wished to call attention to a number of problems that have received only glancing recognition from the field, despite their growing importance for both professional practice and professional education in social work. As the field expands, and as the educational enterprise continues to grow, where will the teachers come from and how will the quality of teaching be maintained and improved? How can the "gateways" to teaching careers be broadened? What kinds of qualifications should the new teachers bring with them? And, if we assume that proficiency in practice is only partly related to skill in teaching, how are we helping young teachers to develop the classroom practices by which they will model the very skills and sensitivities they are purporting to teach?

Second, having defined these problems and pressed their importance, we set out to harvest the ideas, experiences, and practice wisdom of those whose job it is to worry about such things. We assumed that on these, as on any complex problems, there are people in the field—practitioners, teachers, students, administrators—who have thought seriously about them, formulated their concerns in new and creative ways and tried various approaches to their solutions. And we assumed, further, that these ideas, questions, and experiences could serve as springboards for new thinking, new definitions, and new proposals for action.

Third, we hoped to precipitate curiosity and concern about certain specific questions for which technical answers are badly needed. Primarily, we hoped to bring the problems of pedagogy itself to the professional agenda. It is much easier to wax inspirational about the need for great teaching than it is to define the skills involved in the teaching-learning relationship and to build a program for helping young teachers (and old ones) to acquire these skills. As we found students bitter about working with teachers who could not practice the human relations skills they preached, so we also found teachers depressed and angry about having been thrown into the classroom without help or preparation. That the lack of assistance and supervision is often defended in the name of academic freedom makes the new teacher's ordeal no less arduous. And the dilemma of freedom versus structure, of creating a training process that will not damage the teacher's freedom to run his own classroom and teach his own subject, is not, after all, very different from the problem of the student who is trying to develop a helping relationship that enables his client to move more freely and independently.

Finally, we hoped that the Faculty Development Project would touch off new work in many quarters, new attempts and experiments addressed to one or another of the many tasks projected in this analysis. However limited each of these efforts might be, their cumulative effect could be considerable as schools, agencies, professors, students, and the Council on Social Work Education itself, move to direct themselves to new research, new procedures, and new structures related to the problems of recruitment, training, pedagogy, socialization, and other issues.

Whatever else we may accomplish, Dr. Soffen's report is an invitation to share our learnings and our sense of urgency about the problems of faculty development in social work education. To say that these concerns are important is not new; it is not even controversial. But to claim for them a surpassing importance, that is, a high priority in time and resources, does indeed constitute a new proposal. If there are enough who regard such a proposal as timely and relevant, this report may help lead the way to a new achievement in social work education.

WILLIAM SCHWARTZ
Chairman, Advisory Committee
Faculty Development Project

vi

Contents

PART 3—THE PROCESS OF FACULTY DEVELOPMENT

Faculty Development in Professional Education

*Problems of, and Proposals for,
Recruitment, Pre-Service, Induction, and
Continuing Development in Social Work Education.*

The Faculty Development Project

The Faculty Development Project was initiated in July, 1965, by the Council on Social Work Education (CSWE), supported by a grant from the National Institute of Mental Health, Public Health Service, U.S. Department of Health, Education, and Welfare. It proposed to confront the problems of quantity and quality of faculty in graduate education for social work, which have become increasingly insistent in recent years. Its specific purposes were twofold: (1) to clarify the sources of faculty personnel and the routes to positions in social work education; and (2) to develop proposals for sound and realistic patterns in the recruitment and pre-service preparation, induction, and continuing education of faculty.

The rationale for the need for the Project is derived from several readily documented propositions: (1) the need for more social workers is great and increasing; (2) major expansion of social work education is necessary and urgent; and (3) availability of qualified faculty is a key obstacle to expansion of social work education.[1] But imposing as problems of quantity may be, they cannot be attacked meaningfully unless the more elusive answer is available to the haunting question about what is meant by "qualified" faculty. There are many definitions of quality and qualification, but precision of definition apparently has not yet been achieved to a degree which makes possible broad consensus about appropriate routes and preparations. A definition which incorporates all the virtues is relatively easy to formulate; simultaneously it becomes more difficult to find enough personnel who can satisfy that definition. It is clear, therefore, that the Project proposals will need to accord with acceptable definitions of "good teachers" and "good teaching."

The definitions will necessarily change with the times, with the re-

---

[1] See Arnulf M. Pins, in *Social Work Education and Social Welfare Manpower: Present Realities and Future Imperatives* (New York: Council on Social Work Education, 1965), p. 2.

quirements of a dramatically evolving profession, dictated by cumulative wisdom. Any proposals for faculty development—even the selection of pertinent data—are intertwined with issues in social welfare, in social work practice, and in professional education. These issues are heavily value-laden and are not likely now, nor for a long time, to be definitively resolved. No issue which impinges on the concept of faculty development is independent. One cannot discuss preparation and credentials of faculty without reference both to the changing nature of social welfare and social work, and to the changing curricula of the professional schools. Similarly, faculty development for social work education must be placed within a perspective of the realities and demands of the academic community with its own traditions and values, and be congruent with emerging formulations of the purposes and qualities of professional education in general. Surely, the definitions must be based upon accepted educational foundations, learning psychology, and teaching theory.

As a faculty of a school of social work is built, it reflects a particular combination of this host of variables. Obviously, it is necessary to start with an admittedly *ad hoc* frame of reference, certain to change as time and experience and new knowledge dictate. It is necessary to identify the "givens" as points of departure. In turn, the routes and their associated preparations can then be specified. Accordingly, the quantitative and qualitative dimensions are not discrete in the sense that they can be considered separately. Both concerns operate concurrently: our charge calls for appropriately prepared teachers in sufficient numbers.

Two important considerations which are closely associated with quantity and quality are the most efficient deployment of available faculty and the evaluation of their performance. It seems clear that each of these questions becomes more amenable to analysis and action *after* the prior question about what is needed to be a good faculty member is more definitively answered. As this criterion is established, the study of deployment and evaluation can proceed more fruitfully. For the present, therefore, they are beyond the scope of this inquiry. It may not be amiss, however, to note that experimentation in utilization of faculty, such as size of classes, use of assistants, team teaching, the new instructional media, or independent study must also be undertaken. The current sense of crisis will not be eliminated by the most successful outcomes of any one line of attack.

The present report takes as "given" the current curriculum policy of the Council on Social Work Education within which are built the curricula of the more than seventy professional schools in the United States and Canada. It probes at the nature of the problems identified with faculty development, analyzes some of the issues, and presents approaches and proposals for action.

Many of the issues and proposals are relevant to the broader arena of university affairs and to education for other professions. To the extent that they are, an increased awareness of mutuality of values and aims and a consequent interchange may well be a fortunate outcome of the present effort.

Previous Activities Which Generated the Project

A number of forces operating over a period of many years converged to define the scope of the present Project and to give evidence of its timeliness. Concern for the quantitative aspect of faculty development is everywhere obvious—in all the means by which employing institutions seek out prospective faculty, formally and informally. Evidence is to be found in the increasing number of listings in the registry of faculty vacancies maintained by CSWE. More aggressive advertising has appeared than the neutral listing typically to be found in professional journals. The word "raiding" of faculty was introduced into the title of a workshop for Deans and Directors of Schools of Social Work at the CSWE 1967 Annual Program Meeting.

A survey of faculty of graduate schools of social work has been conducted by CSWE, supported by a grant from the Children's Bureau, Welfare Administration, U.S. Department of Health, Education, and Welfare, concurrently with the present Project. Both have been consequent to recommendations of earlier committee work, and data from the faculty survey are drawn upon herein.

The qualitative dimension has been pointed up sharply by Blackey, who says:

> It seems incredible that we have done so little to train teachers for faculties of schools of social work. Our drive toward securing higher qualifications for practitioners has been constant. Our failure in settling for less than the best in the selection of teachers to prepare practitioners is an indictment which we must acknowledge and remove.[2]

The CSWE Committee on Advanced Education has addressed itself to several of the relevant issues. The report of its Subcommittee

---

[2] Eileen Blackey, "Issues in Social Work Education—New and Changing Demands Made of the Profession," *Education for Social Work* (New York: Council on Social Work Education, 1964), p. 86.

on Preparation of Teachers pointed to the need for data about manpower needs in teaching and highlighted the question of advanced and doctoral programs in social work as a source of supply of social work educators. It took the position that:

> Practictioners need help in making the transition from the professional role to the role of teacher. Preparation for teaching that is high in quality needs to consist of much more than technical classroom skills. Knowing what kinds of materials should be included in a given course or sequence, knowing where such materials can be found and how they should be organized, and understanding how students can be helped to integrate their various educational experiences are also part of preparation for teaching.
>
> It is also likely that persons entering teaching have had intensive experience in only a limited number of areas of practice . . . and must acquaint themselves with the literature and the conceptual and practical problems in other fields. Furthermore, the person entering teaching from practice rather than from advanced academic study is likely to find that curricula include materials not included when he received his professional training.
>
> The Subcommittee urges the provision of programs to (1) update a new teacher's technical knowledge; (2) acquaint him with the rationale for current curricula and the Council's recommendations regarding curriculum content; and (3) provide him with the opportunity for studying the principles of learning and teaching which would take into account his new professional role as a teacher.[3]

The report of the CSWE Project on Field Instruction,[4] as it has analyzed the tasks of field instruction in social work education, has restated insistent issues which have implications for the recruitment and preparation of field instructors.

Faculty development has received intensive and continuing attention from the CSWE Committee on Teaching Methodology and Materials. One of the major charges to the Committee has been "to stimulate interest in, encourage cooperation towards, and establish guidelines for improved teaching methodology in the field of social work." Among its activities has been the publication of widely used materials on teaching, e.g., *The Teacher's Compendium, A Source Book of*

---

[3] Elizabeth G. Meier, "Preparation for Teaching Social Work," *Social Work Education Reporter*, XIII, 3 (September, 1965), pp. 14ff. See also, *Some Educational Patterns in Doctoral Programs in Schools of Social Work*, Jeanette Regensburg, ed. (New York: Council on Social Work Education, 1966).

[4] *Field Instruction in Graduate Social Work Education—Old Problems and New Proposals* (New York: Council on Social Work Education, 1966).

Readings on Teaching in Social Work, and *An Annotated Bibliography on Audiovisual Instruction in Professional Education*. There has also been an increasing number of articles on teaching theory in the *Social Work Education Reporter*, and an expansion of "Teaching News-Notes" in this periodical. Several additional source books for teachers are nearing completion, and an annotated bibliography on teaching and learning is also in process. The Committee has begun collecting audio and video tapes of classroom teaching, and increasingly has taken a leadership role in planning sessions and workshops at CSWE Annual Program Meetings. Dramatic evidence of the pressing interest and need for this aspect of faculty development is to be found in the high attendance at these sessions, the number of requests for consultation from CSWE staff, and in the outcomes of the Committee's work.

Faculty Development Defined

Dean Blackey provides an inclusive definition of faculty development when she urges that:

> . . . if we apply to the problem of preparation for social work education the same educational principles which we apply to preparation for practice, we can identify three major stages of learning:
>
> (1) Acquisition of knowledge and experience basic to responsible entry into teaching; (2) sound development in the initial stages of teaching; and (3) continuing education and development toward higher levels of achievement.[5]

Faculty development, then, is a three-phased process which begins with pre-service preparation, continues through induction into full-time responsibility when the individual and the employing institution enter into a contractual relationship with each other, and ideally extends to continuing growth for the individual and the faculty as a whole.

This inclusive definition is not new as a concept of faculty development in higher education. Forward thrusts have been made on one or another of the fronts according to priorities assigned at any given time by any of the sectors. Many fields may be described by the following comments about legal education:

> Faculty development is a major concern . . . but there have been very few formal programs on the subject. There will probably be

[5] Eileen Blackey, "Selection and Preparation of Faculty for Schools of Social Work," *Journal of Education for Social Work*, I: 1 (Spring, 1965), pp. 5-12.

more in the future. A good deal of attention has been given . . .
by some people, but not very much in a formal way.[6]

We have found, on the whole, that the greatest amount of attention
has been focused on pre-service preparation of faculty. On the other
hand, there appears to have been relatively little identification or attention to the induction phase. In some professional fields much concern
has been directed to continuing education of faculty, and we shall
borrow directly from their experience.

That the definition of faculty development should be inclusive is a
premise of this report. Whatever the preparation a new faculty member brings to his academic community is highly significant to those
already on the faculty. What social and personal price is paid if the
potential contribution of the well prepared teacher-scholar must wait
as he struggles inefficiently because he does not know how to use the
available resources of the university! Finally, the teaching to which
we aspire is an ideal toward which one must work for a lifetime. It is
actualized only as basic and appropriate preparation is enriched within
a climate of mutuality among all the members—the new and the old—
of an organic faculty in professional education.

Strategies

To accomplish the Project's purposes different kinds of data were
needed, and a range of strategies was employed. It was necessary to
gain a view of current developments in the field of practice for which
social work education prepares, as well as projections for a reasonable
period ahead. Educational developments in social work had to be
placed within the context of higher education: its history, its current
issues, and the best estimates of future directions. The reality of these
two contexts, the profession of social work and the educational enterprise within which education for social work takes place, gives rise
to some specific issues which need uncovering, ordering, and analysis.
Proposals become a blending of facts and values. For this task several
strategies were employed to secure empirical data and knowledgeable
opinions, preferences, arguments, and judgments from many sources.
(See Appendix IV.)

A major instrumentality of the Project has been its Advisory Committee. Among its eighteen members there were representatives of
social agency practice and administration, social work administrative
and teaching faculty, university administration and education for other
professions and academic disciplines.

---

[6] Letter from Michael H. Cardozo, Executive Director, Association of American
Law Schools, May 9, 1966.

The Advisory Committee met twice, the first time early in the Project period and again near the end. The first meeting uncovered a host of issues about which exploration and subsequent judgments were to be made. Pertinent points of view were sharpened and analyzed. The Committee also participated in explicating the scope of the Project and formulating its operational definitions. Proposed strategies were reviewed. Consultation with members of the Advisory Committee was used by the Project Director during the intervening months, and at the final meeting, the Advisory Committee reacted to a draft of the text of the Report. While each member of the Committee made a significant contribution, responsibility for the total Report rests solely with the writer.

The extensive literature on the history and problems of higher education and professional education was reviewed, insofar as time permitted. The literatures of education for the several professions, e.g., medicine, psychology, nursing, law, gave direction to valuable information, described approaches and programs, and identified persons whose thinking might profitably be exploited. People in the several fields were interviewed, in person when feasible, or through correspondence. Individuals were interviewed in national educational organizations, such as the American Council on Education, the Association of American Colleges, and the Council of Graduate Schools in the United States, and in governmental agencies, such as the U.S. Office of Education and the National Institute of Mental Health, which administer grants and fellowship programs. (See Appendix IV.)

We found, indeed, that social work education does not stand alone in the kinds of problems in faculty development that it has identified. There is questioning and ferment about the *status quo*, much more than had been expected at the outset. There are many issues and responses in higher education, and in education for the professions, often parallel to those to be found in social work education. On the other hand, it is not to be denied that we enter territory which has not been safely charted. Against this backdrop, the literature and expertise of social work can best be viewed.

In addition to the extensive review of the literature, three surveys and two workshops were conducted to provide data specifically about social work education.

A questionnaire was sent to the deans and directors of all the schools of social work which asked for statements about problems and descriptions of current practices with respect to faculty development. In addition, they were asked to "day-dream," as though freed of immediate pressures, and to indicate the direction that they would like to see in the future. (See Appendix I.) This survey followed a "workshop" meeting of deans and directors at the Annual Program Meeting of CSWE in January, 1966, at which problems were explored and information about current practices was exchanged.

An additional questionnaire was sent to the individuals identified by 39 of the schools as having responsibility for faculty development or the *improvement of instruction* within their respective schools. They were asked to describe the scope of their responsibilities, the methods they employed, and examples of how these were operationalized. (See Appendix II.)

In addition to the administrative outlook it seemed appropriate to seek understanding from the point of view of teaching faculty, particularly new faculty. Their experience in becoming faculty could provide a different perspective and a rich source of information. The target group selected consisted of almost 300 individuals who assumed full time classroom or school-based field instruction responsibilities in schools of social work either in 1963 or 1964. Their experience, it was believed, would be recent enough for fresh and vital recall, yet have allowed for a one- or two-year perspective to have developed. There were 175 valid returns in this survey. (See Appendix III.) From this number, 30 were invited to a special workshop, during the same Annual Program Meeting. The participants were selected to provide representation of schools by geography, size, and "newness," as well as degree of interest indicated on the completed questionnaire. During the workshop session, several of the major problems and issues reflected in the written returns were analyzed in greater depth in a face-to-face interchange. (Both the deans' and the new faculty workshop sessions were tape-recorded for subsequent analysis.)

Individual deans and faculty members, in addition to those on the Advisory Committee, were interviewed particularly with reference to doctoral and advanced education as preparation for faculty. Descriptions in school bulletins of advanced educational programs in social work were reviewed. The experience of the Career Teacher Program of the National Institute of Mental Health for social work and other mental health professions was investigated from the points of view of personnel both in the granting agency and in the schools intimately associated with the Program's operations. Staff of the Council helped make available understanding of the developments and activities of the bodies with which they work, as well as their own pertinent judgments and encouragements.

Because the direction of a proposed program for faculty development is tied to the precision with which good teaching can be described, the Advisory Committee suggested that in addition to the "official" sources an attempt be made to see "good teaching" and "poor teaching" as the *student* experiences it. Accordingly, Dr. William Schwartz, Chairman of the Project's Advisory Committee, invited eleven students at the Columbia University School of Social Work to discuss this matter in depth. The students had just completed the two-year masters curriculum, either in casework, group work, or community organization; their degrees were "in hand," and they were free to that extent to delve into an experience still very fresh to them. The three-hour group interview (see Appendix VI for abstract) did in fact confirm some of the "biases" of the interviewer and of the project director, but it also added an incisive quality and fresh formulation not as likely to come from the educator, and which has its own authenticity.

An opportunity became available for the project director to participate with Mrs. Bess Dana, then CSWE educational consultant, as a co-leader of an institute for new faculty on "The Social Worker as a Teacher" in July, 1966, under the auspices of Social Welfare Extension, University of California at Berkeley. This experience provided, in a limited sense, a field test of several of the ideas germinated by the activities of the Project. Needs and priorities of interest identified earlier were measured against the needs and interests identified by the twenty participants in the summer institute.

The surveys and the interviews, with a few exceptions which will be apparent, did not seek quantitative data. Although relative numbers are surely useful in understanding the extent of a problem or a development, the challenge to this Project has been to untangle from among all the known practices and viewpoints those which can be helpful and to put them together in a new and meaningful order. For this challenge, tradition and currency must be understood, but they should not bind. Accordingly, isolated or minority suggestions which offer promise for rising to the challenge were not discounted. Rather they were tested for their substance or their utility.

Tentative formulations were tested at meetings of the CSWE Committee on Teaching Methodology and Materials and the Committee on Advanced Education, as well as of the Advisory Committee, and some of the insights generated in these groups are also reflected. Special acknowledgment is gratefully accorded the executive and staff of the CSWE for help, both with plodding detail and imaginative suggestions, over and beyond the call of duty. Mrs. Bess Dana, Dr. Katherine A. Kendall, Dr. Harold Lewis, Dr. Arnulf M. Pins, Miss Marguerite V. Pohek, and Professor Violet E. Tennant all made an invaluable contribution in their careful reading of the completed manuscript.

We were interested in soliciting ideas and *expertise* in whatever sector and from whichever vantage point fact and wisdom pertinent to our purpose could be found. It is difficult to give acknowledgment commensurate with their contribution to the several hundred persons who were called upon. Whether to complete questionnaires, answer inquiries and send materials, grant interviews, participate in workshops and meetings, all gave more than time, fact, and insight. They consistently supported and reinforced the sense of mutual investment.

The data from all the sources do not fall into neat categories around which chapters are build, but are utilized as the discussion unfolds. In Part I, social work education is placed within the Janus-like perspective of the profession which it serves and the institutional setting within which it operates. In the first chapter, social work education as an enterprise is described briefly, particularly for the non-social-work reader. In Chapter II imperatives for social work education derived from the profession are reviewed, and in Chapter III, some of the realities of professional education within the university, and their associated issues, are considered.

In Part II, the spotlight is focused on the social work educator. What he should know and what he should be expected to be able to do are considered in Chapter IV.

Part III is devoted to the faculty development process. Principles are suggested in Chapter V to serve as guidelines for the analysis and formulation of proposals to follow. Recruitment and preparation during the pre-service period is the subject of Chapter VI; the induction period and continuing development phases follow in Chapters VII and VIII. Specific recommendations are addressed to the schools of social work, to the agencies providing social work services, and to the Council on Social Work Education in Chapter IX.

PART ONE

Faculty Development
in Perspective

CHAPTER 1

The Educational Enterprise
for Social Work

Professional social work is relatively new, and only in recent years has education for the profession become fully integrated into the university. The first schools of social work, established in the early decades of this century, were organized and operated under the auspices of one or a group of agencies in a community, with senior agency staff serving as the educators. These early schools were chiefly independent training centers for family casework agencies in the large cities.[1]

> In 1898 the Charity Organization Society of New York began a summer training course for prospective agency workers. A few years later, this course was expanded into a one-year program given by the New York School of Philanthropy, the forerunner of the New York School of Social Work, which became affiliated with Columbia University in 1940 and in 1942 was renamed the Columbia University School of Social Work. Within the two decades after 1898, educational programs for social workers were developed in other cities. . . . Some of these programs were affiliated with universities; others were operated independently.[2]

As another example:

> The Institute of Social Science, a settlement undertaking and an early experiment in extension work at the University of Chicago in 1901, became the Chicago School of Civics and Philanthropy in

---

[1] See, for example, Chapter I, "Evolution of Social Work Education," in Ernest V. Hollis and Alice L. Taylor, *Social Work Education in the United States* (New York: Columbia University Press, 1951); Rachel B. Marks, "Education for Social Work," in *Encyclopedia of Social Work*, Harry L. Lurie, ed. (New York: National Association of Social Workers, 1965), pp. 277-283. See also, *Contemporary Education for Social Work in the United States* (New York: CSWE, 1966) for a comprehensive overview.

[2] Marks, *Ibid.*, p. 277.

1907. The affiliation of the Chicago School with the University of Chicago marked the first real university sponsorship of a school of social work. Other schools had tenuous university affiliations. . . .[3]

Inexorably, the "importance of association with a university in the development of scientific professional education for social work" became manifest, and in 1924 university affiliation was a condition for membership of new schools in the American Association of Schools of Social Work. "In 1935 AASSW adopted a requirement that only schools established within institutions of higher learning on the approved list of the Association of American Universities could be accredited. All existing schools were so qualified by 1940."[4]

The School of Applied Social Sciences of Western Reserve University opened in 1916 as the first graduate professional school of social work within an American university. Of the 35 schools of social work at the end of the 1920's, 11 were on a graduate basis, 14 offered both graduate and undergraduate courses, and 10 were distinctively undergraduate.[5]

Although the focus of the present Project has been upon graduate social work education, it is appropriate to note that undergraduate social welfare courses and sequences have continued to be developed and offered throughout the years and have recently shown a phenomenal increase. Of 681 institutions which responded in a recently completed study,[6] 529 reported that they are offering at least one course with social welfare content at the undergraduate level, and 232 offer formally defined sequences, majors, or concentrations. The patterns of relationships of undergraduate offerings to graduate programs are diverse. Undergraduate sequences may or may not be associated with graduate schools, and graduate schools may or may not offer undergraduate courses. Where they do, the same faculty may or may not teach at both levels. To the extent that the discussion in the following pages of the needs of graduate faculty is applicable to faculty in other professional education and in undergraduate social welfare sequences, the proposals which are presented may hopefully be found useful by them.

---

[3] Hollis and Taylor, *op. cit.*, p. 9.

[4] Marks, *op. cit.*, p. 278.

[5] James E. Cutler and Maurice R. Davie, *A Study in Professional Education at Western Reserve University* (Cleveland: Western Reserve University Press, 1930), pp. 16-18

[6] Sherman Merle, *Undergraduate Social Welfare Education in the United States: A Survey of Programs, Faculty, and Students* (New York: Council on Social Work Education, 1967).

4

PROFESSIONAL EDUCATION FOR SOCIAL WORK

Since 1939, professional education for social work has been graduate education. The number of graduate schools of social work has increased dramatically: 12 new schools were accredited by the Council on Social Work Education[7] during the past decade, and as of July 1966, there were 63 accredited schools in the United States and 7 in Canada. In addition, 2 schools are open and working toward accreditation, and 4 have firm plans for imminent opening.

Accreditation by the CSWE of a program leading to a master's degree in social work is based, among other requirements, upon a two-year curriculum consistent with the "Official Statement of Curriculum Policy for the Master's Degree Program in Graduate Professional Schools of Social Work."[8] The goals of professional education for social work, as formulated by the "Curriculum Policy" are that the student:

Incorporate the knowledge and values basic to social work as a professional discipline.

Understand the central concepts, principles, and techniques applied in social work practice and their significant variations by method and by field of practice.

Manifest compassionate respect for individuals, and appreciate man's capacity for growth and change.

Attain a level of competence necessary for responsible entry into professional practice and sufficient to serve as a basis for a creative and productive professional career.

Develop the discipline and self awareness of the professional social worker, and accept responsibility for the continued development of his own competence.

---

[7] The Council on Social Work Education was formed in 1952 as the one organization for the United States and Canada responsible for setting and maintaining standards for graduate schools of social work, i.e., accreditation, as well as for giving leadership to developments in curriculum, teaching, educational experimentation, and research in undergraduate, master's degree and doctoral programs, and for spurring the expansion of resources for social work education. The present constituent members of the CSWE include over 40 major public and voluntary national agencies, 196 institutions offering undergraduate social welfare programs, 70 graduate schools of social work, and the National Association of Social Workers.

[8] See "Official Statement of Curriculum Policy for the Master's Degree Program in Graduate Professional Schools of Social Work," adopted by the Board of Directors of the Council on Social Work Education, October 19, 1962.

Recognize the significance of scientific inquiry in advancing professional knowledge and improving standards of practice.

Accept an obligation to contribute responsibly to the achievement of social welfare objectives that express the goals of a democratic society and to the development of the profession that it may increasingly serve society in the prevention and treatment of social problems and the enhancement of social well-being.

Perceive and be able to interpret social work as a profession dedicated to the promotion of individual and social welfare in his own and other societies.

To achieve these objectives, the curriculum of professional education includes major content areas in Social Welfare Policy and Services, Human Behavior and the Social Environment, Methods of Social Work Practice. The learning experiences within all these content areas are provided through classroom courses, field instruction, laboratory exercises, tutorial conferences, and research projects.

The social work curriculum has traditionally had its loci both in the classroom and in the field. Until recent years, an agency oriented supervisor was the "teacher" in the field. More recently, field instruction has emerged with a more inclusive educational function than had previously been allocated to field instruction. Briefly stated, the teacher in the field is now required to convert the experience of practice into concepts and principles that can be taught and learned. He no longer relies upon after-the-fact teaching, but must select and order learning experiences for the student that are consistent with overall learning objectives. He must have within his grasp a repertoire of teaching methodologies that are more inclusive than reliance on traditional supervision as the major method and include, for example, group teaching and the use of written assignments. Like the classroom teacher, he too must support his teaching with theoretical knowledge and with the capacity to conceptualize, and with the commitment to the fact that the field experience, like the classroom experience, must address itself to the transferability of learning.[9] The present demand upon the field teacher is for the application of a curriculum building methodology to field teaching.

This development has resulted in the carving out of new positions more directly responsible to the schools than was true in the past, regardless of current source of support, i.e., university, agency, or grants funds.

---

[9] See Mildred Sikkema, "A Proposal for an Innovation in Field Learning and Teaching," and Jeanette Regensburg, "Report of Exploratory Project in Field Instruction," both in *Field Instruction in Graduate Social Work Education, op. cit.*

The revival of the educational center idea emerged as a logical response to the contemporary task of education for social work. The full time well trained social work educator became the model for clinical teaching as well as classroom instruction.[10]

The teaching hospital as a center for medical education where the teaching function has high priority is well known. Legal education has within the past two decades seen the emergence of the institutionalized legal center, the "Modern Inns of Court in the best traditions of those sixteenth century Inns."

> The centers are attempting to bridge the gap in approach between the legal educator and the practicing attorney, coordinating the efforts of law schools, bar associations, lawyers, and informed laymen to advance the administration of justice.[11]

Kindelsperger suggests that:

> This trend may be interpreted as a growing change in methodolgy; namely, more use of group seminars and, perhaps more important, gradual recognition of what many of us are fully convinced of: the successful field instructor must be a well prepared educator attached to a faculty with appropriate academic rating for his or her position.

> Many hold the opposite view on this issue. The forces leading to this trend are reflected in the new curriculum statement which calls for an increasing breadth in intellectual content, and responsibility for teaching appropriate aspects of the *entire curriculum* in field instruction.

> The more we know about field instruction through research and heuristic observation, the more complicated it appears as a learning process. In fact, within a few years we may have more difficulty with clinical professors (our term at Tulane) then will be true in recruitment of the so-called classroom instructors. . . .

> It is possible that a substantial proportion of content now taught in the class might better be taught in the field. The growing opinions on this subject that I am aware of are particularly impressed with the possibilities of teaching research methodology and human behavior in field settings. Perhaps this is another way of saying what was said above with reference to the requirements of the

---

[10] Walter Kindelsperger and Helen Cassidy, "Social Work Training Centers: Tentative Analysis of the Structure and Learning Environment." (Mimeographed.)

[11] Albert P. Blaustein and Charles O. Porter, *The American Lawyer* (Chicago: University of Chicago Press, 1954), p. 180.

field teachers of the future. I do not mean to imply that the field teachers will be doing all the teaching in these areas noted, but it is quite probable that there will be a greater share of the teaching and that many of the formal distinctions between class and field teaching in these areas will diminish in significance.[12]

On the other hand, there is an extant point of view which questions this trend and the appropriate place of field instruction in the master's social work curriculum, although it has been an integral part of professional education for social work from its inception. Some of the questioning derives from the university tradition and concern that a major segment of the educational program is not completely under the control of the school. Some derives from the pressures of new content and accretions to the curriculum. Some argue forthrightly that the demands of the future dictate a reordering of curricular priorities. Associated with this position are arguments that the most effective impact on the educational program of the school lies in its intellectual rigor, and that the practice objectives will best be achieved by those who will be practitioners under agency control after they receive the master's degree.

It is not within the scope of this Project to deal with these issues, but we must recognize that the ferment about future arrangements has implications for faculty development. If field instruction is to be maintained as part of the curriculum, faculty will continue to need an amalgam of qualities, interests, and preparation that will increasingly differ from those of the academic professor.

The number of graduates from schools of social work has more than doubled in the past decade. In 1955, 1,772 students were graduated, 2,231 in 1960, while in 1966, 3,967 received master's degrees. There were 10,131 students enrolled in master's degree programs as of November 1, 1966, an increase of 13 percent over the previous year.[13] However, these graduates are insufficient in number to fill existing vacant positions, to meet the needs of a growing population, to improve

---

[12] Letter dated Dec. 20, 1965 from Walter Kindelsperger, Dean of the School of Social Work, Tulane University. See also Jean M. Maxwell, "New Settings for Field Instruction," *Social Work Education Reporter*, XIV:3 (Sept. 1966), pp. 30ff. The School of Social Service Administration of the University of Chicago announced, as this manuscript was going to press, the establishment of a Social Services Center to "combine community service and professional education." A pilot educational program is scheduled to begin in the Center in 1967-68.

[13] *Statistics on Social Work Education* (New York: Council on Social Work Education, 1967). See also, "Selected Statistical Highlights on Growth and Change of Social Work Education," Document #66-26-18, dated December 29, 1966, of the Council. (Mimeographed.)

services, or to staff new public and voluntary programs. Most schools of social work are filled to capacity and most of them report turning away qualified applicants.

POST-MASTER'S EDUCATION IN SOCIAL WORK

The non-social work reader is requested to note that the *basic* educational requirement for professional social work is a full-time two-year master's degree. This difference from the more common pattern, whereby a master's degree is earned at the successful completion of one year of full time study, should not be overlooked at the point when education beyond the masters is considered. If there is a rationale for a two-year program, it is presumably because the substance of master's education in social work requires two years, and it would be inconsistent to equate a master's degree in social work with a program that can be completed in one year.

Put another way, the M.A. in many academic or professional disciplines may be the first year of doctoral study, a testing or screening period for further graduate work; the Master of Social Work degree testifies to substantial achievement at the graduate level. Perhaps out of a desire to emphasize the basic professional requirement, social work education has reserved the term "advanced education" for formal study beginning with the third graduate year.

An interest in education beyond the masters was accelerated out of concern for leadership by practitioners who would return to practice, to supervision, to staff development, to research, or to administration in agencies, as well as for the needs of faculty in social work education. Many of the latter have frequently obtained their advanced education in disciplines other than social work, in the expanding social and behavioral sciences, and in education. Doctoral degrees other than in social work have continued to be valued in many quarters.

Currently, 19 schools of social work in the United States and Canada offer advanced education beyond the master's degree. These programs are of two types, non-degree and doctoral. Nine of the 19 offer a "third year," i.e., one year beyond the master's, which may be terminal, or in some schools may serve as the first, residential year of doctoral study. Eighteen offer a doctorate, either a Ph.D. or a degree which uses the nomenclature of a professional degree, e.g., Doctor of Social Work or Doctor of Social Welfare (DSW). Although the degree programs differ in detail, they are essentially of similar calibre and rigor as doctorates offered by their respective universities, and include dissertation

9

requirements.[14] Both the one-year and doctoral programs are intended to serve as preparation for faculty positions.

Although advanced degrees in social work have been offered since 1920, all but four of the present programs have been established since 1945. A total of 74 advanced degrees had been earned between 1920 and 1945, 69 in the decade 1946-1955; and about 275 in the most recent decade. The rate has accelerated, and 64 doctorates were awarded during 1966. Although about 25 percent of this number had taught before starting doctoral study, 68 percent were in teaching immediately after doctoral study.[15] The total number of students in all post-master's programs in social work in that year was 269.[16]

There is an unduplicated total of 4,845 faculty in graduate schools of social work.[17] Of the total, 1,524 are in full-time positions and 3,321 have part-time appointments. These numbers show a 100 percent increase in full-time faculty during the preceding decade, while part-time faculty increased almost 60 percent.[18] Third year programs account for 116 faculty members, and 210 are engaged in doctoral teaching. Most of those who teach in post-master's programs also teach in the master's program.

The Deans' Advisory Committee of the Council on Social Work Education developed in 1966 a detailed statement on how much and how fast social work education can and must expand. The projections call for annual increases in the capacities of existing schools and the establishment and accreditation of over thirty new schools, making possible four times the number of graduates in the next decade as there were in the previous one.

Steps to expand graduate social work education are already under way. A CSWE project for developing new schools of social work was initiated in July, 1966, with NIMH support to stimulate and assist the development of new graduate programs of high quality. The Council is

---

[14] See, Regensburg, *op. cit.*

[15] "Survey of Doctoral Graduates, 1965 and 1966," *Social Work Educational Reporter,* Vol. XV, No. 2, p. 7.

[16] See *Statistics on Social Work Education, op. cit.;* also Marks, *op. cit.,* p. 282. Arnulf M. Pins, in "Education: Its Contribution to the Manpower Equation," *Manpower in Social Welfare: Research Perspectives,* ed., Edward E. Schwartz, identifies the characteristics of the recipients of the degrees, the jobs into which they were absorbed, and future sources of students for advanced programs.

[17] Two sources of data have been used: Richard Onken, *Survey of Faculty in Schools of Social Work* (New York: Council on Social Work Education, 1968); and a survey of faculty who began their teaching careers in 1963 and 1964, conducted for purposes of the present Project.

A brief description of the preparation and deployment of current faculty appears in Chapter VI, and draws from both of these, as well as other sources.

[18] There were at least 138 teaching vacancies for 1966-67 listed with the CSWE in May, 1966.

also taking steps to stimulate and help the expansion of existing schools. In addition, several schools are planning new programs of advanced education and others are taking steps to extend the scope and size of doctoral programs.

It is clear that an adequate supply of properly qualified faculty is a key prerequisite for these expansions. It is difficult to estimate accurately the exact number of new faculty needed. The Deans' Advisory Committee, in this connection, estimated that approximately 1,600 new faculty will be required to achieve the projected expansion of existing graduate schools of social work, the creation of new schools of high quality, and further development and enhancement of post-master's programs in social work. This estimate took into consideration the current and continuing use of part-time faculty, possible improved utilization of faculty in the years ahead through new teaching patterns and educational technology, and a probable 20 percent loss of existing faculty in the next decade due to marriage, motherhood, retirement, and other causes. Faculty for undergraduate social welfare education are not included in this estimate, although their increasing numbers will also be drawn to a considerable extent from the same sources.

We shall be considering all potential sources of faculty, to identify the routes which should be the focus for intensive attention. However, first we shall attempt to place the educational enterprise within a perspective, looking both at the school of social work and the profession, and the school within the university.

CHAPTER 2

The School of Social Work and the Profession

The nature of education for a profession is such that it must be responsive to changing demands from the "front lines," and at the same time give impetus to changing the field itself. The availability of new knowledge for improving skill may have an experiential, pragmatic source such as "the field," or it may come from an academic, "non-clinical" source. The boundaries and content of practice are ever-changing. Thus education for that practice must provide leadership by virtue of its site at the "tower," at the same time balancing that forward look with the realities of the present. Professional education is both reactive and initiative.

There are ancient professions with centuries of experience in learning to live up to this complex role. Yet the educational institutions for medicine, law, and theology, for example, face many of the same quantitative and qualitative issues that confront social work education. This is inevitable by the nature of their mission. Thus, education for professional social work, and specifically the availability, in quantity and quality, of the agents of the educational enterprise, must be placed within the context of a profession expanding in scope and changing in content.

AN EXPANDING AND CHANGING PROFESSION

It is estimated that at the present time there are well over 15,000 budgeted social work positions in health and welfare agencies that are unfilled and many social work jobs requiring the highest level of competence are filled by people who do not have graduate education. Problems resulting from the population explosion, the race revolution, urbanization and automation, recent federal legislation setting up new health and welfare programs, and changes in the nature and scope of voluntary local social welfare programs all call for more social work personnel. The plans for the establishment of community mental health centers alone will require many more social workers than are currently available. The Task Force on Social Work Education and Manpower of the U.S. Department of Health, Education, and Welfare detailed the need for 100,000 new social workers with graduate professional education by 1970 and many personnel for social welfare with only a college degree.[1]

Official recognition of the critical shortage was made by President Johnson in his special message on health and education to Congress in March, 1966, when he called for legislation to make a frontal assault on the shortage, "at a time when we need their [qualified social workers'] skills more than ever before. These workers are important to the success of poverty, health and education programs."

No less significant than the quantitative urgency is the changing nature of social work practice. A qualitatively different kind of practice is now expected even in the most traditional settings. Within a generation, not only has casework became a generic method of practice, but the generic nature of the profession has been rediscovered. The emergence of the National Association of Social Workers as *the* association of one profession reflects this trend, as does the discontinuance of accreditation by specializations, all within the past decade. More dramatically it is widely reported (although we have no hard data immediately available) that many casework positions, for instance, now have expectations for sophisticated group and community skills, as well as skills in working with individuals. (The converse is probably also true.)

---

[1] *Closing the Gap . . . in Social Work Manpower*. Report of the Departmental Task Force on Social Work Education and Manpower (Washington: U.S. Department of Health, Education, and Welfare, 1965). Although the present Project takes graduate education as its frame of reference, the overall problem of numbers and expansion encompasses positions for which, *de facto,* undergraduate specialization represents minimal qualification. Indeed, what should be the boundary lines and the respective qualifications for the "levels" of practice constitute unresolved questions for all concerned with welfare services. As an example of a current approach to this question, the Task Force report offers the following scheme: "It is now possible to staff a program . . . through combined and selective use of social workers with graduate professional social work education, social workers with a college degree and in-service training in social work; and social welfare technicians and ancillary personnel prepared through high school and vocational education for a variety of specific occupations." (p. 9). At any rate, the reader should note that a rapidly increasing number of colleges and universities are initiating undergraduate programs of social welfare and most existing ones are increasing their offerings and enrollment to prepare students for either graduate professional education or employment directly upon graduation for tasks in social welfare not requiring professional education.

13

The rapidly changing society which social work serves is witness to new programs and new emphases, even redefinition of the scope of the function of social work. The expanding "anti-poverty" programs, accentuated interest in corrections and rehabilitation, new services to the mentally ill and retarded, to the educationally disadvantaged, to the aging produce new conceptions of the social worker's role and consequent innovations in practice. These developments require a "broader competence" (a term suggested by Dean Blackey) for characteristic uncertainties in the expectations of social work practice. Social workers are increasingly being called upon to play significant roles in legislation, policy making, and administration of major programs at every echelon within continuing and new structures.

The development of new programs in new settings makes its own special demands. Specific examples of these new settings are deliberately avoided here lest the nature of many of the still-unsettled relationships of social work within these programs obscure the important point. The essence of the present cannot yet have been analyzed and understood in depth. Less so can the validity of any view of the future be claimed. But the nature of the immediate future is not unknown: "Most of the changes necessary to deal with the social problems and modern functions assigned to social work have already been anticipated. . . ."[2] Kindelsperger suggests that:

> . . . various units of government, including the federal government, appear to be moving closer and closer to the statement of a fundamental welfare policy which will include basic, minimum conditions for economic and social living.
>
> Specialization by programs will wither away rapidly, and specialization within diversified agency programs will increase sharply. . . .
>
> Part of the necessary response to public expectancy will be a higher level of competence in all areas of service . . . and less acceptance of "doing the best under the circumstances."

John W. Gardner, Secretary of Health, Education, and Welfare, reviewing the significance of the new social programs made possible by recent legislation such as Medicare and the related provisions of the 1965 Social Security Amendments, the Civil Rights Act, the Older Americans Act, the education bills, the mental health measures, and others, notes that "most of the legislation encourages or makes provi-

---

[2] W. L. Kindelsperger, "Responsible Entry into the Profession—Some Current Issues," *Journal of Education for Social Work,* Vol. 2, No. 1 (Spring, 1966), p. 44.

sion for planned innovation." The future of social work "will certainly be deeply affected by the new programs," he predicts.

Just as the medical schools found it necessary not only to establish ties with the basic biological fields, but to develop their own biomedical research centers, the schools of social work will find that certain lines of research will prosper *only* under their own sponsorship. Standing, as all professional schools must, with one foot in the basic fields and one foot in practice, they will find themselves posing questions that may not even interest investigators in the basic behavior sciences.

In short, the great complex . . . that makes up the University Social Work Center of 1990 will have many laboratories for social research.[3]

Turning to the "interface between the school of social work and the rest of the community," he sees

intimate and continuing ties with the agencies that actually provide social services—but many of those agencies will bear little resemblance to the social agencies of today.

One aspect of the relationship will be much more highly developed than it is today and that is the provision for innovation. . . .

The School of Social Work in 1990 . . . will have made itself a hospitable center and intellectual home for all of the great array of occupations, professional, subprofessional, and technical, that make up the field of social welfare broadly conceived, . . . and with its natural allies . . . fellow professionals such as doctors and teachers.[4]

It is not that social work aggressively seeks new functions to create job opportunities for its overabundance of practitioners. Social work can, even at this stage of its development as a profession, claim significant achievements in theory and skill. It has already had a profound influence on and made a unique contribution to the theory and practice of many of the service professions and to education for the professions. The ethic of any profession is violated to the extent that what it has to contribute is not made readily available in the unending struggle for human betterment.

---

[3] John W. Gardner, "Remarks," *Journal of Social Work Education*, Vol. 2, No. 1 (Spring, 1966), p. 7.

[4] *Ibid.*, p. 7.

IMPERATIVES FROM THE PROFESSION

Several imperatives to the schools of social work are inescapable. They must graduate increasingly larger numbers of social workers, increasingly qualified for changing modes of service. Also, the new graduates as a body must present a heterogeneity of aptitude and skill and special interest. While all must be "thinkers" and "doers," they must also be equipped to be innovators and social statesmen.

Building upon the theme set by Gardner as he envisions social work and the social work education center in the next generation, Kendall has specified that

> We must urge our strongest established schools to move more rapidly into new and experimental patterns of relationship with the basic scientific fields, with allied professions and with social work practice. . . .
>
> We must cultivate at the national level and within each university all possibilities for joint effort with other professional groups, particularly in the fields of health and education, to arrive at co-operative and composite training for all . . . in the fields that "teach, heal, serve or nurture."
>
> We have been much too occupied—and rightly so at this stage in our development—in forging our own distinctive educational program at the graduate level and in finding a recognized place of our own within the university structure to invite or welcome interdisciplinary and interprofessional educational planning. This is a task for the future. . . .[5]

An example of the need for a changed quality of teaching which is already upon us is found in changes in the structuring and teaching of the "methods" courses. In several schools, new patterns are replacing the specialized casework, group work, and community organization practice courses. That these changes may represent a trend is not surprising, for the demands of practice, as it has evolved, no longer fit the earlier boundaries of specialization by method. There may be parallel offerings for all students; there may be primary and secondary concentrations; there may be one integrated methods course. An inte-

---

[5] Katherine A. Kendall, "Choices To Be Made in Social Work Education," in *Social Work Practice, 1966* (New York: National Conference on Social Welfare, 1966), pp. 111, 115.

grated course may come early in the timing sequence of the curriculum followed by specialization, or the specialized sequences may culminate in an integrating course.

Regardless of pattern, however, several implications follow. The students have a broader perspective than did their predecessors. The teachers are required to teach courses with a scope different from the ones they had when they were students. They are teaching for practice which is different from their own practice experience. Teachers of integrated courses may be dealing with content with which they have had little or no previous experience. In instances where team teaching is the pattern, different demands are also made upon each of the team members.

There is another, equally insistent imperative. The accumulated body of professional experience generates voluminous data, new understandings, new insights. The changing boundaries of practice beg for integrated knowledge and new formulations of what has been learned and what is about to be known. This is the knowledge-building function.

> Not only the substantive knowledge itself, but knowledge of how to keep up with the continuing advances in professional knowledge is what the university school seeks to give its students. . . .
>
> Equally important is the university professional school's responsibility for the creation of new and better knowledge on which professional practice can be based. Its university position makes it possible for all members of its staff to be part time scholars and researchers and for some to carry on these activities full time. . . . The better the university professional school, the more likely it is to use resources from the other professional schools in the university and from all the other departments of basic knowledge insofar as they are relevant. In sum, the university professional schools are the leading, though not the sole, innovators and systematizers of ideas for their professions.[6]

Research in social work was described in 1951 as a "long known shortcoming."

> A few schools of social work envisaged the importance of research from the beginning and thus provided the profession with a small corps of research workers. Nevertheless, social work has for the most part depended upon other fields for its research personnel. . . . Students have met the routine standards, including individual

---

[6] Bernard Barber, "Some Problems in the Sociology of the Professions," *Daedalus*, Vol. 92, No. 4 (Fall 1963), pp. 674-5.

thesis research, but more often than not have learned little that contributed to a vital research point of view or that developed effective consumers of research findings.[7]

Regensburg gives an example of the "startlingly high volume of need for competent researchers":

> A few months ago the Director of Research, Welfare Administration, stated that 40 researchers were needed immediately in that department alone. A recent regulation requires that each State Department of Welfare have a Research Director, and these positions are extremely hard to fill under present conditions of short supply. Nor can a Research Director function without a supporting staff. In both governmental and voluntary social agencies the demand is for a wide range of research studies; statistical, operational, and evaluative; and the purpose of such studies may be not only to examine and improve a particular program but also to add to the substance of professional knowledge.[8]

Considerable attention has been directed to this shortcoming in the curricula of the masters programs in social work during the past two decades and the level of research sophistication has improved. The number of individuals in schools and in agencies who have had doctoral training—hence are both consumers and producers of research—has increased even more dramatically. Many of them are, in fact, social work researchers. In very recent years, a social work research concentration at the master's level for a few special students has been introduced on a demonstration basis, i.e., as a tentative innovation at two or three schools. But with the more insistent need, the "shortcoming" has not been eliminated. The imperative from the field is even stronger than any expectation from the university for research leadership and productivity by faculty. It has deep implications for effectiveness of research teaching, and even more pervasively, for research mindedness on the part of the whole faculty.

Two additional imperatives from the field are more significant than the attention given them here would indicate. One is the need for continuing education of previously qualified practitioners. "Where the body of professional knowledge is changing very rapidly, the university professional school may take a direct role in promoting the 'adult' education of members of its profession through post-professional train-

---

[7] Ernest V. Hollis and Alice L. Taylor, *op. cit.* pp. 42-43.

[8] Jeanette Regensburg "Recruitment to Post-Master's Programs in Schools of Social Work" paper presented at Annual Program Meeting, Council on Social Work Education, New York, N. Y., January 26, 1966.

ing courses, seminars, and institutes."[9] The second is the ongoing expectation of agencies that schools will give leadership and individual faculty will be available for consultation as agencies initiate new programs responsive to persistent or changing social problems. In short, the service function.

We have noted briefly that the needs of the profession are urgent, quantitatively and qualitatively. Faculty are needed whose relationship to practice is such that they can teach for change and for innovation. They must also be producers of social work knowledge at or beyond its frontiers. They will need to be "triple threat" men,[10] reflective of the teaching, research, and service expectations of the profession.

The social work profession, as a substantive institution within society, has new expectations set for it by a society characterized by rapid change and beset with increasingly critical social problems. Many of the issues identified with faculty development stem from the expectations and stresses of the current scene. Ten years from now the then-current scene may have different "givens." It is indeed statesmanlike to plan for the future; however, there are many possible futures. Some visions of the future reflect hoped-for outcomes which we would like to influence. Others are clearly beyond us to affect.

Projections to the future, even when based upon the same data, differ from each other because the current vantage point differs. It will therefore be necessary to differentiate between long-term approaches and short-term approaches to faculty development. The immediate approaches must accommodate themselves to the current realities. The longer range projections, freed from the pressure of a sense of crisis, can be formulated to affect, as well as be conditioned by, the man pertinent factors. Before we undertake either, however, we must place social work education within the context of the university.

---

[9] Bernard Barber, *op. cit.*, p. 674.

[10] Term used by Dr. George E. Ruff, Department of Psychiatry, School of Medicine, University of Pennsylvania.

CHAPTER 3

The School of Social Work and the University

As schools of social work have become integral parts of their universities, they have been confronted by issues in higher education which have remained unresolved for almost a century. Now they have become issues for social work education itself. Many of the issues fall beyond the scope of the concerns of this Project, e.g., administrative arrangements, the organization of the university, and the relationships of its component parts to each other. Other major issues with immediate pertinence are: (1) the university and professional cultures, (2) preparation for university careers, and (3) teaching in the university.

THE UNIVERSITY AND PROFESSIONAL CULTURES

Within the universities are to be found centuries-old traditions. Graduate schools, since the nineteenth century, have been developing their *modi operandi* with the university traditions. In contrast, the early schools of social work were developed under the influence of the culture of social agency practice. Their incorporation into universities, in varying relationships to the graduate schools and to other professional schools, brought into direct contact diverse faculty groups and contrasting sets of culture. The differences between these cultures may appear to be overemphasized in a generalized historical context. Fortunately, these cultures are compatible, as the experience of the last few decades demonstrates.

As one of the newer professions, social work has had to struggle for recognition within the status hierarchy of the professions. As recently as 1963, social work has been identified (invidiously it seems to us) as an "emerging or marginal profession, along with pharmacy and accountancy."[1] Similarly, some have noted that the sociology of social workers contrasts with that of academicians and with practitioners in the other professions. Whether there are in fact caste or class differences is immaterial; some perceive them and more feel them, and we shall return to this item in the chapter on Induction. A review of some characteristics of the respective cultures of the graduate and the professional schools may be profitable to our purpose.

Objectives and Orientations—The university is dedicated to scholarship and excellence. The university preserves, transmits, and expands knowledge. Operational objectives typically subsumed under this broad dedication are the transmission of the heritage to the new generation, expansion of the frontiers of knowledge, and outreach to the community through service. These three thrusts may have different intensities from one campus to another, each university finding its own balance among them.

The professional schools are also concerned with the excellence of their activities. Their partialized objectives are parallel to those of their respective universities. Despite the generalized congruence of objectives, contrasting educational orientations between the academic and the professional have been noted.[2] For example (granting hyperbole in the process of contrasting), the academic goal orientation is characterized by "to know" and the professional orientation is characterized by "to do"; the major academic value orientation is "truth," and the major professional value orientation is "service." The academic orientation emphasizes the creation and transmittal of knowledge using theoretical and experimental sources, while the professional orientation turns to the application of knowledge from professional and pragmatic sources. Obviously, the contrasts noted above are extremes.

Noting that "through the years, there has been a great deal of self-scrutiny and controversy over the nature of graduate study," Berelson states as a conclusion that:

> In the nature of the case, there is an inherent clash of interests between service and standards, teaching and research, the university and the college, academic and professional objectives, different classes of institutions, different fields.[3]

---

[1] Bernard Barber, *op. cit.*, p. 676.

[2] Informal paper made available by Alex Rosen, Dean, Graduate School of Social Work, New York University, Interview, August 22, 1966.

[3] Bernard Berelson, *Graduate Education in the United States* (New York: McGraw-Hill Book Co., 1960), p. 217; see also Kenneth J. Little, "Graduate Education," in *Encyclopedia of Educational Research*, Chester Harris, ed. (New York: Macmillan, 1960), pp. 593-602.

Universities generally have similar objectives, but arrange them in varying hierarchal order. In turn, the units within any one university develop emphases which are congruent with the order of objectives of that university. At this time there appears to be at least as much difference among the universities with respect to the ordering of their objectives as there is significant distinction between the professional and the academic. McGlothlin summarizes that "professional education should be directed toward significant objectives including professional competence, understanding of society, ethical behavior, and scholarly concern."[4]

In similar vein, McGrath states that:

> The one generalization which emerges . . . is that the sharp dichotomy which has prevailed for centuries in higher education between liberal and professional studies is no longer useful in advancing the cause of higher education; nor is it consistent with the facts of contemporary academic life in this country. . . . The character and quality of any instruction must be determined by its specific purposes, by its relationship to the whole context of learning. . . .[5]

The purpose of noting these differences lies in the fact that a useful principle is generated; namely, the importance of recognizing the existence and the legitimacy of differing hierarchies of the same objectives among the professional schools. This phenomenon is fortunate, for it assures the availability of varying emphases among the schools, available for matching to the heterogeneity of needs of the profession, outlined in the previous chapter. The principle of heterogeneity also has implications for a balancing of the kind of preparation and interests of faculty, which will be discussed later.

Academic Freedom and Professional Responsibility—Another manifestation of the contrast in cultures is the valued tradition within the university of academic freedom on the one hand, and the tradition of professional responsibility in social agency practice on the other. The duty and the right of the professor to teach the truth as he sees it, to ask questions for research which challenge ancient truths, and to disseminate freely his findings and conclusions are inviolable; they are rights that have been won and rewon in each generation and must

---

[4] William J. McGlothlin, *The Professional Schools* (New York: The Center for Applied Research in Education, 1964), p. 31.

[5] Earl J. McGrath, *Liberal Education in the Professions* (New York: Teachers College, Columbia University, 1959), p. vi. For a brief overview of professional education, see Lloyd E. Blauch, ed., *Education for the Professions* (Washington: U.S. Government Printing Office, 1955).

continually be guarded against infringements.[6] The principle of academic freedom is violated to the extent that the creativity of the teacher and his freedom to experiment or innovate is in any way restricted. To minimize restrictions of any kind, in principle at any rate, structures which suggest administrative hierarchy are deemphasized. The collegium, the community of scholars, is characterized by maximum independence of initiative and activity by each of its members.

In contrast, accountability on behalf of the agency's clients is carefully provided for through a supervisory structure within each social agency. Supervision has been developed in social work theory and practice as a process for freeing the creativity of the practitioner. Supervisory skill is often of such a high level that it enhances the effectiveness and satisfaction of staff. Administrative supervision, however, is characterized by an emphasis of concern for the recipient of service which gives it a bureaucratic quality in sharp contrast to the traditional climate of a university.

The implications of these differences are many. One is associated with the conception of the scholar; there are other implications for the transition of the professional from a practice setting to the university, the operationalizing of administrative concern for academic responsibility and for the relationships of faculty to each other. Each of these implications is recognized at appropriate points in the chapters which follow. At this point it is sufficient to note that the principles of both academic freedom and academic responsibility can and must be safeguarded as complementary values which do not necessarily crowd each other.

DISTINCTIVE CAREER LINES

The contrasting academic and professional orientations suggest an additional contrast, namely that a career in social work education is distinctive from a career in social work practice. The question of the career line arises in a professional school more sharply than in the academic disciplines. The typical career line for the young student who aspires to the "academic life" is a relatively simple one to describe: he pursues graduate study and moves more or less directly into the positions of instructor and professor. Any non-academic work activities, often seen as detours and distractions, are essentially tem-

---

[6] See, for example, Richard Hofstadter and Walter P. Metzger, *The Development of Academic Freedom in the United States* (New York: Columbia University Press, 1955), for a history of academic freedom to the recent past, and the adoption and modification in the United States of the concepts of *Lehrfreiheit* and *Lernfreiheit*.

porary means in the pursuit of academic qualifications. This is also true to some extent for *some* positions in some professional schools.

In social work education, however, most social work teachers in the past have first been identified with practice and saw themselves as practitioners. Until recent years, formal education beyond the master of social work degree (MSW) was not widely required. Accordingly, Wessel has asked: "Do we really identify ourselves as teachers, educators, or as social workers?" For many years she had identified herself as a social worker, and only in later years, in the course of doctoral study, did she find "identification with the changing purposes, problems and processes of the educator" and make a new alignment with the university, this time as a teacher.[7] Jennings has argued that the "social work educator has chosen an alternative career line within the profession of social work."[8]

The prevalent position, currently, is that the social worker who would become a social work educator is not moving from one social work setting to another. The career line for the social work educator is distinctive and substantive, calling for specialized preparation. Blackey has summarized this position:

> Our master's degree program prepares for direct practice, not for education. Too often the assumption is made that a good practitioner will make a good teacher just by virtue of moving from his agency to the classroom. The demands made of teachers today for extended knowledge in the social sciences, for research knowledge and sophistication in conceptualized thinking cannot be met except by additional education beyond the master's degree. Even these requirements fail to take into account the educational base required for the practice of teaching, namely, knowledge and application of learning theory, knowledge and skill in curriculum building and course construction and the development of creativity and skill in the methodology of teaching.[9]

It may be easy to agree that the career line for social work faculty is a substantive one, but it has been difficult to specify the preparation for this career line. Before undertaking this task, however, it is

---

[7] Rosa Wessel, "Practices and Problems in the Selection and Development of Faculty for Schools of Social Work," paper presented at Annual Program Meeting, Council on Social Work Education, Toronto, Canada, January 30, 1964.

[8] Daniel Jennings, "Characteristics of Faculty Members of Graduate Professional Schools of Social Work in the United States and Canada," (Unpublished doctoral dissertation, Catholic University, 1965).

[9] Eileen Blackey, "Issues in Social Work Education—New and Changing Demands Made of the Profession," *op. cit.*, p. 86.

necessary to consider the university context for career preparation. If the host institution were clear about pre-service preparation, there would be only one problem, namely, the development of programs for social work faculty that are congruent with typical patterns. But the reality of the university is extremely complex and perennial issues remain unresolved. To present them may be helpful.

PREPARATION FOR UNIVERSITY CAREERS: THE DOCTORATE

As has been noted, university objectives deal with educating the new generations, expanding the frontiers of knowledge, and reaching out in service to the supporting society. The faculty are primary agents for achieving these objectives. Their activities, taken together, are called scholarship; those who have the capacities and pursue these activities are called scholarly. Theirs is a "community of scholars." However, because individuals differ in their inclinations, because the institutional objectives to which they commit themselves vary at a given moment in the priorities set, because emphases within the several disciplines and the professions change, scholarliness has needed continuing redefinition. It has been partialized in the restatements by terms such as teacher-researcher, research-scholar, and teacher-scholar, each reflecting changing thrusts, and to which we shall return in the next chapter. At this time we shall ask: How does one achieve the qualities of scholarliness?

The institutional response over the years for the preparation of scholars has been the development of a rigorous complex of advanced educational activity designed to give evidence of ability to meet the expectations for the scholar. The successful completion of this activity is symbolized by a doctoral degree. The doctorate has become the official symbol of the "doctor," the teacher, the scholar.

But while the symbol has remained stable in the current century, what it symbolizes and to what it should testify have remained questions about which a vigorous debate has raged. It has become the "glory, jest and riddle of the world of higher learning in America."[10]

There has been continuing concern about the preparation of college faculty throughout this century. The literature of the continuing de-

---

[10] Moody E. Prior, "The Doctor of Philosophy Degree," in Everett Walters, ed., *Graduate Education Today* (Washington, D. C.: American Council on Education, 1965), p. 30.

bate about many of the issues related to preparation—the nature of graduate education and doctoral study as preparation—is copious.[11] The same issues were highlighted by the President's Commission on Higher Education[12] immediately after World War II, and they have continued to receive attention in the national forum until the present.[13] Berelson observes that:

> It is instructive and often entertaining to review the discussions of the AAU (Association of American Universities) in the first few years of its existence (the beginning of the current century). ... There is hardly a topic active today that was not being debated then, and not infrequently in the same terms. Fellowships, the meaning of research, the character of the dissertation, the quality of the students, the foreign language requirement, the major-minor problem at the doctoral level, the proper examinations, the

[11] See, for example, C. R. Pace, "The Preparation of College Teachers," *Review of Educational Research*, 19 (June, 1949), pp. 230-34, which provides a bibliography covering the period 1945-48. See also Edward V. Hollis, ed., *Toward Improving Ph.D. Programs* (Washington: American Council on Education, 1945); Howard Mumford Jones, *Education and World Tragedy* (Cambridge: Harvard University Press, 1946).

[12] *Higher Education for American Democracy, A Report of the President's Commission on Higher Education*, Vol. 4, *Staffing Higher Education* (New York: Harper & Bros., 1947); see also critiques by Harold R. W. Benjamin, "Ph.D.'s Preferred," *Journal of Higher Education*, 19, 4 (April, 1948), pp. 189-93, and Charles W. Jones, "The Truman Report and the Graduate Schools," *Journal of Higher Education*, 20, 7 (October, 1949), pp. 355-59.

[13] See Theodore C. Blegen, "The Graduate Schools and the Education of College Teachers," *Educational Record*, 29 (Jan., 1948), pp. 12-25; Earl J. McGrath, "The Goals of Higher Education," *Journal of Higher Education*, 20:4 (April, 1949), pp. 171-80; Earl J. McGrath, "The Education of College Teachers," *Journal of General Education*, 3 (Jan., 1949), pp. 83-86; Ruth E. Eckert, "Some Neglected Aspects in the Preparation of College Teachers," *Journal of General Education*, 3 (Jan., 1949), pp. 137-44.

See also Report of Conference sponsored by the American Council on Education and the United States Office of Education in 1949, and another ten years later: Theodore C. Blegen and Russell M. Cooper, eds., *The Preparation of College Teachers*, (1950) and Joseph Axelrod, ed., *Graduate Study for Future College Teachers* (1959), both Washington: American Council on Education.

See also position statements presented at meetings of the Association for Higher Education, in *Issues in Higher Education*, Kerry Smith, ed. (Washington: National Education Assn. of U.S., 1959 & 1960).

A conference on "Preparing the College Professor for Liberal Arts Teaching" called in 1965 by the Association of American Colleges and the Council of Graduate Schools in the U.S. considered similar issues.

Also see, *Improving College Teaching*, Calvin B. T. Lee, ed. (Washington: American Council on Education, 1967), which is an outgrowth of the Annual Meeting of the American Council on Education held in October, 1966. Background papers prepared for this meeting correspond at many points to the same perennial issues, and will be referred to specifically at appropriate points in the text.

role of the Master's, preparation for college teaching, all these topics came up in the first years of the AAU.[14]

Some argue that the doctorate is the *sine qua non* for scholarly qualification and for full faculty citizenship. They defend it with conviction about its time-tested values. Wilson asserts that "the degree is right because it joins the concept of present knowing and future learning. In spite of all complaints about the dissertation, the idea is important to good teaching. A teacher who is not probing the unknown may unconsciously convey the impression that knowledge is static—something to be memorized."[15]

Others, with a figurative shrug of the shoulders, agree that though the doctorate may not insure all that is claimed for it, it remains the best we have, that no better alternative is available. Some cynically refer to it as the "immutable Ph.D.,"[16] unresponsive to needed reforms. It has also been challenged as preparation for inappropriate ends, or simply as unnecessary.

> The Ph.D. fetish is an American phenomenon. . . . It is not encountered elsewhere in the university world. . . . It derived originally from the unique American method of accrediting colleges and has persisted . . . probably because accrediting must continue as long as new institutions are being established. . . . The method of insuring quality . . . in the Commonwealth countries is through affiliation of the new institution with established universities to be qualified to operate independently. The matter of advanced degrees is not emphasized. . . . As a result the shortage of college teachers is not so acute.[17]

---

[14] Berelson, *op. cit.*, p. 17.

[15] O. Meredith Wilson, "The Ph.D. Program as Preparation for College Teaching," *Association of American Colleges Bulletin*, 44, 1 (March, 1958), pp. 55-59. See also, R. J. Henle, S.J., "The Soundness of the American Ph.D. Programs," *Improving College Teaching, op. cit.*, pp. 72-76.

[16] See for example, "New Demands, Same Old Response," which includes statements by Everett Walters, "The Immutable Ph.D.," and Frederick W. Ness, "The Case of the Lingering Degree," *Saturday Review* (January 15, 1966), pp. 62ff; also, ongoing debate in *School and Society* by John W. Dykstra, "The Ph.D. Fetish," 86:233 (May 24, 1958), pp. 237-39, and response by James M. Davis, 86:2144 (December 20, 1958), pp. 458-9; also Lewis Leary, "The Scholar as Teacher," 87:2158, pp. 262-3; also I. L. Kandel, "Some Educational Paradoxes," *Educational Forum*, 22:3 (March, 1958), pp. 261-72. See also, James H. Blessing, *Graduate Education, An Annotated Bibliography* (Washington: U.S. Government Printing Office, 1961) which lists literally scores of writings showing continuing concern with these issues throughout the 1950's.

[17] Oliver C. Carmichael, *Graduate Education* (New York: Harper and Bros., 1961), p. 122.

The purposes and methods of doctoral study become more complex with the advent of professional doctorates as distinct from the academic Ph.D. degree. Should there be distinctive professional doctorates? To what extent should they be different? On the one hand, there is the reality of the proliferation of professional degrees; on the other hand, Berelson observes that:

> There has been a mutual infiltration of academic and professional work at the graduate level; the growth of professional fields has meant a growing demand for professional training at the graduate level and at the same time the development of applications in academic disciplines has meant the growth of professional work within them.
>
> Professional fields (other than medicine and law) have constantly increased their programs at the doctoral level and in general have coveted the Ph.D. in preference to setting up their own doctoral degrees, even if that meant conforming to the general standards for the Ph.D. set up by the graduate school for the entire university.[18]

From every vantage point within university life, from administrators and faculty, come suggestions for reform. Some would change the boundaries of advanced study, i.e., upgrade the master's or downgrade the doctorate. Others take the present boundaries as the given and suggest modifications within the established boundaries to strengthen the degrees in one way or another. Of these, some would modify the dissertation requirement more or less radically. Others have suggestions for the language requirements; or for the sequence and timing of the requirements; or for the duration (the "stretch-out") and the ABD (all but the dissertation) phenomenon.[19]

---

[18] Berelson, *op. cit.*, p. 200. For a discussion of the "chaotic situation in the titling of American academic degrees," see W. Gordon Whaley, "American Academic Degrees," *Educational Record*, 47:4 (Fall, 1966), pp. 525-537.

[19] See, for example, Everett Walters, "A New Degree for College Teachers," *Journal of Higher Education*, 31:5 (May, 1960), pp. 282-14 who urges a two-year master of philosophy degree which could become a doctorate after submission of an acceptable dissertation; J. P. Elder, "Reviving the Master's Degree for the Prospective College Teacher," *Journal of Higher Education*, 30:3 (March, 1959) describes a needed master's program; Albert P. Brogan, "Restoring the Master's Degree," *Graduate Journal*, Vol. 1, No. 1, Spring, 1958, pp. 34-40; William Brickman, "Speed Up of the Ph.D. Degree," *School and Society*, 87:2146 (January 31, 1959), p. 51 suggests alternative ways to speed completion of doctoral work without diluting the dissertation; Benjamin J. Wright, "The Ph.D. Stretch-Out and the Scholar-Teacher," in *Vital Issues in Education*, A. E. Traxler, ed. (Washington: American Council on Education, 1957), pp. 140-151, suggests that the Ph.D. be acquired typically by three years of study and research following the bachelor's degree.

Within the main outlines of the present structure there is ample play for modifications in MA and Ph.D. Programs of study, for some redressing of the over-emphasis upon acute specialization in certain fields, for experimentation with new kinds of graduate degrees and for programs of teacher preparation.[20]

THE TEACHING FUNCTION

Why do these questions remain so long unresolved? If they were in fact the heart of the problem, intelligence and rationality should be able to arrive at satisfying determinations. If there were sufficient precision about an objective, whether or not it had been accomplished could be recognized. Skill could be harnessed for determining the best means for achieving the agreed upon ends, without the heat of argument. Surely in the research-oriented culture of university life controls for testing hypotheses can be devised and adequate numbers of subjects are available.

The basic issue, it appears, is the status of teaching, *qua* teaching, within the university. The research function of university faculty is acknowledged, and its product can be recognized. The research contributions of the university community are everywhere in evidence. And the doctorate, whether a Ph.D. or a professional doctorate, generally testifies to a quality of research readiness.[21] Little attention has been given to preparation for community service as a major area of scholarly activity, except in the recently growing literature of adult education. The debate is most frequently joined as though the issue were teaching *versus* research, or teaching *and* research.

The source of uneasiness lies in the fact that Ph.D. programs are not planned to prepare potential faculty members specifically for the teaching they will do.[22] The President's Commission on Higher Education in 1947 obseserved that:

> College teaching is the only major learned profession for which there does not exist a well-defined program of preparation directed

---

[20] Henry David, "What are the Basic Problems in the Preparation of College Teachers?" in *Current Issues in Higher Education*, G. Kerry Smith, ed., *loc. cit.*, 1960, p. 180.

[21] There are a few professional doctorates that are not "research" degrees, for which a research dissertation is not required, but this is not the prevailing pattern.

[22] John S. Diekhoff, *Tomorrow's Professors* (New York: The Fund for the Advancement of Education, n.d.), p. 56.

toward developing the skills which it is essential for the practitioner to possess.[23]

The same message comes through in an address by Sir Eric Ashby, (Master of Clare College, Cambridge, England, founded in 1326, and "entitled to genuine traditionalism") to an assembly on the "University in America" called together by the Center for the Study of Democratic Institutions in May 1966. "What ails American universities might be healed with a basic prescription: 'For the sacred thread of transmission between teacher and pupil, do you perhaps rely more than we do on inexperienced teachers?' he asked in what was not really a question."[24]

As though anticipating our discussion in the next chapter on the social work teacher, Goheen pleads the cause of good teaching:

> The house of intellect, once so relatively tidy, has swollen and burst into fragments . . . not only in the sciences and the social sciences, but also in the humanities, marked changes are discernible in the materials being studied and the approach to these materials. . . . The movement . . . is towards basic principles and fundamental analysis, away from mere memory work and dependence upon fixed segments of subject matter, but it does call for more talented teachers. Rote learning never was much good. Today it is worth even less. The citizen of tomorrow must master the ways of analysis, must search deeply, if he is to cope with the uncertainties and changes of the decades ahead. But this kind of education cannot be offered by second and third rate minds using second and third hand methods of instruction.[25]

---

[23] *Higher Education for American Democracy, A Report of the President's Commission on Higher Education, loc. cit.,* p. 16.

[24] As quoted by Fred M. Hechinger, "What Should a University Be?" *New York Times,* May 16, 1966.

In the introduction to "Is There a Science of Education?" by Josiah Royce, reprinted from *Educational Review,* I (January, 1891), Borrowman's observation is helpful:

The widely held assumption that academic professors . . . were either uninterested in, or actively hostile to, the study of pedagogy may be accurate with respect to the greater number of them. But the conclusion that the professors of education heard no friendly voice from influential colleagues in other departments is clearly false. Perhaps Royce's sympathetic "wait and see" attitude was more representative than is commonly thought. More careful institution-by-institution research may reveal that in many cases, the professors of education started out with considerable support but later alienated their defenders. From *Teacher Education in America: A Documentary History* (New York: Teachers College Columbia University, 1965), p. 101.

[25] Robert F. Goheen, "The Teacher in the University," *School and Society,* Vol. 94, 2276 (April 2, 1966), p. 178.

A similar point of view about the need for teaching ability in professional education is growing, in this instance for medicine:

> Full-time university medicine came into being because of the dawning realization that the teaching of medicine required as much pedagogic skill as the teaching of anything else at the university level. It could not be left to amateurs. The fact that a doctor was a superb clinician did not imply that he was ipso facto a competent teacher nor that he had the requisite ability to organize and administer the various activities of a teaching clinic in a way to make them effective.[26]

A report to the Harvard Faculty of Medicine on September 30, 1966, of a new approach to planning its curriculum asserted:

> It is fully appreciated that changes in the curriculum can at best only facilitiate the learning experience. The essence of education is to bring together the intelligent motivated student with the sources of knowledge. The role of the teacher is to reduce to a minimum the activation barrier separating the two. There is no substitute for knowledge and these ingredients are insufficient. We feel that inadequate attention has been devoted to *teaching the teachers to teach* (italics mine). We hope that some concrete efforts to experiment with teaching clinics, perhaps seeking the advice and assistance of experts in education will be implemented along with a new curriculum with full recognition that the latter can be no better than its teachers.[27]

Although there has been a considerable response to this deficiency within the past two decades we must ask why the issue about the teaching function has persisted. What constitutes readiness for teaching and how doctoral study prepares for it are at once obscure and loaded questions. While few minimize the importance of good teaching, current thinking in the academic community with respect to teaching is, to understate the case, without consensus. For example, Berelson claims that he remains unconvinced that there is in fact an art of teaching, and if there is, that it can be learned. Others believe that there may be an art but are not sure about what it is or at any rate that it can be acquired. On the other hand, Stratemeyer states:

---

[26] James Howard Means, "Homo Medicus Americanus," *Daedalus* (Fall, 1963), p. 710. See also John E. Dietrick and Robert C. Berson, *Medical Schools in the United States at Mid Century* (New York: McGraw Hill Book Co., 1953), pp. 223-4.

[27] Harvard Medical School, Report of Subcommittee on Curriculum Planning, May, 1966. (Mimeographed.)

Teaching, thus, must remain a central function of all college teachers. . . . All college teachers must be *teaching*-scholars and identify with the teaching profession as well as with the disciplines pertinent to their specialization. Recognizing teaching as of first importance is not to deny the role of research. . . . That many college teachers do not hold this view, have not experienced the satisfactions and the challenges of teaching, and do not see the reciprocal relationship between teaching and research, is not difficult to understand. Many college teachers, of both the academic disciplines and of education (for the professions) have included no work . . . relating to the professional dimension of scholarship for the teachers. Others have had a course or two, and a privileged few have had the opportunity to engage in college teaching under guidance; to experience high quality guided teaching at the college level. Here would seem to be an important area of action for graduate schools, both in the academic and the professional areas.[28]

Sometimes it would appear that the issue is research versus teaching, as though one of these flourishes only at the expense of the other.[29] The President of Princeton University, in explicating the reasons why better teaching must be nourished and sustained, notes the "emphasis and glamor now so widely and strongly attached to research," but denies the existence of a valid issue:

Please do not mistake me. The quest for new knowledge in the university and the college, too, is vital. On campuses all over the country, the stepped-up range and tempo of research have strengthened and enlivened instruction far more widely than they have deadened or disabled it: In the . . . university, research and teaching are two poles of the same magnet; neither has much force without the other. This is what the ideal of the teacher-scholar is all about.[30]

That research activities are more easily discerned and more readily rewarded than good teaching is noted in the Report of the Conference on "Preparing the College Professor for Liberal Art Teaching," called

---

[28] Florence Stratemeyer, "Perspective on Action in Teacher Education," *Action for Improvement of Teacher Education,* Eighteenth Yearbook, (Washington, D. C.: American Association of Colleges for Teacher Education, 1965), p. 38.

[29] See, for example, *Higher Education and the Demand for Scientific Manpower in the United States* (Paris, France: Organization for Economic Co-operation and Development, 1963). The discussion in this review on "The Quality of Teaching" (pp. 33-53) is based on the premise of a "conflict between research and teaching."

[30] Goheen, *op cit.,* p. 178.

in 1965 by the Association of American Colleges and the Council of Graduate Schools in the United States.

The liberal arts colleges are dedicated to excellence in both teaching and scholarship. To his colleagues and to the central college administration the excellence in scholarship of a faculty member, as evidenced by published books, articles and learned addresses, is more readily apparent than is the quality of his teaching performance. Consequently, and all too frequently, teaching performance has been largely ignored in decisions on the salary, promotion or tenure of the college teacher.

If excellence in teaching is valued . . . it must be encouraged and rewarded. In so doing the college must maintain a balance between its concern for teaching and its concern for scholarship. The . . . faculty member should meet established standards of performance in both his teaching and his scholarship, but beyond that, the faculty member whose special gifts and concerns are for encouraging, promoting and sustaining student learning should be equally well rewarded as the faculty member who is an outstanding scholar.

Two questions emerge in connection with the desire to encourage and reward good teaching; how is it possible to discern good teaching? What will the rewards be? Numerous devices have been suggested for obtaining estimates of the teaching ability of faculty members including questionnaires completed by current students or alumni, prearranged classroom visitation by senior colleagues on the faculty, and performances in analagous situations such as public lectures, faculty meetings or forums. Although of considerable value, it is possible that none of these devices yield accurate information about teaching effectiveness if the latter is measured in terms of the quality and quantity of student learning. Furthermore, information about teaching performance obtained for the purpose of improving instruction may not be useful for the purpose of providing a sound basis for administrative decisions on salary, tenure, and promotion. Thus, the question of methods of discerning teaching competence must be a matter for more intensive discussion and analysis before appropriate recommendations are made. Unfortunately, major efforts to reward excellence in teaching more adequately must await some resolution of this question.[31]

---

[31] Draft of 1965 Conference Report, reviewed by this writer before its publication, in the offices of the Association.

The best explanation, granted that the dedication to the teaching objective is deep, appears to be that current thinking is based on contradictory philosophies and psychologies of education, each in turn subscribed to with vigor. Policies and practices are equally disparate, some based on different sets of convictions, some based on traditions not subjected to scrutiny, and some without benefit of an *a priori* rationale. There appear to be three polar positions, however, which may be recognized as subject-matter oriented, teacher-oriented, and learner-oriented, each warranting a brief description.

According to the subject-matter view, the good teacher is master of a specified content area. He knows the subtleties, the intricacies, the relationships of ideas indigenous to a field of knowledge. Then follow several variations. He is good *because* he knows, his knowing generates enthusiasm, application, and imagination in the students—all these being the essential ingredients for good teaching. "Technology" for teaching is either incidental technique if it exists, or as some argue, unnecessary baggage because the outcome is accounted for by the knowing and the enthusiasm. Others have a powerful suspicion of the "educationist." They fear that any attention to methodology predisposes to a weakening of quality of content and threatens standards of excellence of subject matter.[32] Another variation grants that there is a differential effect of teachers equally knowledgeable and enthusiastic about the given subject matter. The difference is attributed to "art," whose nature is essentially mystic, neither describable except in charismatic terms, nor transmissable. The problem is disposed of by the phrase that "good teachers are born, not made."

The latter variation bears some resemblance to the second polar position which may be characterized as *teacher-oriented*. This theme proposes that there is in fact an art of teaching but it resides within the teacher himself and can be improved only by the individual teacher. Variations of this theme include the following: teaching experience —on the firing line—is either the only means or the best means by which refinement of skill takes place. Those who feel it is the *only* way have no further problem; the senior teacher is the better teacher because of his longitudinal experience.[33] The teacher who is not going

---

[32] See exchange in *School and Society* between George B. Cutten, "The College Professor as Teacher," 86:2139, October 25, 1958, pp. 372-75, who says that "the criticism of the Ph.D. as a preparation for teaching in colleges is that it implies if a person knows a subject, he can teach it—a false and dangerous assumption," and Lewis Leary, *op. cit.*, pp. 362-3, who notes that it is "equally false and infinitely more dangerous" to imply that "knowledge of subject is not necessary."

[33] Many hold this view for university teaching, while accepting the importance of professional education for teachers of children.

to improve or cannot improve is either not rehired or eliminates himself. Others see the teaching fellowship (or the sometimes misnamed research fellowship) during doctoral study as a useful device for providing a salary and experience (and presumably competence) in teaching, fortuitously serving administrative needs for "covering" class sections at the same time.

The third major position holds that the art and skill of teaching is developmental if it is *student-centered*. It can be transmitted and acquired when the focus is on the learner. If objectives are formulated as learner outcomes rather than as content areas to be "covered," or solely as teacher behaviors, then the selection of learning experiences becomes a rational activity, in which technique *qua* technique has its place in proper perspective. The formulation and selection of objectives, the organization of appropriate content, the understanding of the learner and the psychology of learning, the judicious selection of learning experiences and the design of a curriculum constitute teaching methodology:[34]

> To be designated a professor . . . is . . . evidence that one knows how to teach. If craftsmanship in teaching were merely a matter of knowing how to utilize economically teaching time and energy, it would still be worth cultivating. . . .
>
> But craftsmanship in teaching is much more. The teacher as artist is much more than the teacher as technician. . . . The art . . . is an exciting discipline, mastery of which demands and merits all that a promising young teacher can bring in the way of natural ability and conscientious application.[35]

Noting the "repeated and disheartening examples of the failure of education built upon the content model (i.e., categories of content, subject matter areas) to alter substantially the behavior of practitioners," Miller looks for a teacher who can

> . . . try a different educational model—one built upon solid evidence about the way adults learn rather than upon the long-honored method of teaching them. There is ample evidence to support the view that adult learning is not most efficiently achieved through systematic subject instruction; it is accomplished

---

[34] Marguerite V. Pohek, "Toward a Methodology of Teaching," *Education for Social Work* (New York: Council on Social Work Education, 1964), pp. 149-161.

[35] Joseph Justman, "What Makes a Good College Teacher?" *School and Society*, 70:1827 (December 4, 1949), p. 420.

by involving learners in identifying problems and seeking ways to solve them.[36]

As the necessary understandings and competence are acquired, the territory allocated to the charismatic and to the mystique of the art becomes manageable. That there is room in this view for the unknown and the personal, i.e., the "art," is gratifyingly analogous to the place of "art" in all scientific and professional endeavor.

Among these three orientations there are additional variations. For example, some note that students respond differentially to the same teacher and the same subject matter, i.e., some do better than others. This variation despairs at this time of describing, much less of mastering, the combination of variables which may some day constitute the art and science of teaching adult students. This point of view may grant the emergence of pedagogoical theory and skill for teaching children, but it has less confidence about the imminence of a science for adult learning.

Also there are many who suspect that experience may not be the only or the best means of improving teaching, but they are reluctant to entertain alternatives for one of several reasons. For example, some fear that administrative involvement in the *how* of teaching may become, or be construed, as a threat to academic freedom because the *what* is too easily contaminated by the *how*. Those who subscribe to this position are willing to consider attention to the teaching component in preservice education, but not as part of an inservice program. Here we have two camps. Some believe that attention to the teaching component belongs in the graduate schools as part of doctoral education, either by means of seminars on the teaching function and on educational problems, or some arrangement for supervised teaching. Another position suggests a "way station" whereby the novice (Ph.D. or ABD) gets experience and some degree of supervision after graduate study at another college before his first position as an official faculty member.[37]

Indeed, these are substantive questions which can appropriately claim the best thinking and energies of all who are concerned with the

---

[36] George E. Miller, "Continuing Education for What?" *Journal of Medical Education* 42:4 (April, 1967), p. 321.

[37] Diekhoff, *Domain of the Faculty* (New York: Harper & Bros., 1956), pp. 67-68. Earl J. McGrath, *The Graduate School and the Decline of Liberal Education* (New York: Columbia, University Press, 1959), criticizes the graduate schools for producing "teachers prepared not primarily for their chosen work." George B. Cutten, "The Professor and the Art of Teaching," *op. cit.*, suggests that the university be reorganized to include, among other suggestions, provision for two vice presidents, one as director of teaching and the second as director of research.

continuing quality and vitality of higher education. They would constitute maximum challenges if the only imperatives were purpose and quality of preparation of faculty. But a sense of urgency, of crisis, is generated by the quantitative dimension. There are some differences in the projections for the future about how urgent the crisis of numbers will be.[38] But the reality of the present as a critical one is not in dispute.

> The body of knowledge to be handled by the graduate school is growing and will continue to grow, thus adding problems of complexity and specialization.

> The demand for products of the graduate school is substantial and will grow in the next period of years. "Everyone" wants doctorates—the universities, the colleges, government, industry. . . .[39]

Within social work education, all agree that the faculty crisis is clear, urgent, and growing!

RESPONSES TO THE PROBLEMS OF QUANTITY AND QUALITY IN PREPARATION FOR UNIVERSITY CAREERS

It has been difficult, apparently, to attack the twin problems of quantity and quality simultaneously. Some accept the *status quo* of doctoral programs as the given, i.e., their content and objectives, and concentrate on the problem of numbers: interesting more young people before they make other career commitments to undertake to prepare themselves for academic careers and encouraging them to pursue doctoral work by means of financial assistance. Others have approached the problem of duration of doctoral study, hastening it or shortening it, as a response to the concern for quantity. Another category of response has dealt with aspects of quality of doctoral study, particularly with respect to the teaching component.

---

[38] Although Berelson concluded that "the crisis over having enough college and university teachers in 1970 is generally overstated, the prospects do not constitute a 'dire threat' to the present level of higher education" *op. cit.*, p. 224. In contrast, McGrath was reported in 1960 to predict that the "shortage of teachers may assume crisis proportions within five to ten years." *New York Times,* November 3, 1960.

[39] Berelson, *op. cit.*, p. 219. For a fuller discussion, see Part 3, "College Teachers: Quantity and Quality," in *Improving College Teaching, op. cit.*, which includes Allan M. Cartter's "Future Faculty: Needs and Resources" and commentaries by Berelson and others. (pp. 113-145).

The responses to the many aspects of these two dimensions have been imaginative and ingenious. Attempts to deal with the quantitative problem by the universities themselves (in addition to financial assistance from university funds) are reflected in suggestions for changing the boundaries of advanced study, either to "upgrade" the master's degree or "downgrade" the doctorate. On the current scene, a committee of the University of California, Berkeley, has urged the creation of a new Doctor of Arts degree which would testify to qualification in "all but dissertation" (ABD) and therefore cut down on the duration of doctoral study and eliminate the chronicity of the ABD phenomenon. The never-subdued urging, on the other hand, to restore the status of the master's has recently received new impetus with the announcement by Yale University, the first to offer the Ph.D. in this country over a hundred years ago, of a new Master of Philosophy (M. Phil.) degree, effective for students entering in the fall of 1968.

> The traditional Ph.D. programs are said to place too much emphasis upon research and require too long to complete. As a result it is alleged that the graduate schools are training specialists with neither a concern nor a flair for college teaching. The issues involved are complex and the argument suffers from oversimplification and misunderstanding. But as a first step pointing the way toward meeting the demand for more and better college teachers without debasing the Ph.D. . . . [the M. Phil. will] be awarded to students who have completed all requirements for the Ph.D. except the dissertation.[40]

To what extent either or both of these approaches will prevail is not known. Evidence that they are being considered seriously, however, is that a plenary session of the Sixth Annual Meeting (1966) of the Council of Graduate Schools in the United States was devoted to "The Development of Intermediate Degrees" with panel presentations of the several points of view.

During the past two decades a complex network of stipends, scholarships, and fellowships has developed with the specific intent of supporting more and qualitatively better graduate study for future faculty. The funds come from university, foundation and governmental sources. A few of these are noted briefly as examples of the differing emphases.

A new Ph.D. program which includes two years of teaching experi-

---

[40] John Perry Miller, "The Master of Philosophy: A New Degree is Born," Announcement sent by Dean Miller, Dean of the Graduate School, Yale University, August 4, 1966.

ence is cited from the *Harvard Alumni Bulletin* (October 26, 1963) in *The Flight From Teaching*.[41] In it, the dean of the Harvard Faculty of Arts and Sciences notes both the financial advantage to the institution of finding ways "to make more use of the *best* graduate degree candidates," and the benefit to the graduate student: ". . . teaching experience ought to be a part of training for the Ph.D., and . . . it ought to be undertaken by graduate students not as a chore imposed by financial need but as an invaluable part of their education."

The Woodrow Wilson National Fellowship Foundation Awards Program is a typical approach to "provide a positive stimulus to young men and women to test their possible interest in an academic career." Its long range objective is "recruitment for and improvement in college and university staffs." Each fellowship carries a liberal stipend and payment of tuition fees. During the fifteen-year period ending in 1960, the total number of fellowships was 2,057; 1,000 are now appointed annually.[42] This volume has been made possible by a 25 million dollar appropriation in 1957 from the Ford Foundation for a large-scale extension of this program.

The Ford Foundation has in recent years supported a College Teacher Preparation Program designed "to improve the preparation of college teachers." A characteristic of this program is that it does not specify the doctorate as a symbol of preparation. Its primary thrust is directed at identifying young potential scholars early, to interest them in academic careers by encouraging and supporting them in undertaking graduate study in a special master's degree program. Using variations such as MA-T or MA-3 as symbols, or "scholars" designation, these three-year master's degree programs typically begin in the undergraduate senior year, and may or may not be terminal.[43]

---

[41] *The Flight From Teaching*, (New York: The Carnegie Foundation for the Advancement of Teaching, 1964), pp. 13-14. This summary of a discussion by the trustees of the Carnegie Foundation suggests that "one practical measure open to any university is to set higher stipends for teaching assistantships than research fellowships. The reverse is usually true today, and the ablest students make a beeline for the fellowships." (p. 14).

[42] *Handbook of Fellowship Awards* (Princeton, N. J.: Woodrow Wilson National Fellowships Foundation, 1960), see Preface by Hugh Taylor, President of the Foundation. See also "Foundation-Financed Activities Bearing Upon College Teaching," *Educational Record,* 37:2 (April, 1956), pp. 153-162 for reports on projects supported by grants from the Fund for the Advancement of Education, Ford Foundation, Carnegie Corporation, General Education Board, Danforth Foundation, Russell Sage Foundation, and John Hay Whitney Foundation.

[43] For the purposes of the present study, a survey letter was sent to the 39 institutions which have participated in the Ford Foundation College Teacher Preparation Program. The letter asked for data about the experience of the institution with the special master's program, and solicited evaluative comments. Twenty-one responses

Most recently, the Ford Foundation announced grants of $41.5 million dollars to ten universities for a program which will allocate 200 million dollars in the next seven years to reform the quality of the doctorate and strengthen the preparation of doctoral candidates for teaching careers. "The Ford reforms—through better research-and-dissertation years and through a concerted effort to make teaching a part of doctoral training rather than an incidental chore—promised organizational improvement."[44]

> While each university will work out its own reform procedures, they will typically consist of providing funds for the last year or two of a four- or five-year graduate program when the student is working on his dissertation. They may also provide for a year of full-time, paid teaching internship—freed from any other graduate study requirements.[45]

The significant role of the federal government in providing traineeships for advanced study, both for continuing practitioners and potential faculty, is well known and need not be itemized here. (That the support comes from a variety of sources within the governmental agencies, e.g., The National Institute of Mental Health, the Vocational Rehabilitation Administration, the Children's Bureau, and programs within the Office of Education, is also well known, particularly to the deans of schools of social work who must make separate applications to each of the sources.) As the need for personnel to develop new services becomes critical, and for faculty to educate that personnel, stipends are developed to provide for traineeships for practitioners and for the advanced education of those who are increasingly needed to teach the new trainees.[46]

The National Defense Graduate Fellowships Program (Title IV of the National Defense Education Act) is another example of a major effort undertaken by the United States Government to attack the

---

were received, indicating, in general, evidence of satisfactory achievement and quality of experience. Each institution has developed its own program autonomously, a few provide some experience addressed to the teaching component; most are exclusively subject matter oriented. These programs obviously have no immediate pertinence to preparation of faculty in education for professional social work, but they are noted as evidence of the multidirectional approaches to the quantitative aspect of the problem.

[44] Fred M. Hechinger, "Reappraising the Ph. of the Ph.D.," *New York Times,* April 16, 1967.

[45] *Ibid.*

[46] Grants are awarded for graduate study, both master's and doctoral work, as well as short-term programs to colleges and universities, and include stipends to the students as well as to the institution.

quantitative faculty crisis. To be eligible, an applicant "must be *interested in,* or continuing in, an academic career of teaching in institutions of higher education, [and] . . . intending to enroll in a course of study leading to the doctorate." In fiscal 1966, 180 institutions participated, 6,000 fellowships having been awarded. Thus far, very little interest in this program has been shown by social workers although they are presumably eligible.

As the program operates currently, a dissertation must be an integral part of doctoral study. In the few instances where a professional doctorate rather than a "research" doctorate is under consideration, consultants from that field may specify appropriate substitutes. No official criteria are specified with respect to provision for the teaching function as such, although during the past two years applying institutions have been asked to describe what elements in their doctoral programs are addressed to it, and criteria may eventually be formulated.[47]

On the other hand, there has been a surge of effort in recent years directed toward the teaching component. The framework for this effort is based on the position that there is in fact a high level teaching component which can be learned and improved.

> My view is that the graduate assistant system, as usually administered, does not fill the need, nor will the emulation of senior professors insure adequate preparation for good teaching. If these contentions are admitted, it follows that little improvement may be expected in the quality of college and university instruction until our graduate faculties become convinced that college teaching is an art the practice of which requires special skills and insights in addition to advanced education in a substantive field.[48]

Here again, some feel that this component is accounted for by knowing about, and learning to value, educational foundations, the psychology of learning, or the methodologies of classroom "teaching" and evaluation. Others believe firmly that preparation for the teaching component cannot be satisfied except through "learning by doing" under extremely competent and consciously planned supervision. To add complexity to the patterns, the learning to teach component is

---

[47] Interview with Dr. James Blessing, Division of Graduate Programs, Graduate Academic Programs Branch, Office of Education, Department of Health, Education, and Welfare, Washington: June 14, 1966. See also *National Defense Graduate Fellowships, Graduate Programs 1966-67.* (Washington: United States Department of Health, Education, and Welfare, 1966).

[48] Carl R. Bye, "What Will be the Dimensions of the Ph.D. and the Professional Doctorates?" in *Current Issues in Higher Education,* G. Kerry Smith, ed., *op. cit.,* p. 185.

variously introduced as part of doctoral study, e.g., seminars *about* education and/or teaching internships, or as a post-doctoral experience.

The Danforth Foundation has supported several university projects[49] intended to improve the preparation of college teachers by means of internships for Ph.D. candidates. Each institution has developed its own plans, but typically they include a year during doctoral study during which the candidate has teaching responsibility assigned and received consciously designed supervision of his teaching.

A useful summary of these developments is available in the background paper prepared for the conference on "Preparing the College Professor for Liberal Arts Teaching" referred to earlier.

> The largest number of programs designed to improve the preparation of college teachers which were reported to us are based on varying degrees of supervised teaching experience. Forty such programs were mentioned by our respondents. Eleven institutions reported teaching intern programs which in some cases are arranged with neighboring colleges or with the evening division of the university. Eleven and fourteen universities, respectively, report supervised teaching experiences and supervised experience as a laboratory assistant. The degree of superivsion in these programs varies greatly not only with the program but also with the interest of the senior faculty members assigned to supervise the work of graduate students. Some graduate school deans report that there is "much supervised teaching" because 'close contact with faculty members working with them on course preparation is presumed to be the best preparation" for college teaching. On the other hand, there are institutions such as the one which reported that only "in some departments . . . senior faculty visit the classes conducted by teaching assistant."

> Two universities mentioned seminar courses in which the student has an opportunity to prepare course materials and to present them to a class in a setting which they may profit from constructive criticism. . . .[50]

---

[49] Five institutions listed are: The Department of History Washington University; St. Louis, Missouri; The Graduate School, Yale University; Department of English, Emory University; The Graduate School, Duke University; The Department of History, University of Virginia. Letter from Mr. W. Max Wise, Associate Director, Danforth Foundation, July 8, 1966. See also, W. Max Wise, "Who Teaches the Teachers?", *Improving College Teaching, op. cit.,* pp. 77-89.

[50] Peter H. Armacost and Diane Howland, "Background Materials on Selected Topics for a Conference on 'Preparing the College Professor for Liberal Arts Teaching.' " (Mimeographed. Association of American Colleges, 1965.)

The imperative for this relatively new emphasis, which adds to the period of doctoral study, is argued by Dean Miller as based upon four propositions:

First, the faculty has a responsibility to initiate the more promising graduate students into the art of teaching. Second, this is best done by providing graduate students with limited supervised teaching experience under the guidance of experienced faculty. Third, this experience must be viewed as an opportunity open to those of proven intellectual competence and teaching promise, rather than as a chore necessary for financial support. Fourth, there should be available to the student who wishes it the wisdom of those who are wrestling with issues of higher education as teachers, researchers, and administrators.[51]

Antioch College is currently introducing a post-doctoral internship for individuals who have recently completed Ph.D. degrees to:

. . . strengthen the teaching in the humanities. The program [is] designed to acquaint teaching fellows in the humanities with a variety of effective ways of teaching, expose them to the excitement and rewards of such teaching in a liberal arts context where the humanities flourish, encourage them in the development of their philosophies and styles of teaching, introduce them to the possibilities of continued improvement of teaching, and introduce them to the strengths of interdisciplinary effort in instruction in the humanities.[52]

A recently completed survey[53] reports on programs for the recruitment *and* training of college teachers by means of teaching assistantships during doctoral study in 146 departments and schools in 42 emi-

---

[51] John Perry Miller, "The Teaching Assistantship: Chore or Challenge?" Reprint from *Ventures Magazine of the Yale Graduate School* (Vol. IV, Fall, 1964). In letter from Dean Miller, dated August 4, 1966, he notes that the teaching internship program is not specifically related to the newly announced Master of Philosophy degree (see text above), "although it is clear that we shall have to rethink our program in light of this new degree."

[52] Communication from Dr. Morris Keeton, Academic Vice-President, Antioch College, dated August 5, 1966.

[53] Frank Koen and Stanford C. Ericksen, *An Analysis of the Specific Features which Characterize The More Successful Programs for the Recruitment and Training of College Teachers*, (Ann Arbor: The Center for Research on Learning and Teaching, 1967). The report suggests that "the 'optimal' model that emerges from the survey is composed of three *functional* stages labelled for convenience: apprenticeship, assistantship, and instructorship. Each stage should be defined in terms of the teaching assistant's competence and responsibilities, rather than in terms of time period." (p. 41)

nent universities. In addition to the administrative advantages to the departments, i.e., meeting the need for classroom instructors, the "successful" features of the programs were noted as (1) "satisfaction with the supervised development of neophyte teachers which allowed experienced teachers to pass on skills and ideas to the apprentice instructors," (2) the "centering on the concerns, needs, and characteristics of the assistants themselves and a move away from more direct institutional and logistical interests," and (3) going "beyond teaching *per se* . . . to the benefits which appear to accrue to the undergraduates resulting from the special training given the teaching assistants."[54]

The Career Teacher program of the National Institute of Mental Health (Public Health Service, U.S. Department of Health, Education, and Welfare) is yet another example of an effort to buttress the teaching function of faculty in the several professions related to mental health, i.e., psychology, psychiatry, nursing, and social work. Career teacher awards are made to cooperating schools to enable candidates who have completed doctoral course requirements to spend a year at a cooperating institution (not necessarily the school where they have been studying nor the one in which they will be receiving full-time appointments). They gain experience under the guidance of master teachers before accepting full-time faculty responsibility. A design for improvement of teaching characterizes the experience, and is not associated with work on the dissertation. Each mental health profession develops its own patterns within this general objective.

Parallel to the Career Teacher Programs in mental health are the predoctoral and postdoctoral *research* fellowships of the Public Health Service (HEW). The purpose of the Research Career Program of the National Institutes of Health is to increase the number of stable full-time career opportunities for investigators (not primarily teachers of research) on university faculties relatively early in their careers. The awards may be for relatively long periods, i.e., not necessarily limited to one or two years.

Summary

In this chapter we have noted some of the issues which agitate the academic world. There are differences between the cultures of the university and of the profession with respect to value orientations, emphases among objectives, and relative concern for academic freedom and professional responsibility. The career line in social work education

---

[54] *Ibid.*, p. 32.

is substantive and distinct from the career line within the profession of social work.

A major issue in preparation of university professors is the status of teaching *qua* teaching. The questions raised are of two orders: whether ability to teach can be acquired, and if so, how it can best be acquired. There have been imaginative proposals and innovations throughout the university world for improvement of preparation, particularly with respect to improvement of the teaching function.

The issues associated with the doctorate as preparation for university professors are no nearer resolution today than they were a half century ago. It would be more productive to affirm the boundaries of the requisite advanced education by identifying the components of preparation that are necessary and then to decide upon the appropriate symbol which will attest to evidence of satisfaction of the requisite components.

We have attempted an aerial view of social work education as an enterprise within the context of both the profession it serves and the university base from which it operates. Imperatives from the profession and issues in university teaching that are pertinent to social work education as well as to education in other disciplines and professions have been noted. We turn now to the social work educator who is the immediate object of our concern.

PART TWO

The Social Work Educator

Four Components of Preparation For the Social Work Teacher

What is a good teacher? Each level within the education hierarchy—the administrator, the teacher, the student—has an idealized model, a teacher who is creative, contributing, inspiring. Deans want these qualities in their faculties; teachers want to have them; and students look for them. As one new teacher at a workshop put it: he wants to become a good teacher, to be creative and make his contribution, but he is not ready to accept the model that he sees around him. (While there is some hyperbole in his last phrase, is not its essential truth, in fact, the rationale for the existence of the Project?)

The centrality of questions about good teachers and good teaching has been evident throughout. Whether in the meetings of the Project's Advisory Committee, in the workshops of new teachers and of administrative officials of the schools, or in interviews with educational leaders, the discussions inexorably led to consideration of these pivotal concepts. The issues were joined and sharpened only as these were examined.

There must be clarity about the kind of teacher to be developed in order to give direction to a program of faculty development. What are the demands of his total range of responsibilities? What should he know and what should he be able to do? It is appropriate therefore to review the extant models and to identify the qualities for which to strive. Then it will be possible to suggest preparations designed to achieve them.

THE SCHOLAR AND THE SCHOLARLY
PROFESSIONAL

There is no dearth of truly inspiring descriptions of good teaching. Each generation in the history of man has known good teachers and described their qualities so that others might aspire to emulate them. All too frequently, each generation has known poor teaching. Definitions of a good teacher are often lofty descriptions of an ideal, but an operational definition has continued to be elusive. Some have approached the question by describing *attributes* of a good *teacher,* others the *qualities* of good *teaching;* some probe for the essence of creativity. Some are confident that the definition of good teaching will emerge as we gain greater understanding of good learning. Perhaps a good teacher does more than good teaching. Gardner is reassuring when he observes that "the mercurial spirit of great teaching and great scholarship cannot be organized, rationalized, delegated, or processed."[1] Without presuming to review all that has been said about good teachers and good teaching, we should note briefly a few sources which may be representative of the current state of the question before adjusting the focus on the social work teacher.

Diekhoff conceives of "scholar teachers" who may be "productive scholars" and others who may be "productive teachers":

> If his love of learning results in the continuing increase of [his own] knowledge, that is as it should be. If it leads him to increase not only his own but also the world's knowledge, he is what we call a "productive scholar." If his love of learning leads him to share his knowledge and his love of it with others, we may call him a "productive teacher."

> It is commonplace to regard productive scholarship and productive teaching as mutually exclusive accomplishments, perhaps no product of the graduate school is more likely to be an effective college teacher than the productive scholar, not because "productive scholarship" is a condition of good teaching but because love of learning is a condition of both scholarship and teaching. The real enthusiast for knowledge will pursue it and will communicate it, in books and articles or in the classroom, or by both means.

> Of course there are scholars who do not publish. We have called them "productive teachers." They may be the best teachers

---

[1] John Gardner, *Self-Renewal: The Individual and the Innovative Society* (New York: Harper and Row, 1963), p. 82.

we have. But failure to publish is not what makes them good teachers, and it does not follow that a faculty member is a good teacher because he does not publish. He is not likely to be a good teacher unless he shares the enthusiasm for knowledge of the productive scholar.[2]

Lamenting what he observes to be a decline in the role of the teacher-scholar for whom there is "less and less prestige," Reisman describes him as

> . . . a person who regards himself as a reflective and civilized student of his subject without feeling he must do extensive research in it. There never were many such people on the American academic scene, and the majority of professors . . . who claimed to be scholars were either ham actors, or pedants, or both. But the *scholar* is not . . . part of an academic production line so much as the man who reads and reflects and enjoys learning and in the continuing debate on research versus teaching, this particular species tends to drop from view.[3]

Apparently, with the same model in mind, Brown lists as the attributes of the creative teacher-scholar: an inquiring mind, the powers of analysis and accumulation, intuition, self-discipline, and a tendency toward perfectionism. The last attribute may be expected to be associated with tendencies to introspection and to resistance to external authority.[4]

In an incisive critique of American higher education, Sanford uses an anthropological frame of reference to classify teachers. For example, the teacher as "shaman" may be "vain or exhibitionistic . . . [or] withdrawn, diffident, even humble. Essentially, however, he keeps the audience's attention focused on himself. He invites us to observe the personality in its encounter with the subject matter. . . . When this orientation is combined with unusual gifts, we have a charismatic teacher . . . marked by power, energy, and commitment." The teacher as priest "stresses not his personal virtues, but his membership in a powerful or admirable collectivity, e.g., physics, psychoanalysis, classical scholarship. . . . [He] says: 'I am valuable for what I belong to. I represent and personify a collective identity.' " A third type is classified

---

[2] Diekhoff, *The Domain of the Faculty, op. cit.,* pp. 52-53.

[3] David Reisman, "Alterations in Institutional Attitudes and Behavior," in Logan Wilson, ed., *Emerging Patterns in American Higher Education,* (Washington, D. C.: American Council on Education, 1965), p. 68.

[4] J. Douglas Brown, "The Development of Creative Teacher-Scholars," *Daedalus,* Summer, 1965, pp. 615-631.

51

as "mystic healer" who is "altruistic," who "concentrates neither on himself, nor on the subject matter, nor the discipline, but on the student saying 'I will help you become what you are.' . . . [He] keeps his own achievement and personality secondary; he works to help the student find what is best and most essential within himself."[5]

Goheen sharpens the concept that it is an attribute of the good teacher to focus upon the learner and to interact with him:

> Each great teacher has his own unique way. Yet, more often than not, two particular attributes will be found in the successful teacher. One is an ability to awaken and stimulate delight in the use of the mind. The second is attention to the effort to do so, together with a belief in its value to the student *in his own right*. . . .
>
> There is another role that the good teacher plays. He is interpreter in the house of learning. Now, the word interpret has several connotations: to explain—to construe. All involve the making of a connection. This is what the teacher does. He puts the student *in connection* with the problem at hand and leads him to seek and press an engagement with it.[6]

As we turn to the teacher in professional education, we will see some of the qualities of the model of the academic scholar, sometimes in the same terms, sometimes recast.

The Scholarly Professional—These attributes are sharpened, and additional ones are introduced by the unique character of professional education. Thus, the teaching function in legal education according to Freund must be reflective of the following formulation of objectives:

> . . . the transitoriness of a large part of the informational content has forced the schools to a sharper appreciation of what they have always professed, that their mission is not to produce lawyers, but minds trained for law. More specifically, there is an intensified effort to explore fields of law by sinking shafts rather than covering the ground. More basically there is encouragement to seek for common or unifying principles that will help consolidate and simplify. . . .[7]

Or, in nursing education, "the single purpose . . . is to prepare professional nurse practitioners who can command a growing body of

---

[5] Nevitt Sanford, *The American College* (New York: John Wiley and Sons, 1962), pp. 407-412.

[6] Robert F. Goheen, *op. cit.*, p. 177.

[7] Paul A. Freund, "The Legal Profession," *Daedalus*, (Fall, 1963), p. 698.

knowledge in their nursing practice, clinical care, and services and are able to share, with the physicians and members of the allied professions, a greater responsibility for the welfare of patients and the health of families."[8]

To provide a "perspective on teaching-scholarship" in *teacher education,* Sratemeyer outlines the following dimensions: understanding the power of knowledge to open doors; having insight into significant relationships among ideas, phenomena, and events; differentiating between intensive and extensive study, between awareness as contrasted with understanding-in-depth of situations of human importance. But "to use knowledge intelligently requires more knowing. . . . [It] means zeal for constructive action based on meaningful *inter-relating of thinking, feeling, and behaving.* The relationship between intention and action, insight and courage, vision and drive are factors vital to scholarship today, and mandatory in teaching-scholarship." She adds as a "unique professional dimension" scholarship that includes "having insight into helping others—individuals and groups—develop competence and genuine interest in learning. This characteristic distinguishes teaching-scholarship from that of other professionals."[9]

The teacher-scholar "has the ability to bring personal meaning to the world of ideas. He possesses his own unique framework, he has his own good reasons for learning what he decides to learn. . . . He is able to select and build upon significant ideas, observe relationships and distinguish essential matters from irrelevant and incidental ones."[10]

THE SOCIAL WORK TEACHER

Although the social work curriculum (see Chapter I) aims at integration of its subject areas, each area has its own characteristics. In turn, faculty members may become identified with one or another of the curricular areas. Ideally each will not only see the relationship of his area to the whole but help the student see the mutual interrelationships of the social work methods, social-psychological, social welfare

---

[8] Frances Reiter, "The Generic Program of the Graduate School of Nursing of the New York Medical College," in *Nursing Education—Creative, Continuing, Experimental,* papers presented at the Twentieth Conference of the Council of Member Agencies of the Department of Baccalaureate and Higher Degree Programs (New York: National League for Nursing, 1966), p. 11.

[9] Florence B. Stratemeyer, *op. cit.,* pp. 23-41.

[10] Dean Corrigan, "The Personal Dimension in the Education of American Teachers," paper prepared for the conference honoring Florence B. Stratemeyer, French Lick, Indiana, June 10-12, 1965.

policy, and research sequences. The question remains, however, whether differential preparation and experience is appropriate or whether there should be one typology.

Boehm conjectures about alternative patterns, patterns analogous to those developing in other professional schools.

> Should social work faculty members be engaged in teaching what may in time become the basic social work sciences, as well as social work values and the social work methods, or should different faculty personnel be employed for these two components of the curriculum? Certainly a case could be made for either pattern.
>
> . . . Conceivably two sets of social work faculty might be developed, both recruited from social work, with one group teaching in the foundation component, and the other group in the methods components of the curriculum.[11]

He suggests two additional possible patterns: "that social work personnel teach the methods courses, and that the basic social science areas be taught by faculty recruited from those fields . . ."; or, that "there be clinical teachers who would collaborate in their clinical teaching with scientific personnel drawn partly from social work and partly from the underlying social and biological sciences."

Jennings found four current types of social work faculty, models partly synthesized from the ideal types described in the general literature of higher education. The four types are: the teacher-social worker; the academic scholar; the research-consultant; and the professor-administrant.[12]

The goals of the social work curriculum place a high level of expectation on the educator.

> Educators [for the profession] endeavor to develop a high level of competence for immediate use. . . . It is a characteristic of professional education that it teaches a body of principles and concepts for differential use. It should foster . . . the inclination to understand these principles beyond the confines of the profession. In short, it endeavors to set in operation a learning process that will endure and wax strong throughout the years of professional activity.
>
> Thus professional education trains for professional self-

---

[11] Werner W. Boehm, ed., *Objectives of the Social Work Curriculum*, Vol. 1, Social Work Curriculum Study (New York: Council on Social Work Education, 1959), pp. 214-215.

[12] Jennings, *op. cit.*, pp. 52-53.

dependence. There cannot be an admixture of limited goals and high goals. . . .[13]

Towle partializes these high goals into five categories of aims

To develop in students the capacity to think critically and analytically and to synthesize and to generalize. . . .

To develop feelings and attitudes that will make it possible for the student to think and act appropriately. . . .

To develop a capacity for establishing and sustaining purposeful working relationships. . . .

To develop social consciousness and social conscience . . . to which are subsidiary a critical, rather than worshipful, attitude toward the profession's rationale and instruments . . . a constructively critical attitude both toward society's response to the profession and toward the profession's principles and instruments. . . .

To develop an orientation to the place of the profession in the society in which it operates. . . .[14]

"The creation of a graduate school atmosphere in which students could take the initiative and responsibility for their own education" is a "central guiding concept" which Somers suggests for social work teaching.[15]

As though in response to the challenge of these aims, Smalley has answered the question "What are we looking for in social work educators?" by first listing five desirable attributes for *all teachers in graduate schools:* an "interesting" self in lively possession of its own uniqueness as an individual; scholarly qualities; skill in teaching and commitment to teaching; interest, motivation and capacity for continuing the development of himself as a teacher; and capacity to function as a member of a faculty—to develop his own knowledge and his own teaching skill, to make his own contribution as an individual but as part of a whole working toward a shared and common purpose.

For *social work* faculty, she adds: identification with the profession for which the school is preparing; knowledge of range and depth with-

---

[13] Charlotte Towle, *The Learner in Education for the Professions* (Chicago: University of Chicago Press, 1954), pp. 5-6.

[14] *Ibid.,* pp. 6-17.

[15] Mary Louise Somers, "Toward the Improvement of Social Work Teaching Methods and Materials," *Social Work Education Reporter,* XIV:4 (December, 1966), p. 28ff. Dr. Somers cites Milton J. Horowitz, *Educating Tomorrow's Doctors* (New York: Appleton Century Crofts, 1964), for the quotation.

in a particular core subject area or sequence; commitment to the use and continuing development of skill in the generic principles of social work method. . . .[16]

Identifying "an ability to create the conditions in which learning takes place" as an essential quality of skill in teaching for social work, Younghusband asserts:

> Any fruitful educational institution is a society in which students and teachers are both learning together.
>
> It is such institutions which make education a continuing process of growth in succeeding years. This level of education in turn produces some people who always want to learn more, to use old knowledge as a springboard for new knowledge, who are eternally curious . . ., who begin to know what are the right questions to ask and the way to search for answers, who are able to remain flexible, humble, imaginative, and capable of surprise. This is indeed to have the intellectual integrity which in due time may lead to wisdom.[17]

Finally, since "the process of discovering knowledge, not the acquiring of authorized information" must be one of the outcomes of social work education, "we must enable our students to learn the process of learning in order to contribute effectively, not merely to survive. . . ."[18]

The listing of aims and the formulation of categories of attributes are a useful beginning. But it is essential to take the next, more difficult step before proposing how these attributes are to be achieved. It is necessary to be precise about *what the social work educator must know* and *how much*, and *what he must be able to do* and *how well*. (The reader may agree with our conclusion that the continuing debates about preparation for teaching in higher education, to which we have referred, have been unresolved precisely because of the surprising lack of attention given to this essential intermediate step.)

Two sets of attributes are noted but need no further discussion here. The first set deals with the personal, charismatic qualities, e.g., enthusiasm, individuality, "personality," magnetism. They may be considera-

---

[16] Ruth E. Smalley, "The Attributes of a Social Work Educator," *Social Work Education Reporter*, 13:2 (June, 1965), p. 10ff.

[17] Dame Eileen L. Younghusband, "Developing the Faculty: The Opportunities and Demands of Teaching," paper delivered to the XIIIth International Congress of Schools of Social Work, Washington, D. C., August 31-September 3, 1966, pp. 5-6.

[18] William H. Barber, "Keynote Address," in *Remaking the World of the Career Teacher* (Washington, D. C.: National Education Association of the United States, 1966), pp. 35-36.

tions in choosing a faculty career or in being selected for one, but they are possibly end products of a depth of knowing and wisdom about which we are not sufficiently knowledgeable,[19] and therefore are not included as a component of preparation. Similarly, the value system that a social work educator brings to his university calling must be appropriate and beyond question. When more is known about how professional values are acquired and strengthened, these may well be included as a component of preparation. For the time being, a high degree of assurance is to be found in the fact that the social worker brings with him a system of professional values congruent with those of the professional educator. At any rate, the questions of "how much" of professional values and "for whom" do not require discussion; the answers are obvious.

There are, however, four components other than the charismatic and values components which constitute the preparatory equipment of the social work teacher. The four components are 1) the subject matter areas of social work and social welfare, 2) the practice of social work, 3) research in social work and social work education, and 4) teaching. These categories have been somewhat arbitrarily formulated for convenience of exposition.

Each of the component areas must further be partialized. There are degrees of knowledge—knowledge about an area of subject matter, knowledge in depth, and knowledge for use. Upon the latter, choices based on values are made, and priorities are set. There is wisdom, which is knowledge tested in the crucible of experience. Each component has analogous levels. There is knowledge about practice, skill in practice (with its own several levels), and practice wisdom. One can be a sophisticated consumer of research, he can understand research methodology, or he may have research skill. The teaching component, similarly, has knowledge and attitudinal ingredients as well as skill. Professional wisdom is therefore a blending of knowledge, values, and skills not confined to one area of subject matter. The partialization which follows, as an intermediate stop for purposes of description, admittedly does violence to the organic quality of the living essence of the great teacher.

The Subject Matter Component

The teaching-learning transaction cannot be conceived of as taking place with inadequate currency in subject matter. The objectives of

---

[19] See, for example, *Daedalus* (Summer, 1965), especially articles by David Hawkins, "The Informed Vision," pp. 538-52, and Jerome Kagan, "Personality and the Learning Process," pp. 553-563.

professional education deal with intellectual as well as attitudinal and skill outcomes. There can be no debate about the place of knowledge in the equipment of the educator. No one responsibly fails to value the subject matter component.

It is also easy to agree that social work knowledge is increasing in our day at an unmanageable pace and is no longer to be encompassed even by the rare intellect, let alone by most. The unanswered questions then become *what* knowledge, as well as *how much,* and for *whom?* On this matter, we come face to face with the same issues, such as breadth vs. depth, as are agitating education for all disciplines and professions. What stance can we take about these questions within our own house?

The wisdom and the conceptualization needed to help the learner is not necessarily acquired exclusively during a period of practice after the masters degree has been earned. Data to support this statement have been provided by new teachers.[20] Since new teachers come to their new career positions by different routes, they identify this need in varying terms. For example, some identify the problem as "conceptual teaching." Another puts it directly as "many social science concepts have been added. . . ." (As the converse, those who recently received doctorates, describe difficulty with "decisions about level appropriate" for master's degree students after their own doctoral study. However, this is a teaching component problem, and is discussed later.)

Bruner's concept of the "structure of subject matter" is useful at this juncture:

> In order for a person to be able to recognize the applicability or inapplicability of an idea to a new situation and to broaden his learning thereby, he must have clearly in mind the general nature of the phenomenon with which he is dealing. The more fundamental or basic is the idea . . . the greater will be its breadth of applicability to new problems.[21]

No argument can be made that the learnings testified to by the masters degree in social work in themselves provide the degree of substantive breadth and depth which is called upon by one who would teach to that program's objectives.

Professional education, to be truly professional, must be based upon a theoretical system of knowledge, as well as attitudes and

---

[20] New teachers are those who responded to the Survey of New Faculty, or those who participated in the Berkeley Institute, both described in the Introduction. Deans who were interviewed also spoke strongly to this point.

[21] Jerome S. Bruner, *The Process of Education* (Cambridge: Harvard University Press, 1962), p. 18.

values. . . . This becomes the foundation for education within the profession. It does not consist of an inventory of practice and techniques. This is why professional educators became increasingly responsible for the theoretical clarification and definition of what is "generic" in our practice. It was this recognition . . . which . . . made this practice teachable as a profession. The subject matter of the profession must assume a transformation which makes it conform to basic requirements of professional education.[22]

The inevitable conclusion is that whether the new faculty member is to meet classroom or field responsibilities, or whether he comes with little or a great deal of experience in practice, he will be handicapped in measuring up to expectations without additional formal substantive education. He will need it to find an effective, creative, and satisfying role for himself on a social work faculty, either for the present or the future. The depth of content will depend upon the area of specialization.

This conclusion does not to any degree imply disrespect for current senior faculty who may not have had formal advanced education. They have, in fact, been among the pioneers and the creators of the new knowledge which now requires additional study by the younger generations.

How much and for whom are questions that are best answered by recognizing that all faculty cannot be expected to be equally prepared in all areas of content. Depth or specialization is inevitable and desirable. Two points are being postulated here: field instructors and teachers of practice need advanced substantive content as well as do teachers in other subject areas. This content cannot currently be acquired either at the masters level or as practice wisdom alone.

The Practice Component[23]

Historically, most social work educators came directly from many years of practice, and the practice component has been taken for granted as basic to the preparation of social work educators. (The conviction in social work education about the importance of this component may, in fact, be one of its contributions to the design for education in other professions.) Despite the accomplishments within social work education, the practice-before-teaching dictum has been re-

---

[22] Jennings, op. cit., p. 24.

[23] This component is referred to as "clinical" in several of the professions, especially those dealing with dysfunction and pathology. In social work, some associate clinical with casework practice rather than group work or community organization.

opened for questioning on the current scene. Some of the questioning may be the result of the pressure for more teachers, and schools have been forced to recruit individuals with very few years of practice experience. The economic consideration should not be discounted; after a few years of experience, the type of social worker who attracts the attention of a school as a potential recruit will have advanced in salary to a point which cannot readily be matched by university salaries for the lower ranks.

The critical question remains how much of the practice component in the preparation for which faculty? Here we find a myriad of positions. One position holds strongly that most, if not all, faculty in education for social work must have a clinical qualification, i.e., an MSW degree and experience in practice. Erudite and otherwise qualified academicians may be able to absorb an approximation of practice sophistication, but it is at best a compromise. Another position partializes, and while it values the practice-oriented professor, agrees that he is not essential in some areas of curriculum. Surely the teachers in the "Social Work Methods" sequences must have had practice experience, but the scientist, from the academic disciplines which now comprise social work knowledge, has major contributions to make, even without a clinical identification.

As has already been noted, one prediction is that the inevitable curriculum of the future will de-emphasize clinical experience, at the same time as another sees the emergence of the clinical professor who does his clinical teaching in educational centers, similar to the teaching hospital in medical and nursing education. On the current scene we are witnessing *de facto* applications of each of these positions. Surely it is not our prerogative to foreclose on these developments; none of these positions will (or should) be written off for the foreseeable future. The essential conclusion is that the practice component must be included in planning for the preparation of a not inconsiderable number of the social work educators who will be needed in the future as in the present.

There is currently no evidence about how much practice experience is optimum as a pre-service requirement before beginning teaching. Most of the schools currently induct and will continue to induct new faculty with a range of practice experience. They use different rationales. One point of view notes that the two years of experience in field work which is accounted for at the master's level of professional education should not be discounted. Another point of view is based on the belief that clinical experience can appropriately be allocated to the in-service period of faculty development. At any rate, here lies an opportunity, indeed an imperative, to design carefully a study of the experiences of the schools, in which innovations in the provision of amount and timing of practice experience are variables subject to experimental testing.

The Research Component

There is a desperate need for research skill and significant research activity if social work schools are to fulfill their mission for the field and take their appropriate place in the university community. Unfortunately, this postulate is too often presented in a manner which appears either to deny the importance of other educational functions, or to claim that research skill is inclusive of any of the other skills. Again, we must ask: how much research and for whom?

We do not know whether good practitioners can be good researchers or whether good researchers can be good practitioners; whether the skills are independent, whether they complement or crowd each other. The answer may depend on the kind of research one has in mind.

In the light of the pressing needs for research activity and a research orientation in the field, the following observation has implications for our consideration of the research component for faculty. Arguing the need for research orientation in residencies in psychiatry, a working paper of the Group for the Advancement of Psychiatry observes that:

> If those responsible for training are engaged in research, residents will tend to identify with them and adopt their attitudes. A recent study of the careers of psychiatrists who had their residency in a large hospital showed that the career choices were in part determined by the hospital setting, but most importantly by their teachers. At one time there was an exceptionally strong research interest in the hospital; subsequently, the percentage of residents who became involved in research doubled.[24]

This is a vulnerable point in social work education, as noted by Regensburg in a review of three studies about the career aspirations and choices of social workers, namely *the very small percentage in all three studies who expressed an interest in research.*[25]

The GAP manuscript cited above, noting that "ideally, the psychiat-

---

[24] Unpublished paper circulated among members of the GAP in 1966.

[25] Regensburg, "Recruitment to Post-Master's Programs . . . " *op. cit.* The three studies are (1) a survey in 1962 of over 2000 students then in their second year of the masters program to learn of their interest in advanced education; (2) a survey by Kidneigh and Crane of the highest ranking students who had obtained their masters degrees in 1961-1964; and (3) a survey in 1964 by French of students who had left school in 1957.

ric teacher should be skilled in diagnosing and treating patients, in communicating his knowledge to residents, and in conducting research," adds that "few will be able to carry on all of these activities with equal effectiveness."

Schools of social work will continue to need both gifted practitioner-teachers and also faculty who are imaginative and skilled researchers. In other words, there is a need for a range of research skills within a faculty; research skill is no more an absolute quality than is any of the other components. Some members of a faculty are expected to be able to initiate major research projects of their own, others to teach research to their students. However, even those who teach in curricular areas other than research, will need basic research sophistication if they are to fulfill the expectations set for them by the social work curriculum for educating practitioners:

> The advancement of learning demands research, ingrained as an attitude of mind in all members and developed as a special skill in some. A research approach to the solution of a problem enables the practitioner to learn through experience and to convey what he learns. Certain knowledge of research and disciplined thinking will make for intelligent interpretation and use of the work of those who are specifically engaged in it. The development within a profession of its own research both improves its service and bespeaks the maturation of the field of endeavor. Sound research proceeds from and contributes to sound practice.[26]

Following through on this line of reasoning, all faculty will in the future need basic research skill and sophistication beyond that attained at the master's level. All will be consumers of research. All will participate in research as teachers, in action-research. The research specialists, the initiators and the independent researchers, will obviously need skill of a much different order.

Neither the basic nor the more advanced levels of knowledge and skill in research, of the quality needed for productive performance by a faculty member, has been assured at the masters level in the past, nor have "third year" programs stressed this objective. Very few individuals acquire research skill exclusively in agency work. A few schools are currently introducing a research specialization at the masters level (innovations approved by CSWE through its accrediting process) for a small number of students who come with social agency experience, with social work practice skill, a beginning knowledge of research methodology, and with a manifest interest in social work re-

---

[26] Towle, *op. cit.,* p. 6.

search as a career objective. It is too early to know what the level of research attainment will be. At any rate, the number of future teachers coming through this route is not likely to be large. The argument clearly leads to the conclusion that the several levels of research skill will need to be acquired through educational programs beyond the masters.

In addition to the research courses in advanced and doctoral programs, the dissertation is the traditional means by which research skill is acquired and demonstrated. If it is under attack in certain quarters, it is either because it sometimes does not achieve functionally the research objective, or more frequently because objectives are claimed for the dissertation with which it should not be burdened. It is, probably an effective means for achieving some research objectives, but *it does not differentiate between objectives for the several levels of research skill needed by the schools.* We take no position about whether it is the only means, or the best means. More important is the fact that it does not deal with the other component objectives of advanced education.

The Teaching Component

The literature is replete with inspirational descriptions of the good teacher.[27] The new teacher, eager to fulfill his calling, may know about the attributes, he may be inspired by the exhortations to want to be a good teacher, but they cannot in themselves make him one. They do not tell him what to do so that these can also be *his* attributes.

Granted that the faculty member is adequately prepared with respect to the amount and depth of knowledge which he has made his own, with practice wisdom for making vital that knowledge, and with research sophistication which makes knowledge and wisdom progressive, explorative and expanding. He must also have the ability to make these resources—which *he* possesses available for use by his students. It is difficult to find a term to delineate this ability. As has been noted in the previous chapter, some see teaching as essentially an art, and deny that it can be learned. Others are confident that it can, that the ability to teach is both teachable and learnable. They point to the tremendous accretion of understanding about the teacher-learner transaction, an understanding whose frontier is constantly being expanded. Some of this group therefore call it a science, while others who also see teach-

---

27 See Helen Harris Perlman, ". . . And Gladly Teach," *Journal of Education for Social Work*, Vol. 3, No. 1 (Spring, 1967) pp. 41-51. In this moving tribute to Charlotte Towle, who was a member of the Project's Advisory Committee when she died, Mrs. Perlman documents the nature of the blended quality of skill and humanity which is teaching.

ing ability based on a growing body of knowledge are reluctant to attach the scientific label to it. Still others hyphenate both art *and* science. For our purposes, however, the concept encompasses much more than mechanics or technical skills. It refers to an ability built upon: (1) philosophical foundations, i.e., the purposes and issues of educational thought, (2) psychological foundations, i.e., how the learner learns,[28] and (3) knowledge and skill in communication, in the organization of curriculum, and in the appropriate use of a range of teaching-learning methodologies. Too often taken for granted, but explicitly to be subsumed under these broad formulations of foundations are, for example: the making of perceptive choices among many worthy objectives; sensitivity to the strengths, the special problems, the styles of learning of the adult learner; and the development of a style for teaching which has integrity for each individual, who in turn must learn to work with his colleagues toward the integration of the whole curriculum.

But we have already begged part of the question, for by this definition we deny that subject matter enthusiasm and expertise in the teacher is self-igniting, able to provide and sustain its own thrust. Wise puts it as a question:

> Does the content of Ph.D. study in a discipline provide a sufficient basis for the prospective teacher to select subject matter appropriate to the courses he will teach, and does it prepare him for the intelligent exercise of his responsibilities as a member of a college faculty which must make decisions about both purposes and procedures. . . . [29]

Burns states the issue sharply, as follows:

> Even for those who obtain the doctorate, such advanced study is in most cases only a partial preparation for faculty participation. Equipped with new content, with an increased ability to manage new knowledge, with the methodology of research, the new doctor emerging from an advanced program has not of necessity had any experience or participation or education in *what is involved in the*

---

[28] The learner in our context is an adult. It is perhaps *obiter dictum* to point out that there is a growing body of knowledge based on research which deals specifically with adult learners. The psychological foundations for use by the teacher in the education of professionals include, as well, borrowing and modifying, as necessary for his purposes, the already extensive body of "pedagogical" knowledge developed for education of the young.

[29] W. Max Wise, "Who Teaches the Teachers?", *Improving College Teaching, op. cit.,* p. 79.

organization of content for consumption by others, or in the methodology of conveying it.[30]

Nearly a generation has passed since Reynolds

> . . . advanced the point of view that learning involves the whole person, and that it has important emotional and social as well as intellectual motivations. If this is true, the process of learning can only be understood in the light of all the sciences, biological, psychological and social, which are concerned with the dynamics of the adaptation of human beings to their physical and social world.[31]

It is a "synthesis of all these sciences" which constitutes the educational foundations for teaching.

That the importance of this component is increasingly being recognized in higher education in general, and in education for other professions, has been noted in the previous chapter. There has been a parallel growing concern about the lack of attention to provision for this component in the preparation of social work educators. The recommendations of the Subcommittee on Preparation of Teachers of the CSWE Advisory Committee on Advanced Education, has already been mentioned. Noting the demands set by the current curriculum policy for social work education, Witte has observed:

> But how we shall teach it, *why* we shall teach it in one way rather than another, and which changes we hope to bring about in those whom we are teaching in preparation for their entry into the profession—all these are questions to which the answers are far less clear. Yet they are insistent questions which must be answered if we are to teach effectively.[32]

The question about how much teaching ability can best be answered by analyzing needs as they are formulated by new teachers and by

---

[30] Mary E. Burns, "Advanced Curriculum and the Faculty Manpower Problem," paper presented at the Annual Program Meeting, Council on Social Work Education, New York, January 26, 1966, p. 5. See also Lewis Leary, "The Scholar as Teacher," *op. cit.*, who calls the Ph.D. a "reminder that the aim of education is knowledge and of teaching the communication of knowledge."

[31] Bertha Capen Reynolds, *Learning and Teaching in the Practice of Social Work* (New York: Rinehart and Company, 1942), p. 62.

[32] Ernest F. Witte in "Foreword" to the *Teacher's Compendium*, Marguerite V. Pohek, ed. (New York: Council on Social Work Education, 1963), p. v. There has been an unexpectedly great market for the modest attempt made in the *Compendium* to present introductory content for developing teaching ability, which can be explained as an indicator of widespread recognition of the need.

recent students at the receiving end of both good and poor teaching.

Responses to the survey of the present Project indicate that new teachers have differential needs, depending upon whether they come from practice or from advanced study, although most of the latter have also been practitioners, supervisors, or administrators. They need help with setting course objectives, designing courses, planning individual class sessions, and articulating content of their course with the rest of the curriculum. They seek for clarification of objectives, suggested by the following excerpts from their responses:

... education, not casework thinking
... transformation and assimilation of practice content to classroom
... from graduate school to professional school emphases

They list problems of appropriate role, which relate both to clarity of objectives as well as to methodologies:

... not social work helper
... teacher versus social worker
... transformation to role of faculty advisor

Not surprisingly, there is a consistent request for help with teaching methodologies and specific techniques:

... use of lecture and class discussion
... role playing
... new techniques
... assignment of reading
... use of evaluative tools

Students who had just completed the two years of graduate study were asked in the group interview conducted by Dr. Schwartz to describe what in their recently completed encounter with teachers had helped and what had militated against their learning. In addition to documenting ideas about good teaching with which there is probably widespread agreement, and dividing on issues similar to those which divide many educators, the students presented some insights not likely to originate with the educators.

They took it for granted that the teacher "knew his content"—his position on the faculty of the school stipulated to this component. If he did no know specific facts, that in itself was not disconcerting. In fact, students were ready to be less demanding of a new teacher, and to bide with him in his initial floundering. True, they said, many teachers "steeped in their material" create an interest and powerful enthusiasm by their knowing, but others, equally knowledgeable, "somehow, just don't come through." Some students were upset when, with their admitted naivete about practice, too much burden was put on them to use the theoretical material, to see the implications for practice. A few questioned the clinical wisdom of the teacher when his orientation to practice differed from the reality as the student knew it.

But most important, the students were concerned with a quality which they called "honesty" and which has different forms of expression operationally. When a basic honesty comes through, it frees the student to think and to work. He is motivated. However, as an example of what happens when this quality is absent: the teacher asks members of the class for their opinions, "but you don't dare speak up, you'll be exposed"; or "when he asks for discussion but if you don't say what he expects, he cuts off the discussion." Finally, students ask: "Why do so many teachers need (seek, beg for) approval from the class? As good practitioners, they don't have the same need for approval from their clients—and they are supposed to be teaching that to us."[33]

The formulations of the new teachers and of the students differ, but the message is the same: a good practitioner may become a good teacher, but he is not a good teacher merely by virtue of the fact that he has been a good practitioner. The orientations, the skills, the "know-how" are different. Although social work practice and teaching should have and do have clearly differentiated purposes and methods, certain skills are associated with all professional behavior. The transfer of skills in problem solving or in planning, for example, is readily accomplished. That there is a generic base in the social work and the educational processes should not be minimized.

The reader may have noted that in the itemization of problems above, particulalry as listed by the new teachers, understanding the learner was not included. This should not be surprising, since social work practice is also based upon psychological foundations. The practitioner-turned-teacher has a base available to him and he may be expected to call upon pertinent knowledge and competence he has acquired as a social worker. "In her attempts to orient educational methods to the dynamics of behavior, I believe that the social casework educator has arrived at some sound methodology."[34] (Some of us feel, in fact, that the conscientious use of this body of knowledge and experience from social work practice, transferred appropriately to educational purposes, has enriched, and can further enrich, general educational theory and practice.) The person coming to teaching with skill in

---

[33] An abstract of the group interview will be found in Appendix VI.
[34] Towle, *op. cit.,* p. xvii.

social work practice has assets which he can claim for his educational role. This gives him an advantage over other prospective university professors.

There has unfortunately been some confusion about what part of social work competence is transferable to educational purposes, which Towle pinpoints:

> Adaptation of casework learning to education has also implied a shift from studying and helping individuals engulfed by a life-situation beyond their integrative capacity to studying individuals with relatively high integrative capacity in a goal-striving situation. In those instances where the goal has been appropriate in terms of the student's abilities and disposition, the situation has afforded bountiful opportunity for the nurture of the ego for growth. The problem has been that of selecting, pacing and timing the opportunities with reference to developmental norms.[35]

Social workers turned educators know deep "in their bones" the *importance* of the professional relationship which fuels the process in social work helping. They also know *how to use* the relationship between the professional self and the client. They will therefore recognize the same concept, as it has been developed for the educational process as useful:

> Just as we have had to shift our understanding of the learning process from the process to the learner, so we are now discovering the understanding of teaching is not to be found in methods but in the teacher. The teacher is first and foremost a person, a self. He is not a library, not a machine, not a disseminator of knowledge. He is a human being interacting with other human beings in a very human process. Learning to teach is not a question of learning to *do* something; it is a matter of learning to be *something*.[36]

Although referring to the professional social worker, Schwartz has given precision to the concept of interaction and relationship which is also applicable in the learning process:

> From our experience we can testify that there are "knowers," who cannot help anybody, and there are "feelers," who cannot put their feelings to use in the service of people. Ultimately, both cognition

---

[35] *Ibid.*

[36] Arthur W. Combs, "Teachers Too Are Individuals," *The Self in Growth, Teaching and Learning*, Don E. Hamachek, ed. (Englewood Cliffs, N. J.: Prentice-Hall, 1965), p. 458.

and affect must be transmuted into ways of listening and responding, and it is these operations, consistently reproduced, that represent the educational payoff in any profession.[37]

Looking back on more than three decades of teaching, Wessel con-
templates "a very old and familiar conflict of values in which the
teacher becomes entangled."

> It is the controversy over the relative value of man's two inescap-
> able motives—the practical and the contemplative. Which is more
> noble—to do or to think? . . . to act (to teach) or to contemplate
> (to search for and discover new knowledge).

For herself, she concludes:

> Those of us who teach where both motives are thus valued, who
> are privileged to work in this "perfection of unity" are blessed,
> indeed . . .

> I can tell you that it is purest joy to feel yourself kindling into
> being the students' intellectual interests, liberating their minds to
> become engaged in new discovery of themselves and their world;
> and liberating their feelings, towards finding fresh and deeper
> insights.

> It is also pure aesthetic pleasure to feel yourself, each time,
> re-creating and re-inventing the whole process and content, the
> whole drama, in teaching a class, no matter how many times you
> have taught the course before.[38]

At the first meeting of the Advisory Committee for the present Project the following statements for which there was high consensus were
formulated:

> The teacher organizes—he is responsible for organizing experi-
> ences so that the *student* can become activaetd.

> The teacher is *not* a lecturer with primary responsibility for
> *transmitting* content which he has mastered to the student.

> He clarifies learning goals . . . helps students with learning
> goals, not with acquiring content.

---

[37] William Schwartz, "The Classroom Teaching of Social Work with Groups: Some
Central Problems," *A Conceptual Framework for the Teaching of the Social Group
Work Method in the Classroom* (New York: Council on Social Work Education,
1964) p. 6.
[38] Rosa Wessel, "Response," on receiving award on the occasion of her retirement,
April 29, 1966. (Mimeographed.)

The teacher *unleashes* the capacities of the student. The student must do the "digging," the teacher helping him find the places to "dig."

The teacher differentiates between the situation where he is needed and the one where the student should be left on his own.

The Advisory Committee also urged that in thinking about good teaching, room be allowed for the master teacher, the great *doctor*, the unusual and unique teacher with his own style, which he may not have learned and which may not be replicable by anyone else. Echoing this plea, Combs reminds us that "teachers are unique human beings. . . . No good teacher is like any other. The good teacher is no carbon copy. He is an individual who has learned to use his particular self in effective and efficient ways. . . . Every good teacher will necessarily behave in ways that are individual and unique."[39] Perlman defines teaching as having essentially two components, namely, the organization of knowledge, and method—*for style*.[40] These positions are a far cry from the placebo that "good teachers are born, not made."

We have not differentiated, in this discussion of the need for ability to teach, between classroom and field teachers. Their methodologies vary, as has been clarified by Towle and Schwartz.[41] However, the field instructor must also have preparation for his teaching function.

The shift from practitioner to educator is a complex one. . . . Training must prepare him to perform this new role competently. The field instructor must have a thorough understanding of available educational concepts regarding learning patterns and teaching methods and of ways to interrelate the two; . . . in learning to use his knowledge of personality dynamics and treatment procedures in order to make educational diagnoses and teaching plans.[42]

---

[39] Arthur W. Combs, *op. cit.*, p. 458.

[40] From a joint interview with Helen Harris Perlman and Mary MacDonald, June 1, 1966. Professors Perlman and MacDonald have had responsibility for at least eleven career teachers under the NIMH Program (described earlier) during the past decade. Attributes of their "model" teacher include: wanting to know more, liking to help others "catch on"—a nurturing quality, ability to reorganize subject matter reflective of individual wisdom, self-awareness, and a sense of the spirit of the *collegium* with ability to live up to that spirit.

[41] Charlotte Towle, *The Case Method in Teaching Social Work.* (New York: National Association of Social Workers, 1959.) That field teaching has a distinct function which has its own effective methodology is further explicated by William Schwartz, *op. cit.* The methodology of field instruction is increasingly being studied in a systematic manner. See, *Field Instruction in Graduate Social Work Education—Old Problems and New Proposals, op. cit.*

[42] Aleanor Merrifield, "Changing Patterns and Programs in Field Instruction," *Social Service Review,* Vol. XXXVII, No. 31, (September, 1963), p. 278.

If the future will see more "clinical professorships" in social work education, with classroom teachers placed in field assignments as suggested by Kadushin,[43] or if there will be more teaching centers, as suggested by Kindelsperger, preparation to *teach* in these settings will increasingly be needed.

Educational enterprise is derelict if it does not develop standards for good teaching that can be recognized and valued. One can learn how to teach, and an intuitively good teacher can become a better one. There is a growing body of educational knowledge—philosophy, psychology, and "know-how"—which is available to those who would exploit it. To ignore it is to short-change the profession. True, some master teachers never had an "education course," many teachers are good teachers with only native qualities, and many have learned to be good teachers out of their own firing line experience. (This line of reasoning might also be used to denigrate the importance of education for professional practice: all professions, however, while valuing the "natural" and the intuitive individual, and granting that experience too is a teacher, nevertheless require the same formal credentials from all.)[44] That we cannot settle for anything less than the best expresses our concern for increasing, improving, and maximally using the scarce and valued social work educator.

> The nature and quality of college teaching directly affect the educative or miseducative quality of the student's experience. The nature of the learning opportunity can be as potent a factor as the substantive being studied.[45]

Summary

Four components of preparation have been specified. Additional questions have also been asked: How much of each component and for whom? To ask these questions obviously suggests that all faculty cannot and should not be expected to be equally prepared in all areas of content, be equally steeped in practice wisdom or skill, be equally active in research. Just as there must be specialization of content, so is

---

[43] Alfred Kadushin, "Two Problems of the Graduate Program: Level and Content," *Journal of Education for Social Work*, Vol. 1, No. 1 (Spring, 1965), p. 41.

[44] Pohek recalls that "this dialogue rings a familiar bell. Is it not strangely reminiscent of the early days of casework, when fear was . . . expressed lest natural skill in relationship be submerged in concern with . . . method and the art of helping be lost in scientific technique?" See Marguerite V. Pohek, "Toward a Methodology of Teaching," in *Education for Social Work* (New York: Council on Social Work Education, 1964), p. 154.

[45] Florence B. Stratemeyer, *op. cit.*, p. 38.

it appropriate to recognize gradations and specialization within the practice and research components.

There are many gradations of the practice component, ranging from a basic orientation which is quite different from deep skill and practice wisdom. Similarly, many levels of research, understanding, and skill can be identified, from research mindedness—valuing research and knowing how to use research findings in teaching—to ability to participate in sophisticated research activities, and finally, imaginative and initiating research skill. All members of a faculty need a basic level of research mindedness if they are to fulfill the expectations set for them by the curriculum. Some must be able to initiate and to teach research. Research skill is no more an absolute quality than is any of the other components.

The faculty member must be a generalist in the sense that he qualifies, at least at a basic level, both in practice and in research. Granted that there will be special instances—as distinct from the general criteria—such as the social scientist whose contribution to the curriculum has its own rationale. All should be specialists in an area of curriculum content, as well as in either practice or research. (Specialists in both practice and research just don't come very often!) But all must have the ability to teach.

The needs of the field, the mission of the university and of its professional schools, and the "given" inherent in the nature of faculty—the human component—each of these stipulates difference. The arena for social welfare activities was never unitary; today its complexity is staggering, and the outlines of its future are not fully known. Objectives and emphases are ordered differently from university to university and from school to school, as they should continue to be. The "human condition" of difference is a strength as well as a necessity. In short, it seems wise to avoid aiming either for the "model teacher" or the "model faculty." Each faculty will usefully have its own face. As Perlman teasingly notes, a faculty can be "oddly assorted" or "richly diverse."[46]

The charge to the Project has been to develop proposals for the recruitment, preparation, induction, and continuing development of faculty in social work education. Issues about which a stance must be taken and problems which must be attacked to assure soundness and realism have been reviewed. In Part III guidelines are explicated, followed by an analysis and proposals for pre-service and in-service development.

---

[46] Perlman. "—— And Gladly Teach," *op. cit.*

PART THREE

The Process of Faculty Development

CHAPTER 5

Guiding Principles for
Faculty Development

The multitude of issues and complexities that form the context for a consideration of quantitative and qualitative faculty development has been reviewed. A review, however, is productive to the extent that it leads to an accretion, a new insight, a plan for action. In one sense, these insights are conclusions; as stimulators of action they are guiding principles, setting the ground rules for action. In this chapter guidelines for action proposals have been extrapolated from the perspectives within which the discussion has thus far taken place.

The first principle is strategic; it actually suggested itself early in the period of the Project activities. *It states that proposals for this Project be mutually consistent, but not necessarily packaged.* To insist upon a unitary package, would require a too-limiting base of consensus.

This principle is based on the expectation and the granting of legitimacy to alternative value bases. Different orientations based on different starting points probably cannot be reconciled within our generation, nor should consensus be sought. For consensus forged even by reasonable men, without an additional generation in time to do sophisticated experimentation, will not necessarily bring us nearer to wisdom. The sought-for wisdom may reside in an orientation—a configuration of values—not yet conceived. For our time, we have our work cut out for us. The more enthusiastically and aggressively specific objectives are pursued, the more likely the ultimate wisdom will emerge. But most important, by avoiding a bargaining climate of *quid pro quo,* long cherished convictions can be sorted out and examined deliberately rather than polemically and classified according to which are supported by evidence and which by high-sounding folk lore.

The open acknowledgement of difference rather than its sublimation may prove to be productive. Social welfare as an enterprise and professional education for that enterprise need imaginative and divergent approaches consistent with professional responsibility. It would be surprising to expect within our institution less of the valued heterogeneity than in American society itself. Obviously, any conclusions or proposals that flow from assumptions that are unacceptable to many will not have much value and cannot hope for support. To aim for proposals based only on a given for which broad consensus is assured is also not wise. There are many inherent issues that cannot now be universally resolved, and a base for consensus would be too restricted. It appears wise, therefore, not to insist upon an "all or nothing" package. It may be possible to partialize the proposals so that those who can accept with conviction only some of the proposals are free to do so. Each sector of the field—the front-line service agencies, the schools of social work, and the Council on Social Work Education—and each of *their* constituent units may set their own priorities. The one outcome that is not tenable is to continue noting the complexities of the problem without taking some affirmative action.

This approach can provide a degree of freedom not possible if consensus and a "package" were set as a condition. We aim our sights high, preferable to an across-the-board attack based upon the least-common-denominator of agreement.

The second guideline is closely related, and differentiates between the *reality and the ideal*. The need for this principle is derived from the fortunate human approach to virtue. Everyone is for it. At the point where a model of any sort is under consideration, the formulation is likely to be expressed in optimal terms. *All* the *desiderata* are listed. That is what a model is—an idealization which is to serve as a pattern. The problem inherent in model building, however, is that because of the "human condition" compromises with the ideal are inevitable. The individual who can satisfy all listed criteria is too rare. Consequently, much energy is consumed rationalizing the compromises and distinguishing between *desiderata* and expedience. For example, although the doctorate is often stipulated, the ABD (all but the dissertation) is accepted in consolation. Similarly, many new faculty members start with little more than the MSW and "promise." While a gap between the reality and the ideal is inevitable—we would worry if our ideal were set so low that it was too easily attainable—the amount of current gap creates its own pyschological problems of guilt, defensiveness, and double talk.

The present uneasiness in the university is revealed in a paradoxical tension between how things are and how they ought to be. This is shown by the answers of the deans, the graduate faculty, and the recent recipients to the identical question put to each group.[1]

An alternate approach is to start with the "human condition" and to identify the direction from that starting point, recognizing that the ultimate point on the line thus sketched is not to be fixed for all times, but reflects at any moment the parameters of reality at that moment. In other words, we suggest a basic set of the most rigorous criteria with which we cannot compromise. For the gap to serve as a dynamic for constructive action, it seems necessary to approach the present assignment on *two different planes, separating the ideal from the current reality*. For the immediate period ahead, *we should specify a floor below which we may not drop* and place priority on evidence of potential for moving upward. Anything above the floor becomes a fringe benefit to be used as resource for the deliberative building of the firmly documented positions. By using this principle we do not endanger an orientation toward the ideal; we hasten its attainment.

The reality-based starting point will specify a number of essential criteria, for some of which there may be alternatives. If essentials are specified, alternatives by which these essentials may be satisfied, and what is and what is not interchangeable, can be approached deliberately.

The use of a starting point and the specifying of alternatives are not necessarily as radical as might appear at first glance. The models used throughout professional practice are all the result of a development process, reflecting day to day decisions growing out of an immediate reality. Eventually they become structured and institutionalized. Better to build by means of a rational process rather than to build an *ex post facto* rationale.

The third guideline is closely related to the second and urges the use of both *long term and short term approaches*. It is important for two different, but compelling reasons. No matter how promising a set of proposals for achieving an objective, and regardless of the enthusiasm with which they are undertaken, complex problems are not solved overnight. Until the longer term goals can be realized, the flow of everyday business must continue and decisions must be made that fall short of the ideal. More specifically, new faculty will be hired for next year and for several years to come whose preparation can hardly have been influenced by strictures or proposals from this Project. A morato-

---

[1] Berelson, *op. cit.*, p. 85.

rium cannot be called on hiring faculty from among the prospects currently available. Yet they will be required to meet the demands for an educational responsibility for which they may not have been prepared. In this sense it is wise to recognize immediate urgencies and provide for them alongside ultimate sights for faculty development.

But in a more complicated sense, extremely rapid changes are taking place: this is a given of the modern world. The social work profession, as a substantive institution in society, has new expectations set for it by a beset society, and, in turn, it changes its stance to meet those expectations. Many of the problems of faculty development in education for the social work profession stem from the stresses of the current scene. Ten years from now, the then current scene may have different "givens." It is indeed statesman-like to look ahead and to plan for the future. But there are many possible futures. Some visions of the future reflect hoped-for outcomes which we would like to influence. Others are clearly the products of forces which may be beyond us to affect. Projections to the future, even when based upon the same data, differ from each other because the current vantage point differs.

Any plan for faculty development impinges upon almost every other aspect of social work education. For example, a discussion of optimum preparation of faculty cannot be dissociated from a given position with reference to the ideal curriculum; in turn, the curricula of social work education are constantly changing, affected by and influencing the nature of the practice of social work in the future. Similarly, a career line for the social work educator cannot be discussed without reference to career lines in practice and in the university. Each of these variables is at the moment "the given," and yet each is constantly evolving in directions being determined by a complex of interrelated forces. The immediate approaches must accommodate themselves to the current realities. The longer range projections, freed from the pressure and a sense of crisis, can be formulated to affect, as well as be conditioned by, the many related factors. A differentiation between long and short term approaches provides a basis for planned allocation of resources. If sights are set high, as they should be, long term goals will take time to accomplish. The best way to get started for the "long haul" is to cover the first leg of the journey, especially if the ultimate route may need to be modified. Some short term proposals will have a remedial flavor. Others will give impetus to movement in the direction suggested.

An additional principle specifies that the *boundaries of the requisite advanced education be determined by the component areas needed by faculty in social work education.* This principle is based on the conclusion that the Ph.D. as a symbol currently testifies to different achievements.[2] If we start with the symbol, the debate, which has continued for more than half a century, will continue unabated, as each sector interprets what it means or should mean. More helpful, it would seem, is to affirm the boundaries of advanced education and then find an appropriate symbol. That social work education is not alone in this orientation to the symbol has been documented but warrants recall:

> Yale's break with tradition gambles boldly on the expectation that other high-quality institutions would join. But progress in American higher education has always been determined by the power of the few prestigious style-makers and pace-setters.

> If one or two other Ivy League universities or the equivalent and a few high-prestige state universities follow Yale's example, history will have been made. It would not be out of character. Slightly more than 100 years ago, Yale awarded the first Ph.D. degrees in the United States to let American scholars get their doctorates without having to go to Europe.[3]

Not only Yale, but other prestigious universities and professions, are modifying their educational arrangements, either within the boundaries of the traditional Ph.D.—narrowing or broadening them—or going beyond the boundaries. It is encouraging to remember that universities and degrees are constantly in flux, and there is no "immutable law" against change. The principle, however, deals with what components are needed, not with what degree is needed.

With specific reference to social work education, Stein has recently stated that:

> We have, however, occasionally over-compensated and identified with academic form rather than substance. . . .

> Doctoral degree programs are essential for the proper growth of our teaching faculties. . . . We should, nevertheless, be prepared to look at other sources as well for some of our class teaching faculty . . . *provided they have demonstrated scholarly capacity and aptitude for teaching, are willing to invest in new learning, and can adjust to university life.*[4]

---

[2] For a full discussion of this point, see *Graduate Study for Future College Teachers,* Joseph Axelrod, ed. (Washington: American Council on Education, 1959), Topic I: "Is the Ph.D. the Best Degree for College Teachers?"

[3] Fred M. Hechinger, "What Should a University Be?" *New York Times,* May 15, 1966.

[4] Herman D. Stein, "Cross-Currents in Practice, Undergraduate and Graduate Education in Social Work," *Journal of Education for Social Work,* 1:1 (Spring, 1965), pp. 59-60.

That this principle includes the component dealing with ability to teach should be particularly noted. It is based on the conviction that effective teaching is crucial, and that to teach effectively can be learned. It is also based on a view of professional responsibility that denies that academic freedom is not involved in requiring evidence of the ability, whether acquired in pre-service education, through the use of a "way station," or as an in-service requirement under appropriate controls.

The final principle deals with *faculty heterogeneity*. The spectrum of objectives toward which the university and its schools work has been noted. These objectives, however, are ordered differently from school to school. Each school of social work will presumably match its university's ordering of objectives. For example, in the accreditation process for professional social work education, each school is asked not only its objectives, but also the objectives of the university within which the school finds itself, giving full recognition both to the *de facto* and *de jure* heterogeneity of objectives among the universities. Further, the specific hierarchy reflects each school's priority decisions made out of the confluence of its own history and the appraisal of its current mission. Therefore, the profile of the faculty of each school will be uniquely its own.

The "human condition" of difference is a strength as well as a necessity. Although referring to another context, Coyle reminds us that:

> . . . some of us as faculty members, as I observe us, are in fact better at one or another of these phases of the profession. Some of us focus more naturally on "must know," i.e., on intellectual mastery; some on "must do," i.e., professional skills; some on "must be," and "feel." These differences I think are quite natural and inevitable and in fact represent that variety of emphasis and temperament necessary within any faculty to get the blend and balance for the whole.[5]

There is no final preferred model of a professional social worker, nor should there be. The older professions are in constant flux, because of the changing nature of the society in which they practice. As an emerging profession—emerging relative to the older ones—social work is subject to the same currents of change and to its own pressures. To know

---

[5] Grace Coyle, "The Role of the Teacher in the Creation of an Integrated Curriculum," originally presented at the Annual Meeting of the American Association of Schools of Social Work, New York, February 1, 1952. Published in *Social Work Journal*, 33:2 (April, 1955). Reissued by Council on Social Work Education, in a *Source Book of Readings on Teaching in Social Work* (New York: Council on Social Work Education, 1965).

this and to accept it is reassuring. Given the framework set by the objectives of the Curriculum Policy Statement of 1962, uniqueness should surely be valued and encouraged. Out of differences, as much as out of a common base, will come the dynamic for continuing probing and the achievement of quality in depth.

In short, each faculty will have its own face, and these profiles will differ from one school to another. Taking into account the range of strengths, the loci of instruction, and the different constellations of objectives among the schools, responsive to society's call, it seems wise to avoid aiming for the "model teacher" or the "model faculty."

It is this value system, freedom from traditional models where they do not coincide with our own imperatives, that permeates the proposals that are now being formulated. The tempering of these formulations by further debate and challenge will insure that the projected orbit will be held to a center of reality.

CHAPTER 6

The Pre-Service Phase:
Recruitment and Preparation

There are 4,845 faculty in graduate schools of social work (GFS),* of whom 1,524 have full-time, and 3,321 have part-time appointments. Full-time faculty may be grouped as follows: 63 percent have classroom or administrative responsibilities or combinations of these; 24 percent are full-time field instructors, and 13 percent have combinations of classroom and field instruction assignments. Nine percent of the part-time positions are for classroom instruction and 91 percent for field instruction (GFS). Forty percent of new faculty have the classroom as the primary locus of their initial assignments, an additional 20 percent do both class and field instruction, and 40 percent are primarily field instructors (NFS).

The proportions are generally the same in both surveys for the several curricular areas in which they teach: about 60 percent in the practice sequences (31 percent in casework, 13 percent in group work, and 12 percent in community organization); about 10 percent teach research courses or serve as advisors for student research projects; 26 percent in social welfare policy and services sequences; and 28 percent in the human behavior and the social environment sequence. Of new faculty who have classroom teaching responsibilities, 60 percent teach in more than one curricular area (NFS).

---

* Two primary sources of quantitative data are used in this chapter. Richard Onken, *op. cit.*, reports on the recently completed Survey of Graduate Faculty (GFS). The Survey of New Faculty (NFS) was undertaken for the specific purposes of the present Project. A questionnaire was sent to 294 individuals whose names appeared on rosters of faculty appointments in 1963 and 1964. As expected, some of the appointments were of people returning to teaching or otherwise not within the definition of the NFS population, namely, individuals who were new to teaching in 1963 or 1964 either as classroom or field instructors. The response rate was over 66 percent, and almost all of the schools open during these years which had new faculty are represented in the returns.

ROUTES TO FACULTY POSITIONS AND
POINTS OF ENTRY

Individuals who are now on social work faculties have come to these positions by one of several routes, each with its own associated backgrounds and preparations. Of new faculty, most of the individuals decided upon teaching as a career at some point after completing their master's degree; only 12 percent before or during their master's study. All who had completed their doctorates decided firmly upon teaching during their doctoral study (NFS).

The education and practice experience, and consequently the points of entry and routes followed to current positions are all characterized by considerable variation. For example, both NFS and GFS surveys show their undergraduate majors: 55 percent in the social sciences (11 percent in Psychology); 8 percent in English and Literature; 6 percent each in Social Welfare and in Education, and the remainder in Chemistry, Biology, Fine Arts, Premedical, Law, Engineering, and Business Administration. Some reported more than one undergraduate major.

Almost 90 percent of all faculty have master's degrees in social work; the non-social work master's degrees are in sociology, psychology, and education (NFS). The largest number of those who do not have a social work degree teach in areas of the curriculum other than the practice sequences.

Although a doctorate is increasingly being stipulated for university appointment, the exceptions to this requirement are extremely numerous.[1] Of the total current faculty population, 10 percent have doctoral degrees. Of these, 52 percent are Ph.D.s, 27 percent are D.S.W.s, 5 percent are Ed.D.s, 10 percent are M.D.s, and 5 percent are other doctoral degrees. Forty-five percent of the doctorates are in Social Work, 13 percent in Sociology, 10 percent in Medicine, 8 percent in Psychology, and 7 percent in Education (GFS).

New faculty included 15 percent who had doctorates when they first began teaching or earned them within two years, having begun to teach while completing their dissertations. (NFS). That this new group has a larger percentage than does the total faculty population, namely 10 percent, is not surprising, reflecting the fact that the total faculty population includes large numbers of senior faculty for whom a doctorate was not required when they began their teaching careers.

---

[1] The percentage of new staff with doctorates in all U.S. institutions was 25.8 in 1960-61, ranging from 17 percent in the small private colleges to 29.7 in the state universities and 35.9 in the private universities. The percentage of staff with doctorates had decreased during the previous decade. See *Higher Education and the Demand for Scientific Manpower in the United States, op. cit.,* p. 45.

The proportion of doctorates held, however, may be viewed from another vantage point. Forty percent of full-time classroom and administrative faculty have doctorates, as do 35 percent of all part-time classroom instructors. Noteworthy is the fact that 7 percent of those who have combinations of class and field instruction responsibilities, and less than 1 percent of full-time and part-time field instructors have doctoral degrees.

Thirty percent of all faculty have studied in post-master's programs but have not earned doctorates; 74 percent had been in full-time programs, and 53 percent of these individuals had been in programs which could lead to doctorates (GFS). Of new faculty, 50 percent had completed a year of post-master's study or were "working toward" a doctorate (NFS).

The routes by which these faculty members have come to faculty positions may be roughly classified as (1) the professional route, (2) the academic route, and (3) the acculturation route. Again, the doctorate is not identified as a discrete route, because it may be associated with any of the three major routes. Within these routes, however, there are different points of entry, of which the doctorate may be one.

The Professional Route

The traditional and most frequently used route has been movement by MSWs to a school-based position after a period of professional practice. In the past, a typical point of entry occurred when there was a vacancy on the faculty of a school and a field work supervisor who had come to the favorable attention of school personnel was invited to join the school-based faculty. Jennings found that half of his study population had not actively sought a faculty appointment.[2] More recently, an increasingly large cadre of field instructors has come directly from all ranks of agency personnel, some within a year or two after receiving the MSW degree. In contrast, there are women who had left agency positions to raise families and who later are ready to return to professional activity and prefer the more flexible hours of the university setting. There are also mature and experienced social work practitioners or

---

[2] Daniel Jennings, unpublished doctoral dissertation, Catholic University, 1965. A paper based on this dissertation may be found in "Characteristics of Social Work Faculty Members," *Social Work Education Reporter*, XIV, 3 (September, 1966), p. 23 ff. (Later references in this Report refer to the dissertation text.)

executives who want a new career to which they have long aspired but could not previously realize.[3]

The period of practice varies from one year to several decades. Of recently appointed faculty (NFS), 20 percent had more than 15 years in practice before joining a school faculty; 54 percent, four to fifteen years; and 26 percent less than four years.[4] (The number of years is calculated from the earning of the MSW degree and the classifications do not reflect experience before the degree.) In 1966, 2 percent of all faculty had earned the MSW degree within the preceding three years (GFS).

There is an apparent qualitative difference among those who use the several points of entry within the professional route: those with more than fifteen years, for example, come to a new career in their professional maturity; the larger number use the period of practice before committing themselves to careers in education; and finally there are increasingly large numbers who have spent very few years in a social agency.

Within the practice to teaching route, there are additional points of entry. There are variations in the amount and timing of post-master's education. Some complete a "third year" before starting teaching, other return to advanced study after a period of years of teaching. Relatively few have completed their doctoral work before beginning full-time teaching careers. Nine of those who received doctorates in social work during the academic year 1964-65 had been teaching prior to doctoral study. Most of those who eventually receive the doctorate complete their dissertations after having assumed full-time teaching responsibilities. Of the 23 in the new faculty survey who received doctorates by 1965, at least one-third did so after having begun full-time teaching one or two years earlier.

There are at least two different point of entry represented in the experience of those who complete the doctorate. For example, 38 individuals were awarded doctorates in social work in 1964-65; of these, 24 were then employed in schools of social work, but nine of them had been teaching prior to doctoral study. The doctorate is not a point of entry for those who had been teaching previously.

---

[3] Edgar Perretz, Social Work Training Branch, National Institute of Mental Health, has suggested the term "mid-career" shift to make the distinction between the younger person who becomes a teacher earlier than the one who is, in fact, entering into a second career after a major career in practice.

[4] Only 17 percent of Jennings' Study population had less than ten years of professional social work practice experience prior to entering teaching. This discrepancy with our findings may be explained by the fact that a large number of field instructors appointed during the recent years are younger and less experienced than had earlier been true.

Field instruction positions may be viewed as an emerging point of entry in the sense that they are being filled by some individuals who do not initially see themselves as having made a firm choice for a new career. Some bring less experience, and possibly different qualities, interests, and career expectations to their new appointment. We have already noted that almost all the doctorates are held by classroom faculty. Of new classroom faculty in 1963 and 1964, 29 percent had doctorate and 59 percent were working toward the degree, while only 3 percent of field faculty had doctorates and only 39 percent were working toward the doctorate.

Part-time instruction has long been a point of entry into full-time educational careers. Part-time instructors have taught in all parts of the curriculum while retaining full-time agency or other responsibilities. After a period of time, some who began as part time instructors eventually became full-time faculty. These changes were not seen as qualitative career alternatives as much as change in social work setting, and no additional formal requirements were set. In fact, the experience factor was highly valued.

About 50 percent of current part-time faculty have taught one or two years, 22 percent three to five years, and more than 15 percent have taught more than five years. Prior to their recent appointment, over 40 percent of new faculty had taught social work on a part-time basis, some in undergraduate courses but most in graduate programs or agency-based supervision of graduate students (NFS).

No data are available about the relative number of "returnees," i.e., those who join faculties after a period of temporary "retirement" in order to raise their families.

The Academic Route

Although the professional route has been the preferred one in social work education, a small number of new faculty have used the route typical for other disciplines within the university. In the academic route, one decides upon an academic career either before or early in his graduate study. Earning the doctorate and entering into teaching are immediate goals; the candidate identifies himself early with the academic community and its mores.

An insistent point of view has been acted upon by a few schools of social work. They have "nurtured" young people directly into social work education by assigning them undergraduate teaching responsibilities or research assistantships while they complete their doctoral work. This point of view is reflected in the few programs of advanced education in social work which do not emphasize prior clinical experience as a pre-requisite for admission to the doctoral program.

Five of the eighteen new faculty who earned their doctorates in 1963, 1964, and 1965 (NFS) received the MSW after 1955, and more than half had less than four years of practice experience.

The Acculturation Route

The acculturation route has been coined by the writer to describe the route used by those who teach in schools of social work who are not social workers by education and experience. Not infrequently, for example, psychiatrists teach courses in the human development and social environment sequences while continuing their private practices. Some have appointments in other departments or schools within the university. Part-time appointments in some of these cases eventuate in full-time appointments by the school of social work or in joint appointments with another school. Seven percent of new faculty (NFS) had been full-time faculty in programs other than social work, such as in schools of nursing or staff members in research centers.

The percent of the total current faculty who do not have master's degrees in social work are presumably those who used the acculturation route. Of those who had earned their doctorates by 1965 (NFS), four did not have MSW degrees. Their areas of specialization were in sociology, human development, research, and medicine. Some acculturation presumably takes place in those doctoral programs which are offered jointly with other disciplines.

Obviously, each of these groupings and subgroupings, depending upon the point of entry and the route used, has different strengths and qualities of experience. New faculty are in many respects a heterogeneous collectivity who bring a range of richness of knowledge and experience to the educational scene. They also bring a variety of differential needs, sometimes with gaps in readiness for assuming major educational responsibilities.

Some of the routes are conceivably more desirable, others simply expedient. Since our purpose is to widen the "gateways," we do not envision abandoning those currently in use. In the discussion which follows, both long range and more immediate planning are considered separately.

The long range view is deliberately placed before the section dealing with "in-the-meantime" responses to a crisis for two reasons. The short range programs and activities find their greater significance and can more efficiently be selected within the context of the long view. Second, because a long haul is inevitable to effect a comprehensive plan, there is no better time to start implementation than the present.

87

THE LONG HAUL

The problems with which we are concerned have both quantitative and qualitative dimensions. It is not satisfactory to treat quantity and quality as though each were discrete; consideration of either dimension is meaningless without reference to the other, although specific proposals may deal with one at a time. The first major proposal for faculty profiling, sets the stage for proposals addressed both to an increase in the potential numbers and in the quality of preparation of faculty.

Faculty Profiles

As a first step it is essential to de-globalize the approach to numbers. Projections about how many additional faculty are needed do not provide a basis for the potential recruit to see the implication for him or to plan appropriately. One is not likely to be recruited to choose a career line which is described in vague terms; he has known teachers all his life and social work teachers in his professional education, but does he know much about the range of professional activities which constitute the academic career? At best, he knows that some teachers "do research" and that they "teach classes." He knows that doctoral education is expected for a professorial appointment, yet he is vague about a career in social work education and planning for it.

It is probably even more important from the point of view of the schools that they know not only how many faculty they need or in what curricular areas they are needed, but also the range and balance of component strengths they need for their *collegium.*

It is wise to avoid aiming for the "model teacher" or "model faculty," favoring instead the concept of faculty heterogeneity. That a faculty of a school of social work cannot and should not be monolithic is based on the view that the needs of the field, the mission of the university and its professional schools, and the "given" inherent in the nature of faculty—the human component, all require difference.

> Teachers may be differentiated on the basis of the specific nature of the teaching functions they perform. Some of them have to be creative scholars to fulfill their teaching assignments . . . many college teachers spend many of their lectures or direct and supervise research. I wonder whether we have gone far enough in our concern with teacher preparation to recognize the different function and skills which we tend to lump together under the magic word "teaching."[5]

[5] Henry David, *op. cit.,* p. 181.

All faculty cannot and should not be expected to be equally prepared in all areas of content, be equally steeped in practice wisdom or skill, be equally active in research. Instead, the faculty as a collectivity will probably be constituted with individuals who are at once both generalists and specialists. Some will be generalists in practice orientation or in research sophistication. They will be specialists in an area of curriculum content, or in practice, or in research with skill of a high order. *All will equally need to show evidence of ability to teach.* A distinction is thus made between curricular areas with which a faculty member is identified as specialist (as in current usage) and a profile of the balance of his strengths which avoids highly desirable global qualifications which most individuals cannot satisfy anyway.

The argument for precision in academic job analysis assumes that the profiles will continue to be developmental, responding to changing conditions and imaginative adjustments, and that as much freedom of movement within faculties as now exists will continue. In one sense, the plea is that academic administration exploit what is already known from administrative theory about the value of specificity for operationalizing programatic intent.

Applying this approach, ultimately there will be available a number of profiles for social work education. They will be sufficiently similar to each other to belong to the same genus, yet provide a legitimate range of opportunities for exploiting the unique qualities of the many individuals who should be finding a place for their potential contributions to social work education. Consequently, the composite of profiles for any one school will reflect the character and emphasis of this school.

Recruitment

There has of course been continuous recruitment to the educational enterprise, but it has been individualistic, informal, and "low key." (We do not have hard data about the nature and extent of recruitment, especially by the individual schools, and depend for this statement on impressionistic evidence.) That recruitment in the past has been informal is not surprising; the rapid acceleration in the growth of social work education has taken place within the past decade. Further, the change to an educational career has not occasioned long term planning. An informal registry of open faculty positions has been maintained by the CSWE, used primarily at Annual Program Meetings, but its existence has not been widely known. Recruitment was everyone's responsibility, but there was no organized effort. It may not be too indelicate at this point to note that we refer to field-wide recruitment:

The topic "Successful Practices for Recruiting College Faculty" could mean two things: It could mean the successful efforts of a college to recruit members for its own staff (gathering rosebuds where it may) or it could mean the successful efforts of an institution to encourage its graduates to enter the profession of college teaching.[6]

There is reason to believe that a planned effort can be productive.[7] The range of activities which have successfully been used in other sectors is well known. It is not unreasonable to claim that the efforts of the National Commission for Social Work Careers, jointly sponsored by the CSWE and the National Association of Social Workers, are to a considerable extent accountable for the rapid increase in the number of applicants to schools of social work. The varied routes to educational careers have not been previously described, and there was no official basis to serve as a guide for planning.

The development of faculty profiles and an inventory of the range of faculty positions may be expected to help individuals make appropriate career decisions and plan accordingly. In this connection, it should be noted that the point is increasingly being made that promising students at the master's level be identified and encouraged to plan for educational careers.

Regensburg's observations about recruitment for advanced education as a step in preparation for faculty positions, call attention to the fact that in the Kidneigh-Crane study, 35 percent of high ranking master's degree graduates reported an interest in teaching.

> How early they should be approached and by whom are matters to be decided. . . . There is currently no general plan for recruitment to advanced programs; not that individual schools fail to make their own plans but . . . the profession has not at this time considered or attempted a concerted plan.

She concludes, however, that

> . . . there are hopeful signs of an untapped reservoir for recruitment and alternative ways of recruiting in a coordinated and systematic way.[8]

---

[6] Frederic W. Ness in *Current Issues in Higher Education*, G. Kerry Smith, ed. (Washington: National Education Association, 1959), p. 77.

[7] The attendance of well over 100 persons at sessions on "Career Opportunities in Social Work Education: Requirements, Preparation and Rewards of Teaching," during the National Conference of Social Welfare in 1966 and 1967, gave encouraging evidence of potential value of such programs.

[8] Regensburg, "Recruitment to Post-Master's Programs in Schools of Social Work," *op. cit.*

The agency will continue to be an operative gateway. This concept rejects the notion that a faculty member recruited *by a school* represents a loss to the cooperative agency. It calls upon the agency to help identify the promising educator based on his interest and experience with the many educational functions associated with agency life. Although there may appear to be loss to the agency immediately, ultimately both the field and the agency will gain.

Advanced Education and Alternate Preparations

The professional route will probably continue to be the major one in social work. It may also be expected, however, that with the availability of faculty profiles, schools will better be able to seek individuals from the lesser-used points of entry and the lesser-used academic and acculturation routes. The increased use of these sources will have implications for adjustments in the means by which the essential balance of components of preparation can be achieved. The implications are discussed in the context of the next set of proposals dealing with advanced education and alternate preparations.

The social work educator career line is sufficiently substantive at this time so that it can be stipulated that advanced education will become a prerequisite for full citizenship in the faculty of the future. Many schools are now governed or guided by this criterion. Nineteen schools of social work currently offer advanced education at either the "third year" or the doctoral level. Expansion of the number of advanced education programs by more schools is an implicit outcome if these proposals gain widespread acceptance. As new programs are added they will be guided in the determination of their objectives and the characteristics of their programs by needs which are at least accounted for by current programs.

There are different legitimate and desirable points of entry and routes. In one sense there are also different destinations, i.e., faculty positions within the school faculty profiles. There will therefore need to be alternative preparations based on more than expediency or improvisation. To this extent the preparations which constitute advanced education will be individualized. Enough detail will be given to clarify intent without presuming to direct the individual schools which offer advanced programs with operational decisions which are properly their prerogative.

Advanced education will insure evidence of achievement in each of the four component areas: subject matter, practice, research, and teaching. How these expectations may be satisfied must now be considered. In the discussion that follows, the implications for providing

91

the subject matter and practice components for the several points of entry within the professional, academic, and acculturation routes are explored first, followed by consideration of the research component in all three routes. The provision of the teaching component for all faculty is then considered separately.

The Professional Route—The social worker with a number of years of experience in practice who is stimulated by the questions of other learners and enjoys stimulating them may decide that a career as a social work educator is one he wishes to pursue. Whether he pursues that new career within the social agency in a staff development function where he is also needed or under university auspice may be a matter of preference. But one thing will be clear. He will seek additional formal post-master's education. He will seek programs where he will have opportunity to affirm what he knows and can do, to challenge his firmest beliefs and skills, and to reformulate his understanding of social work knowledge. He will inevitably need to understand the role of research in expanding professional knowledge and to develop skill for participation in research. He will want to know how he learns, how others learn, and how to assist that process. Assuming qualification in the practice component, his advanced education will provide for the subject matter, research, and teaching components.

The qualitatively different nature of the point of entry used by the most mature individuals who are seeking a second career, as distinct from those who embark earlier on education as an alternate career, has been noted. The "second career" subgroup are gifted social workers who have accumulated many years of professional service and who have yearned for the day when developments in their personal lives would permit them an opportunity for an alternate career. They have not in earlier years been able to prepare for a teaching career while financial and other responsibilities were paramount. The older group brings a wealth of experience, worldly and professional wisdom, which can surely enrich the educational setting. Tenure and rank are of somewhat lesser concern to them in their current life cycle.

However, to gain what this group has to offer, some adjustments in current thinking are necessary so that they can appropriately be attracted to educational careers in the university and take their rightful places in the collegium. Is it appropriate to urge the legitimacy of granting academic credit (as is increasingly being done throughout higher education) in recognition of the quality of wisdom which such a person brings? It then would be possible to arrange individualized programs for the more mature person so that he too can aspire to full citizenship within the academic community.

At least 40 percent of current faculty come through the field instruction point of entry. Herein lies an opportunity that should be exploited. Screening of the able is built into the time limited contracts under which many field instructors are hired. Many in recent years are young, and have only a few years of agency experience. This group represents an excellent target for encouraging the planning for advanced education. Their career lines are in flux, and with administrative interest addressed to helping them do deliberate planning, they may become a major source of the kind of faculty needed. Attention to this group is warranted lest an opportunity be lost: almost none of the new field instructors has a doctorate, very few have begun doctoral study, and many indicate uncertainty about their plans.

The part-time point of entry has been a useful one for new faculty. They had taught social work on a part-time basis, some in undergraduate courses, but most in graduate programs or in agency-based field instruction of graduate students. No implication is intended that schools increase the proportion of part-time personnel, for such a development would be against their best educational purpose. However, the social worker who teaches one or two courses at a local school of social work brings enrichment to his teaching and to the whole curriculum. The arrangement provides an extremely valuable resource, administratively, i.e., as a means by which positions that cannot be budgeted as full time are filled. Since many part-time instructors will eventually become full-time, it would be wise to urge planning for advanced education as early as possible.

The Academic Route—The route that has been least exploited in the past yet that offers potential not to be minimized is the one that more nearly resembles the traditional academic pattern. It is proposed that the young, promising social work master's degree student (the undergraduate should remain the target for recruitment to the profession of social work) be identified by faculty and agency personnel because he shows interest and aptitude in teaching or research. He may be helped to identify social work education as an appropriate career line for himself.

The one who chooses this route early will obviously have a longer educational pre-service period ahead and can realistically look forward to several additional years of study.

The practice component in this instance is deferred until most or all of the advanced study requirements have been completed. There may be objection to this deferment by those who prefer the professional route whereby one proves himself in a field of practice before becoming a teacher. The objector is reminded that the professional route has been based on a conception of teaching in social work which has in the past been heavily weighted with the "methods" sequences. Should

93

one not choose to be a specialist in curricular areas other than methods only after he knows *what* he is not choosing, may be asked. And in response, the answer may be given that few career choices and specializations are made out of an all-encompassing perspective from all available possibilities. All in all, a certain amount of self-selection must be assumed to take place by those who choose this route.

The deferment of provision for the clinical component has precedent and is realistic. For example, recruiting psychologists to the academic setting has been much less of a problem than in social work. The NIMH Career Teacher Program in psychology, analagous to the Career Teacher Programs in social work, psychiatric nursing, and psychiatry, was started in 1955 but closed in 1960 because there was no need to use it as a recruiting device. However, it was reactivated in 1965 as a faculty development resource to provide opportunities for junior faculty to strengthen their clinical orientation in balance with the research emphasis of their advanced education.[9]

A recent innovation is making opportunities for the deferred practice experience increasingly available. The Welfare Administration of the Department of Health, Education, and Welfare is encouraging opportunities for summer employment for faculty members in state departments of welfare and in federal programs. "Through these programs, faculty members are providing skilled professional assistance . . . while at the same time gaining valuable field experience for future classroom use."[10] Such arrangements will involve administrative responsibility and cooperation by the agencies and the schools. It is desirable, however, that this block of experience be stipulated as part of an orderly approach to preparation for the educational career.

The route described here, the "academic plus practice" route, has a variation which has, in fact, been used in the past. The student in the MSW program who has inquired about teaching has been told that he would do well to gain a few years of experience in practice and then seek to qualify by means of advanced education. Some will consider this variation as preferable, and it will undoubtedly continue to be used. The problem has been that with rapid advancement in the field available to the alert and the able, returning to school as a student and beginning a long period of advanced education becomes increasingly difficult.

---

[9] Interview with Dr. Forrest Tyler, Training Specialist in Psychology, Training and Manpower Resources Branch, National Institute of Mental Health, June 15, 1966.

[10] *Social Work Education Reporter*, Vol. XIV, No. 2, June, 1966. Several deans who were interviewed indicated agreement with the usefulness and feasibility of the deferred practice experience.

It should be noted that some resources currently available for the support of advanced study are not being used by candidates in social work. There has been almost a complete absence of applications for National Defense Education Awards either by schools of social work or by potential candidates, although there appears to be no identifiable block to their eligibility.[11] This type of resource should be increasingly used.

The Acculturation Route—When faculty profiles specifying the component areas of preparation become available and are known, it can be expected that they will attract a certain number of individuals who have committed themselves to doctoral study in other disciplines and who come to social work as a "minor" in their programs. With the provision of opportunities for satisfaction of the practice component in social work for those individuals, an additional cadre of potential faculty for social work education with specialized knowledge and research competence will come into being.

Increased use of faculty on joint appointment with other departments of the university may be desirable. Educators from other fields provide an enriching resource for social work education. The move toward recognition of common learning objectives and needs among members of the helping professions gives strong support to this approach. Increased use of the acculturation route is consistent with developments pointing toward inter-disciplinary education.

The subject matter and practice components have been accounted for in these sketchy outlines for increased use of the several routes through the medium of post-master's education and practice experiences. A word is now necessary about the research component.

Research—The distinction has earlier been made about the levels within the research component, ranging from knowledge of research for use in teaching to advanced skill needed for initiating and carrying through major research projects. It is imperative to strengthen the research component within social work faculties. It seems realistic to set the basic level of research sophistication as an essential criterion, and as an objective of all post-master's education for all faculty in social work, and reserve the objective of higher level research skill for some programs.

The highest level of research imagination and mastery will increas-

---

[11] An announcement in *Social Work Education Reporter* 14:3, (September, 1966), p. 11, that two schools have applied for grants under Title IV of the National Defense Education Act confirms the neglect in using this resource until now. Unfortunately, the level of some grant stipends has been too low to be used by individuals with family responsibilities and has undoubtedly been a factor in their under-use.

ingly be needed. For this purpose there are resources for postdoctoral research fellowships which have been little used by social work educators in the past. It can be envisioned that as faculty profiles identify positions for which *research* career development opportunities[12] are appropriate, greater use will be made of these for the benefit of both the faculty member and the school.

Research has been identified as a major route for faculty in departments of psychiatry. The bright resident may be interested in research career and incidentally takes on a teaching function. "He may be started on a project, and if that works out he may be taken on as a full faculty member."[13] Research may become increasingly a point of entry in social work education as its research centers undertake major research projects and faculty become increasingly research-oriented.

The Teaching Component and the Career Teacher Internship

The theoretical issues about the teaching component in university education have long been debated, as has been reviewed in Chapter III.

The position that social work teachers need to be able to teach is summarized by Burns in a straightforward statement:

> Even for those who obtain the doctorate, [our context is advanced study, not necessarily the doctorate], such advanced study is in most cases only a partial preparation. Equipped with new content, with an increased ability to manage new knowledge, with the methodology of research, the new doctor emerging from an advanced program has not of necessity had any experience or participation or education in what is involved in the organization of content for consumption by others, or in the methodology of conveying it.[14]

Since the individual who has previously acquired the ability to teach will continue to be the exception, regardless of the route he has used, it follows that the need for this component will be fairly universal. Of the nineteen programs[15] of post-masters' education in social work, slightly more than half offer courses with content about educational problems and issues, e.g., seminars in professional education, history,

---

12 An example of these opportunities is the Research Career Program of the NIMH, referred to in Chapter III. It is this program which we have been told has been underused by social work. Other opportunities have not been investigated.

13 Interview with Dr. George Ruff, cited above.

14 Burns, *op. cit.*

15 The data for this paragraph are taken from a review of the 1965-66 programs of post-master's education in the bulletins of the 19 schools.

trends, organization and administration of social work education. Education courses include: Principles and Methods in Field Teaching, Learning Theory, Principles of Consultation and Interdisciplinary Teaching, Educational Methods in Teaching Casework, and Teaching in Social Work. In several schools, candidates are encouraged to take education courses in the school of education on the campus. From preliminary data of the Survey of Graduate Faculty,[16] less than half of all faculty who had been enrolled in programs of post-master's education had taken any education or curriculum courses. For direct experience in teaching, a few schools offer teaching assistantships in undergraduate or graduate programs, either under the direction of a senior faculty member or as junior members of a faculty group which teaches several sections of the same course. One school provides a practice experience in teaching as field instruction either at that school or at others for prospective social work teachers.

Where does responsibility to provide the necessary learning experiences for improving teaching ability rest, with the advanced education program (i.e., in the pre-service period), with an intermediate "way station," between graduate study and the first full time job, or with the first employing institution (i.e., at induction)? To answer this question categorically is to make a choice based on a number of variables, some of which are value judgments and some are reality considerations. With preferences based on values it is difficult to argue. At best, one can aim to understand the different bases.

Some who believe that this component is appropriately a responsibility of pre-service advanced education do so because they see it as a component of *preparation* on a par with any of the other components. Others prefer that it be included in the pre-service period, or in an intermediate period, because they fear that if it is structured for the in-service period, the controls for the protection of the academic atmosphere of freedom may not be adequate to the administrative necessities of evaluation and promotion. Finally, there are those who would postpone the teaching component until one begins full-time teaching, either because they hesitate to add to the duration of advanced study or because they are convinced that the teacher best learns to teach at what is for him the "teaching moment."

All these positions find support in the literature of higher education. Diekhoff describes all three approaches as possibilities but appears to be identified with a post-degree position.[17] In the same vein, Berelson[18]

---

[16] Onken, *op. cit.*

[17] Diekhoff, *The Domain of the Faculty,* Chapter 3, and *Tomorrow's Professors, op. cit.*

[18] Berelson, *op. cit.,* p. 225.

argues that the teaching component is the responsibility of the institution in which the faculty member teaches. Cartter is reported to advocate a "track system" in which students in graduate school, after their first year of study, will be placed according to whether they are going into teaching or into other careers. "That failing, special training in teaching skills should be 'relegated' to an immediate post-doctoral period."[19] On the other hand, McCutcheon takes the position that room can be found in the Ph.D. program for preparing candidates who are going into college teaching with the teaching component "without endangering the admitted excellence of the present product and without prolonging the time required for the degree."[20]

Morgen offers the thesis that "every graduate student . . . perform as a graduate teaching assistant, both as part of his own educational experience and as a service to the teaching of undergraduate students." He bases this thesis on two assumptions:

> 1) That any university faculty has equal responsibility for teaching and for the advancement of knowledge. . . . The graduate student must learn both the methods of teaching and research, and 2) That the highest form of teaching is the association that a faculty member has with his graduate student in guiding him towards the advancement of knowledge in his area of competence.[21]

The preferences are to some extent associated with different conceptions of the most appropriate learning experiences for increasing ability to teach. Specifically, is a seminar on problems of college teaching, or on the history of higher education, or on the psychology of adult learning sufficient? Is an opportunity to teach under certain controls, such as a limited teaching load, adequate, or is some arrangement necessary for supervision of the intern's teaching by one accomplished in teaching himself, who wants to make the investment and knows how to help the novice?

Each of these conceptions of what is needed is to be found in the

---

[19] M. A. Farber, *New York Times,* October 16, 1966, in a report of the annual meeting of the American Council on Education, of which Dr. Cartter, Chancellor of New York University, is a former vice-president.

[20] Roger P. McCutcheon, "The Preparation of College Teachers," *Graduate Journal,* Vol. 1 (Fall, 1958), pp. 139-43.

[21] Ralph A. Morgen, "The Graduate Teaching Assistantship—Slave Labor or Required Course?", *Proceedings* of the Fifth Annual Meeting, Council of Graduate Schools in the United States, Theme, *The Graduate Student,* James N. Eshelman, ed., (Washington, D. C., December 2-4, 1965), p. 81.

variety of innovations for providing the teaching component. The practice which candidates working on their dissertations are hired as instructors is well known and frequently used in all sectors as well as in social work.[22] The Faculty Internship Program supported by the Fund for the Advancement of Education during the years 1953-58 introduced many innovations which have since been incorporated into the operating routines of the universities which first undertook them on a demonstration basis.[23] A course in college teaching may be combined with an internship, under a departmental professor, and seminar discussion of teaching problems.[24]

A notable exception to the absence of pre-service education for teaching is the Career Teaching Program of the National Institute of Mental Health (see Chapter III). The program of financial support for social work educators is separate from doctoral study in the sense that it is no way within the purview of the institution in which the degree will be granted, although to be eligible for a career teacher award the candidate must have completed all degree requirements other than the dissertation. Since there is no commitment between the institution in which the career teaching year is placed and the career teacher about future employment, the pattern of this program is essentially that of the intermediate station. The year is devoted to teaching under the guidance of a master teacher and is not intended as a means of support for completing the dissertation. In a few instances career teacher appointees have pursued two years of this program.

However, fewer than 75 individuals have utilized the grants available under the NIMH program during the past twelve years. Among the reasons for the quantitatively small numbers may be an overly rigorous battery of criteria for qualifying for an award on the one hand; but there is also a lack of interest in the award. There are obvious reasons. The career teacher year, as an optional addition to the long period of doctoral study, gives the one who chooses it no advantage if this

---

[22] See, for example, "Career Instructors at University of Massachusetts," *School and Society*, 86:2132 (May, 1858), pp. 227-229. Several social work deans reported arrangements of this kind at the Project workshop described in the Introduction.

[23] Diekhoff, *Tomorrow's Professors, op. cit.*; see also, for example, Harold B. Dunkel, "Training College Teachers: A Progress Report from the University of Chicago," *Journal of Higher Education*, Vol. 29:1, (January, 1958), pp. 57-58.

[24] Particia Kozacik, "Future Professors, Coming Up," *College and University*, Vol. 34, No. 1 (Winter, 1959), pp. 205-7. See also, George Fahey and Paul Masoner, "An Interdisciplinary Seminar in College Teaching," *Journal of Teacher Education*, Vol. 11, No. 3, pp. 391-97 for a description of a seminar for graduate students and faculty in all academic and professional fields; or Jean Wellington and C. Burleigh Wellington, "Method for College Teachers," *School and Society*, Vol. 87, No. 2158, pp. 363-64, on a seminar in method for advanced doctoral study.

qualification is not officially recognized, let alone required, at the point of seeking a regular appointment. It may actually be disadvantageous to the extent that one who does not stop at the "way station" for the career teacher experience has an additional year of seniority over his colleague who has done so.

If an inclusive definition of the scope of learning how to teach is used, an internship as an integral part of advanced education is to be preferred. (We shall be returning later to a modified career teacher year for the short range perspective.) By making the experience an integral part of the advanced educational program it will be regularized, expected, and consequently valued. The experience will include *both* "learning about," (through courses and seminars) *and* learning "by doing" (through a field experience under the supervision of one who not only knows how to teach, but who is interested in, and knows how to help, others to develop skill and their own teaching styles).

The concept of class and field as loci for developing skill is well known and widely accepted.[25] Both are integrated in the social work education at the master's level. However, a definitive term to describe this concept for acquiring teaching skill in higher education is lacking. It may be possible to borrow "career teacher" as a generic term (on the assumption that it does not introduce confusion with the NIMH programs). As a term "career teacher internship" expresses the commitment to *learning to be a teacher.*

A word is necessary here about possible adjustments for utilization of the career teacher plan for individuals coming through some of the specialized points of entry. For example, if the part-time point of entry is to be maximally exploited, it is important that the teaching done by the part-time instructor be skilled teaching. Therefore, the first year of part time teaching should be treated as a career teacher year, with an official mentor assigned. Hopefully, course work in education will be planfully taken during a period prior to appointment. These arrangements will probably mean that a partial leave of absence must be obtained from the agency and a considerable investment of senior faculty time made in the beginning part-time teacher. But these adjustments

---

[25] We note an analogous development of one year internships for administrators in higher education reflecting today's "critical" need to increase the number of competent men and women who serve in the ranks of administration in higher education. See Lanier Cox, "The American Council on Education Academic Administration Internship Program," *Educational Record*, Vol. 47, No. 2 (Spring, 1966), pp. 163-172. See also, Ellis L. Phillips, Jr., "Toward More Effective Administration in Higher Education," *Educational Record*, 47:2 (Spring, 1966), pp. 148-162, for a description of programs for the improvement of the administrative component, parallel to the focus in this Project on the development of teaching faculty.

and investments must be made by the agency, the school, and the individual, if the educational activity is taken seriously.

There may be a major additional advantage to this type of investment. The full significance of the teaching assignment can be realized by the new part-time teacher with much less left to chance than is true now. He will more quickly derive the satisfactions which come from good teaching. Most important, the potentially good teacher may more readily be able to choose to make a long term commitment to a full-time educational career.

An adjusted advanced educational program for the individual who is making a mid-career shift, i.e., the mature person with more than the typical amount of practice experience and wisdom might provide that his first year, in effect, be a career teacher internship. The academic requirements for an advanced degree should then be met within a specified period of time, e.g., through planned half-year periods of leave plus part-time study. The innovation lies primarily in the granting of credit for knowledge and wisdom, which is what academic credit should symbolize, and in modifying the structure of advanced education to the extent which is educationally defensible.

Similarly, for professors who may have earned their doctorates in other fields and have come to social work education by way of the acculturation route, or by way of joint appointments, it is important to keep the teaching component in mind. Granted that they are qualified in their subject matter areas, they too must be good teachers. It may be difficult to introduce the use of a mentor from the school of social work for a senior professor on a new joint appointment. It would not be surprising that within a climate where good teaching is administratively supported even senior professors might welcome opportunities to learn more about their teaching effectiveness.

To operationalize the career teacher concept will require additional decisions. The internship can either be provided for within existing doctoral programs, be associated with shorter advanced educational programs, or be included in planning for alternative advanced education to which we turn in the next section. It is important to stress, however, that there be some provision for the teaching component. The career teacher internship provides a frame of reference for improvement of teaching through class and field experience, through flexible application in pre-service or in-service designs. If the field experience cannot, for whatever reason, be effected, then perhaps the course work will be. That would be an improvement over the current situation in which, as has already been noted, half of those who have had advanced, including doctoral, education have had neither course nor field experience in learning how to teach.

101

Alternate Doctoral Degree Programs

Preparation by doctoral study should, of course, continue to be used. But Ph.D. and D.S.W. programs will continue to provide a relatively small number of qualified faculty. Clearly that number will be inadequate. The problems associated with duration of time for completing the degree, the high number of ABDs, and the nature of the dissertation and problems associated with the latter are universal ones.

However, in addition to the quantitative inadequacy and the well-known problems, there are other aspects of the traditional doctorate that merit review. It is a fallacy to offer the all-too-simple prescription of somehow trying to produce more doctorates.

"If doctoral education cannot meet the demands for faculty manpower, what steps can be taken to retain and raise the scholarly level of faculties by appropriate education and preparation of new members?"[26] Burns has responded to this question by suggesting "three possible modes of advanced education," the first of which deals with remedying some of the problems associated with the present "third year" formulations. (The second and third modes will be appearing as we come to the short-range perspective.) She notes the greater accessibility of one year of advanced education, but pinpoints the inevitably lower, second class status of a non-degree program.

A proposal for a two year doctorate may at first glance appear to be radical (one step less radical if it is remembered that the MSW has already provided two full years of graduate education). There is a growing body of thinking in higher education which specifically points in this direction, proposed by influential educators. Cartter's approving reference to this alternative has been noted earlier. On the reasoning that among college teachers who are not publishing researchers (not synonymous with being scholarly) are many intelligent and able teachers, Woodring concludes that a program of graduate work should be devised which is specifically intended for this group, and the Ph.D. should be the degree for the researchers.[27] Taking this reasoning further, Bent points to the *professionalization* of the Ph.D. degree, and concludes that we

> . . . might clarify our thinking on the professionalization of the Doctor's degree by recognizing that the Ph.D. is training of the scholar and scientist, and in this restricted sense is training for a profession. This does not imply that it trains for any profession

[26] Regensburg, "Recruitment to Post-Master's Programs in Schools of Social Work," *op. cit.*

[27] Paul Woodring, "The Profession of College Teaching," *Journal of Higher Education,* 31:5 (May, 1960), pp. 280-282.

which a scholar or scientist may enter. It is preparation for a career involving to a large extent the organization and performing of original research. . .[28]

The Doctor of Social Science degree at Syracuse University for prospective faculty has been evaluated as "an outstanding example of professionalized doctoral work in the best sense of the term."[29] Similarly, to supply the needs of faculty in nursing education, that field has turned to doctoral degrees which are both clinically *and* educationally oriented.[30]

A two-year sequential period in addition to the two-year MSW for faculty in social work education leading to a professional educator's doctorate is proposed not as a compromise between the longer and shorter modes of advanced education. Broad outlines for achieving the essential objectives which have been outlined suggest themselves: each of the two years has its distinctive characteristics and is addressed to relatively specific goals.

The first year will have two primary objectives, namely, expansion with depth in a content area and development of basic research sophistication. It will be a residential year and resemble the current residential programs in many respects. It will differ from current programs primarily in its specificity and selectivity of objectives.

There is no equally desirable alternative to a period of full-time study in order to become and immerse oneself as a learner. Whether this period should be longer is unknown, but a one year residential period has survived long enough in many places to suggest that many schools do have conviction that it is essential and useful. One year may in fact be an optimum period in the life of a person who has already achieved as a professional and who approaches his learning after having been screened for maturity, aptitude, and accomplishment.

It is to be envisioned that among the schools offering advanced education in social work, different emphases will be available. As current advanced education programs are freed of the onus of "buckshot" objectives, they will in turn be able to develop their own emphases and reputations for specialization as is true in graduate education in other fields. Some schools will presumably continue their emphasis upon practice and the clinical component at the advanced level. Others will emphasize the social science research, or social policy components.

---

[28] Henry E. Bent, "Professionalization of the Ph.D. Degree," *Journal of Higher Education,* 30:3 (March, 1959), p. 145.

[29] R. H. Eckelberry, "A New Study of a Notable Graduate Program," *Journal of Higher Education,* 30:6 (June, 1959), p. 343.

[30] Interview with Dr. Esther Garrison, Training Branch, Nursing Section, NIMH, June 16, 1966.

There will thus be an array of advanced programs from which the future career educator can choose in accordance with his interest. All the programs, however, will make available, in common, social work content specialization and broad curricular foundations in basic research and in education.

The second "non-residential" year will be built around a career teacher internship plan and should be relatively easy to implement. During this year, the candidate will carry the typical responsibilities of a full-time faculty member, but will have less than the full number of classes usually assigned. He will also have assigned to him a mentor, a qualified senior professor who will be responsible for helping the novice develop his teaching skills and style. He will be able to participate in concurrent seminars on the foundations and problems of higher and professional education offered either by the school of social work or elsewhere on the campus. Because this is a pre-service educational program, the question of academic freedom does not arise.

An additional innovative characteristic of the career-teacher year is that it can be offered at any school, not necessarily the same school where the residential year work was pursued. Many schools which do not have advanced programs, can offer a qualitative experience; good teaching also takes place at new and small schools which offer only MSW programs. The arrangement is made with the approval of the school that will be granting the degree and will require the assignment of qualified "supervision." Presumably the degree granting schools will want to provide a number of career teacher positions for their own candidates, and will be willing to enter into arrangements with other schools which do not have advanced programs for additional career teacher positions.

There are substantial advantages to the latter in making themselves available for providing career teacher internships. Small schools may well appreciate opportunities to have career teacher candidates on their faculties for one year fresh from advanced study. This may be a particular boon to schools in sparsely populated areas that want to avoid ingrown faculty. Finally, although this plan is not motivated as a recruitment device, a career teacher candidate and the school each have an ideal opportunity to use the year to screen each other in action, with an eye to long-term commitment. In the past, the schools with doctoral programs have had first choice from among their doctoral graduates.

The school offering the residential year of study is responsible for

---

[31] See "A Proposed Curriculum with a Practice Emphasis in Doctoral Programs," based on a report of the Subcommittee on Clinical Emphasis in Advanced Education of the Committee on Advanced Education in Social Work, *Social Work Education Reporter*, XIV: 3 (September, 1966), pp. 33ff., as an example.

awarding the degree. However, we continue to be faced with the perplexing question about the name of the degree which will testify to these achievements. Obviously, as long as the Ph.D. continues to testify to research specialization it may not be an appropriate symbol for programs which do not emphasize high level research skill. There is an overwhelming amount of evidence of the need for a more precise designation for the academically and experientially qualified *professional* educator.

For those who are concerned that social work education not separate itself further from the mainstream of academic tradition, it can be pointed out that social work is not alone. There are many allies among the most prestigious disciplines and professions, and even more ferment in circles where the traditional facade has not yet been broken. It is essentially a matter of conviction: even if we did not have allies throughout academia already giving leadership to planned change, it would be our responsibility to enunciate clearly our values, our ends, and the means to achieve them. The social work tradition pioneered in the implementation of a clinical master's degree which may have had an impact on other professional education in greater measure than is usually credited to it.

Financing the two years of study for the proposed degree does not appear to be an insurmountable problem. In addition to the support now available from public, university, and foundation sources there are resources not yet fully exploited which could become available. In addition to potentially increased support now available from the Career Teacher Program, the second, career teacher year, is almost self-supporting, for the career teacher position is, in fact, a partial position which schools can readily justify in their budgets by classes and educational functions accounted for. There is also the university investment in the upgrading of the profession. (If the argument holds for the field agency, it also holds for the university.)

Summary

For the long haul, then, several thrusts have been proposed, but the direction is clear. A faculty career will be planned, it will not "just happen." The schools and the establishment will need to specify the elements of preparation that are important to them and make these specifications known. The potential recruit will be expected to prepare himself for a faculty career.

The long-term proposals, then, urge the development of faculty profiles with specification of the balance of the four components. This will result in more precise description of faculty positions for which one may prepare. Existing advanced education programs may then need to be adjusted to the demonstrated need for balance among the components, and new curricula developed. Alternative plans for pursuing these curricula will depend upon the different routes and points of entry which faculty will increasingly be using and the specialized quality of their chosen career lines. The teaching component of preparation will be officially accounted for in the curricular scheme through seminars dealing with the knowledge base of educational philosophy, learning-teaching, and methodologies.

Opportunities for the enhancement of skill in teaching are accounted for in variations of a career teacher internship.

SHORT RANGE PERSPECTIVE

We come now to a series of proposals that have an "in-the-meantime" flavor in contrast to the recommendations that will inevitably take several years to implement and that have been generated by a longer look ahead. No implication is intended, however, that the shorter range tasks are less important. They are, in fact, essential and can furnish a base of experience for a forward thrust upon the long-view recommendations.

For several years to come schools will be looking for new faculty who have traversed the routes currently available. Many will have had no advanced education and a relatively small number of ABDs, Ph.D.s and D.S.W.s. An investment in maximizing their potential contribution as rapidly as possible warrants consideration.

The discussion below is focused first on alternative approaches to the needs of the 50 percent of current new faculty who begin with little or no post mortem education; an approach to new faculty, otherwise qualified, whose ability to teach is not known is discussed next; finally the specific problem of the ABD cannot be ignored.

Short-Term Advanced Education: Regional Centers

Twenty-six graduate schools of social work announced summer offerings for 1967, an increase from 20 in 1966, and 14 in 1965.[32] Totals of

---

[32] "Summer Offerings Reported by the Graduate Schools of Social Work," document 65-6-2 (March 24, 1965), document 66-5-10 (April 14, 1966), and document 67-5-4 (April 19, 1967). The CSWE annually prepares these documents which list summer offerings reported by the graduate schools of social work. The most recent also lists summer institutes for faculty in undergraduate programs in social welfare sponsored in cooperation with the CSWE, regional institutes of the National Association of Social Workers, and international seminars, but these have not been included in the analysis.

more than 250 institutes, workshops, seminars, and short-term courses were listed for the summers of 1966 and 1967, again an increase from 194 for 1965. Most of the summer offerings are for two-week periods, although they range from three days to six weeks. However, fewer than 40 of those announced for 1967 (and fewer than 30 in each of the two previous years) were announced at six of the campuses as being at the post-master's level, i.e., by the requirement that participants have earned the master's degree in social work. Of the advanced level offerings, most appear to deal with advanced social work practice, e.g., family treatment, socio-behavioral theory, and use of groups; very few appear to fall within the research component. In each of the three years there were about six offerings associated with the teaching component, e.g., *The Social Worker as Teacher, Educational Methods in Teaching Casework, Professional Education,* or *Supervision.* In this context, the "question may be raised whether our educational resources are being used to the best advantage."[33]

Burns also suggests the expansion of resources for study on an advanced level. She notes, however, their limitations:

> The problem with institutes, however, is two-fold. Institutes are very time limited. The amount of content which can be covered in them likewise is limited . . .
>
>   . . . I am impressed by the fact that many beginning teachers say that they know their content but they don't know how to teach it. . . . I am unhappy when I see or hear such statements, because practically no one knows all the relevant content in his or her particular area, and keeping on top of emerging relevant content is an everlasting struggle which one practically never wins. To be truly advanced study, such a venture would of necessity have to select and convey much substantive content already found in doctoral programs, and add to this the newest and best knowledge we have about methods by which to select content and teach it. . . .[34]

There are several implications to these misgivings: one is that more short-term opportunities at the advanced level be available. The second is that they be of long enough duration to provide for substantive learning. If they are of sufficient substance, a summer experience can serve well, in one sense, as a psychological point of entry to a more

---

[33] Regensburg, "Recruitment to Post-Master's Programs in School of Social Work," *op. cit.*

[34] Burns, *op. cit.*

comprehensive program of advanced education. It can generate respect and readiness for more study, even enthusiasm; if it is not substantive, the opposite effect may occur. Most important, there must be some sense of sequence, a rationale to the summer offerings so that they can have the desired outcomes.

The potential interest and value of alternative short-term structures such as institutes and workshops, whether during summer sessions or in evening sessions, is well known and does not need to be documented here. They are an integral part of the educational milieu both in social work and in all phases of academic effort.

In addition to one and two-week institutes, which usually provide twenty to thirty hours of sessions, regional centers for a full summer of advanced study in residence offer special advantages.

Dean Kidneigh is credited by Burns as having suggested that:

> . . . with the large number of faculty entering their academic experience each year, it should be possible to establish a full summer advanced educational venture which would be focused on . . . new substantive content, on reconceptualizations of old content and of practice experience, on relating these two sources of content, and finally on selecting, organizing and presenting content. . . .[35]

There is a qualitative difference in the nature of a two-week, thirty-hour course, and a full summer quarter. It takes almost two weeks freed of ongoing job responsibilities to immerse oneself as a learner. This is a point of conviction which has led the Center for the Study of Medical Education, University of Illinois to lengthen the duration of their institutes for medical educators from two weeks to a forty day period.[36]

Several of the schools of social work have well established summer sessions and they currently serve as regional, even national centers, in the sense that they attract students who come from long distances. That they should continue in this role is unquestioned. But to the extent that the small number can not be expected to meet the total need, the desirability of having *additional* regional opportunities is indicated, especially if greater expectation is to be placed on advanced study and

[35] *Ibid.*

[36] Interview with Dr. George Miller, Director of the Center. See also, Edwin F. Rosinski and George E. Miller, "A Study of Medical School Faculty Attitudes," *Journal of Medical Education*, Vol. 37 (February, 1962), pp. 112-123; and Rosinski and Miller, "Seminars on Medical Teaching," *loc. cit.* (March, 1962), pp. 177-184.

greater administrative support is given to faculty already recruited to pursue it.

The establishment of an Institute, created by CSWE and attached to a university, for a five-year period has been urged by Schwartz[37] to deal with the immediate crisis. Arguing that "doctoral student production for teaching should not be depended upon," he suggests a "national vehicle for recruiting and training teachers for schools of social work, graduate and undergraduate." The curriculum of the proposed Institute would be addressed to the components of preparation for social work educators, and the earning of a certificate from the Institute would be recognized by schools as advanced education, and possibly considered as credits towards a doctorate. A host of educational policy issues and operational problems are inherent in this proposal; their solution, however, may be achievable in view of the urgency and the readiness of the field for bold ventures.

The summer period as a short-term structure is available for practice experience as well as for advanced level study in the content, research, and teaching components. Reference has been made earlier to the increased availability of opportunities for summer employment in practice settings for faculty entering by way of the research point of entry along the academic or acculturation routes. Summer employment may well be a means, within the short range perspective as well as in the longer view, for providing short-term basic practice experiences for those who have not had them.

First Year as a Career Teacher Internship

The Career Teacher internship was introduced earlier as an approach to providing for the necessary experiences in the development or enhancement of teaching ability. Many will be coming to faculty responsibilities during the next several years, regardless of how quickly the long-term recommendations are operationalized, without having qualified in this component area. If this component is valued, a solution suggests itself. The first appointment can be made for a one-year period as a career teacher year, with all the controls designed to enhance the opportunity to learn to teach. Where there is no need to make the distinction between pre-service and in-service commitments, the appointment need not be limited to one year. The essential consid-

---

[37] Memorandum from Meyer Schwartz, Associate Dean, Graduate School of Social Work, University of Pittsburgh, dated April 21, 1967. We note also a proposal for initiating a preparatory semester for recruits to positions in social work education, in the discussion stage at Tulane University.

eration is that the investment, in this case falling upon the school, be seen as sufficiently valued that it can become a standard procedure.

Shortening the ABD Stretchout

The problem of the ABD stretchout period for completing the dissertation after all other requirements for the doctoral degree have been satisfied is well known. In current experience in social work the period averages more than two years and is often much longer. Full-time teaching responsibilities undertaken by the ABD compete with the time and energy needed by him to complete the dissertation. Aside from the personal frustration and sense of incompleteness, the school fails to get maximum return from the potential that such an individual has to offer. This loss can be minimized in direct relationship to the shortening of the period. Formal understandings for protected teaching loads during the first year of service on behalf of administration, and for commitment to deliberate speed and concentration on completion of the dissertation on the part of the student seem warranted. True, this represents an investment by the school, but the investment is no greater than the quality of risk and inefficiency which delay encourages. Data are not available to indicate how widespread is current policy with respect to this problem; unfortunately, hearsay evidence indicates that at best there are occasional informal understandings which often give way to exigencies. But there is also no evidence that such policies, if operative, would not be effective. It would not take many years to learn definitively whether this approach can be helpful in avoiding loss of momentum when faculty accept their first appointment or return to positions after doctoral study but have not completed their dissertations.

Summary

The "short haul" proposals are based on the same analysis and are guided by the same principles as are the more comprehensive plans discussed earlier. They are intended to demonstrate the usefulness of specialized advanced education in the components of faculty preparation. They are not intended to substitute for long-term planning and development. In fact, they will provide a base in experience for the long process of improving the quantity and quality of opportunities available for the preparation of social work faculty.

An increase is urged in the availability of short-term educational opportunities at the post-master's level at more graduate schools and at regional and national centers. For those who have not had preparation for teaching, it is proposed that their first year provide for the qualities of a career teacher internship. An investment in shortening the ABD stretch-out period will be of mutual benefit to the individual and to the schools' purpose.

CHAPTER 7

The In-Service Period: Induction

The movement of an individual in a new role into the routines and activities of an ongoing enterprise is a universal process. Structures that affect the process may be informal and happenstance or even non-existent, or they may be designed to help the inductee psychologically and functionally. For a long time schools have recognized the importance of the induction period for their students and agencies for their staffs. That less attention has been paid to this phase in university life can probably be explained simply on the basis that in the academic model, doctoral study while in a graduate school has been considered the locus and the timing for induction into a university career.[1]

The induction period commences when the faculty member—even the seasoned teacher who transfers from another school—and the institution with which he is to be affiliated enter into a contractual relationship and continues until he is able to assume full creative responsibility. There are many who believe that the induction period covers a three-year span, although the pace and manifestations may differ within that period. (One wonders whether the typical pattern of initial three-year appointments in the university is not a structure that reflects the fact and the extent of the induction period.)

What are the problems associated with induction that are faced by new faculty? What are current practices for dealing with these problems? Approached in this way, we shall then be able to consider a design for dealing both with universal induction needs, including those whose preparation meets all the specified criteria, and with special needs that stem from many new faculty continuing to have other than the indicated necessary preparation.

Two primary sources of data about the needs of new faculty—new

---

[1] See Mark Ingraham, "Graduate Training for College Teaching: A Panel Discussion," *Bulletin of American Association of University Professors*, 46 (September, 1960), pp. 294-99.

faculty themselves, and administrative officials of the schools of social work—have been described earlier. (See Introduction.) In addition, the questionnaire to faculty responsible for the continuing faculty development at their schools yielded additional information about the induction phase.

The questionnaire to new faculty asked:

a) What experiences were available to you before or during your first year of full-time teaching in schools of social work to help you in the transition to social work educator? Were they: formal or informal, planned or fortuitous? Courses? Administrative structures? etc.

b) What were the major problems (if any) associated with this transition?

c) What experiences, administrative structures, or other resources would you have liked to have had provided, or would you recommend for the next generation? Would you be interested or willing to pursue this question further? (e.g., at a workshop, if it can be arranged?)

The deans of graduate schools of social work were asked to respond to the following items in a questionnaire and in a workshop:

a) Describe what your school is doing, what experiences are planned before or during their first year of full-time teaching to help new faculty as they move into social work education.

b) What experiences, administrative structures, or other resources would you consider to be appropriate or desirable under optimum circumstances? (This question legitimizes daydreaming.)

PROBLEMS SEEN BY NEW FACULTY

Some of the 176 new faculty who replied recall their induction problems as minimal, no greater and different in quality than those associated with *any* change of setting. The larger number list problems which fall into three broad categories, namely, those associated with the transition itself; the teaching function; and role diversity and role ambiguity. That the teaching function should appear is not surprising since we have already noted that the teaching component is lacking in the preparation of most new faculty, even those who have had post master's education. Two universal problems are the transition (i.e., the socialization of all new faculty) and the clarification and learning of

113

new roles. In turn, socialization has three dimensions: to the university, to the school of social work, and to the field of social work education.

Entering into social work education represents a change in career line. A large proportion of new faculty come from positions in social work practice where their competence was unquestioned. In fact, they were selected because of their status or recognized performance. They come to positions which have major and immediate expectations set for them, or which *they feel* have been set for them, with less than complete conviction about their adequacy for meeting these expectations. These problems are of a level different from the anxieties attendant upon any change from one job setting to another; they are uniquely associated with the expectations set for a university professor. Some of these expectations are self imposed; some imposed by the institution and its administration; some by colleagues in the School of Social Work or in other departments of the university. Students also set expectations for faculty.

Berg had earlier described the "long journey" from an agency career to a school career, even for one who knew the school intimately and had been a unit field instructor for that school.

> Coming with this much teaching experience and with so many years of association with the University of Pennsylvania School of Social Work as an agency colleague and a part-time faculty member, I did not anticipate much dislocation in moving into full-time teaching. I was wrong. I found there was a great difference . . . as I am still learning. . . .
>
> Making the transition . . . involves taking on a new set of imperatives. In an agency, every activity finds purpose, meaning, direction, from the agency's reason for existence: Every activity in a school must, of course, relate itself to the school's central purpose. . . . This means different content, different emphasis, different pressures, a different rhythm to one's work life—a whole new orientation.[2]

Recalling his experience as a faculty member moving to a new school after eight years of teaching experience in another school of social work, Soffen notes twofold anxieties: in effect, will *I* find a psychological home in the new organization, and will what I feel prepared to contribute be valued within that organization? He suggests that

---

[2] Renee Berg, "Practices and Problems in the Selection and Development of Faculty for Schools of Social Work," presented at Annual Program Meeting, Council on Social Work Education, Toronto, January 30, 1964.

the new member is changed during this transition and, "correspond-ingly, the ingroup must acknowledge unto itself that as it incorporates new members into its body, it too will be changing." This transition is not easy, as "almost imperceptibly, the predominant use of the pro-noun 'you' which marks the earlier stages is replaced by the pronoun 'we.' "[3] Jenkins has put it: "How can I be accepted by this group that will put all sorts of pressures on me to be like them?"[4] The "we" feeling is surely important as a goal for the new faculty member.

> The final and most difficult task facing those who would foster good teaching among young instructors . . . is to develop in them a professional commitment to the institution as great as the pledge they have already made to their discipline.[5]

It has also been noted that social work practitioners and new faculty may not be as homogeneous a group sociologically as appears on the surface. Among their ranks are individuals coming from "both sides of the track" and from a variety of subcultures, each with its own per-ceptions of the university as a place to work, of the status of educa-tional endeavor in general, and of the professor, in particular. In addi-tion to the new social work faculty member's perceptions, the percep-tions of the rest of the academic community of the social work educator are in operation. How is his identity *as a social worker* seen by others? Does he take on the burden of any status differences in the perceptions of professional education and social work education, by those in the more prestigeful disciplines within the university?

Some new faculty found that the concept of the university professor as a master in his classroom, relying upon his own intuitive method, is *not* freeing. Others report that exchange among colleagues freezes when a question is raised about teaching methodology. Many had anticipated that they would appreciate the freedom of the university classroom and the absence of supervision as they had known it in the agency. However, although they found this absence less satisfying than anticipated, they do not want to have supervision as they know it from social work practice.

Referring to students beginning doctoral study in preparation for educational careers, Schottland proposes that "the experience of un-learning as well as learning, of developing a new self-image which fits

---

[3] Joseph Soffen, "Practices and Problems in the Selection and Development of Faculty for Schools of Social Work," presented at Annual Program Meeting, Council on Social Work Education, Toronto, January 30, 1964.

[4] David Jenkins, at the first meeting of the Advisory Committee.

[5] Mark Beach, "Promoting Good Teaching in the Microversity," *Journal of Higher Education*, 37:6 (June, 1966), p. 305.

the new roles for which the student is preparing, frequently involves a major reorientation."[6] Perhaps some of the reorientation can be accomplished during doctoral study, perhaps some of it must await the "teachable moment."

With reference to role diversity and role ambiguity, a new faculty member knows that he is becoming a part of an institution new for him and that he is expected to carry new roles, but the roles are not clear. He has an idealized image of the scholar role but has no experience for fulfilling this role except through imitation of scholars he has known. He expects and seeks a structure for the "continued enrichment" and growth necessary for being a scholar. How does one get started on research projects? How does he select community service activities? Does the school have guidelines for these?

There is also a new "colleague role" with professors from other departments of the university. The role as liaison between school and agency, such as in the field advising, is a new one. There are new role expectations of a faculty member in his memberships in community groups and professional associations. Are there university or school policies by which he may be guided in setting priorities for his participation in community service activites?

He sometimes finds different expectations for different faculty; at times he senses different levels of citizenship between field and classroom faculty. There are uncertainties about the ground rules. Some of the problems arise from the expectations in a professional school different from those in the traditional academic departments. The competencies for which faculty are currently being selected appear to be differently distributed.

This summary of what new faculty say about role diversity and role ambiguity documents the point made by Milton and Shoben:

> Oddly enough, the catalogue of professorial tasks is not a small one. Over time, the college instructor has been called upon to extend the frontiers of human knowledge, to resynthesize and reinterpret knowledge, to impart significant information and ideas to young people, (i.e., relative novices . . .) to furnish personal counsel to students, to play a part in the determination of policy and in the management of his department and occasionally in his institution, to render various forms of intellectually based public service, to represent the professional concerns of his special discipline to his institution and to the public at large, and many more. Obviously, these functions have never been equally weighted. . . . The

---

[6] As quoted in Jennings, *op. cit.*

point, however, is that a professor plays many roles and occupies a deceptively complex niche in the hall of the professions.[7]

For the social work educator, Rosen has enumerated the following role relationships arising out of assigned responsibilities: with fellow teachers in the same sequence, with students in his class, with individual advisees, with teachers in other sequences, with field instructors of his advisees, with administrative officials of his school. Additional subtle roles include relationships with faculty in other departments and disciplines, and with students not in his classes.[8]

A useful conceptualization of the distinctive demands for role clarity made by the university is offered by Blau, who points out several characteristics that distinguish universities from other complex organizations. For example, the relationship between staff and line is reversed in the university: administrative authority and professional staff relationships are more difficult to show in a hierarchal arrangement than in most other bureaucracies. Secondly, "whereas most formal organizations tend to draw clear boundaries between the members of the organization and its public, this is not true of the universities." Most intriguing is the characteristics of universities, which:

> . . . are institutional arrangements for regular production of two ingredients of social change. The first is original ideas and the second is men to implement these ideas and produce others. . . . Universities have the functions of developing both new ideas and the producers of new ideas; merely communicating the most recent results of research and training men to apply them could be done in separate institutions.[9]

Some new faculty claim that the socialization and role indentifications presented a minimal problem to them, and that if a problem exists it is inconsequential, easily mastered by a population who have been adequate to much more demanding developmental tasks in their life histories. It is hardly our intention to raise anxieties for them. On

---

[7] Quoted from prepublication copy of chapter entitled, "To Disenthrall Ourselves," by Edward J. Shoben, Jr., in *Learning and Professors,* by O. Milton and E. J. Shoben, Jr., eds., (forthcoming publication).

[8] Information furnished by Alex Rosen, Dean, Graduate School of Social Work, New York University.

[9] Peter M. Blau, "The University as a Distinctive Organization," in *Institutional Backgrounds of Adult Education,* R. J. Ingham, ed. (Boston: Center for the Study of Liberal Education for Adults at Boston University, 1966), p. 98. See also, Logan Wilson, "The Professor and His Roles," *Improving College Teaching, loc. cit.,* pp. 99-109.

the other hand, the larger number identified these as problems with both informational and psychological dimensions.

PROBLEMS SEEN BY ADMINISTRATORS

The problems of new faculty as identified by the deans, directors, or other administrative personnel who attended the special workshop or responded to the survey questionnaire are generally analogous to those described by new faculty themselves, possibly at one level of abstraction higher than as given by new faculty.[10] For example, the administrators identified the clash of cultures, the culture of practice, and the culture of the university. The competence for which a faculty member has been selected may not be as valued by the university as his record of publications. The differences in expectations in an academic discipline from those in a professional school also appear to be a source of confusion.

The teaching component loomed large. New teachers are expected to participate in curriculum decisions without preparation for this task. Some subscribe to the point of view that just as the social worker has to have a sound base for understanding human behavior and the social environment, so must the teacher have a firm foundation for teaching from the extensive body of knowledge about teaching and learning.

The Advisory Committee of the Project also noted that new teachers directly from doctoral study may lose sight of the fact that their students have to learn *to become* makers of social policy, *to become* caseworkers or groupworkers, and not only to be taught *about* social policy or *about* practice. If they expect that they should be preparing social statesmen, they then feel guilty because they find that they cannot achieve this unrealistic goal. Working under the handicap of an inappropriate or insufficiently sharp image with which to identify, teachers may fail to build upon skill for teaching they may already have, and to develop styles which have integrity for them.

---

[10] Some schools were represented both at the Dean's workshop and in the responses to the survey; others in one or the other. An exact check is not possible because the attendance record at the workshop is not complete (43 names were recorded) and 35 response letters were received. In addition, there were responses from six additional schools to the continuing development questionnaire (Chapter VIII) which included data about induction problems and practices. It seems safe to conclude that information from over 75% of the schools is available. Sixty of the schools (87%) were represented in responses to the Survey of New Faculty.

CURRENT INDUCTION PRACTICES

The inventory of induction activities and experiences reported by both new faculty and administrators is impressive. The range of activities is broad and there is a scatter of modes. Many new faculty spoke of the fortuitous availability of a more experienced colleague, others recalled a sense of isolation in a "sink or swim" atmosphere. Many had found planned conferences with the dean or with a senior faculty member either on a regular or "as needed" basis to be useful. There was a sense of agreement among both faculty and administrators that many schools rely upon the dynamics of the informal system which operates in a faculty, and upon the power of this system. There was considerable agreement about the need for explicating the institutional and professional expectations while retaining and maximally exploiting the values of the colleagual, i.e., informal system.

Interestingly, only structures found to be helpful were reported, perhaps because of the wording of the inquiry. The more formalized structures and activities fall into three broad categories, corresponding generally to the three areas of problem identified by new faculty. They are addressed to the newness of the experience, to the procedural aspects of particular assignments, e.g., advising students, and to the content and method of teaching. An additional chronological basis for classification is also suggested, namely, pre-service activities between the time that there is a formal understanding of contract and actual assumption of duties, and in-service activities after the time of entry.

The pre-service activities reported by almost 35 percent of the responding schools include combinations of the following:

1. A prospective faculty member serves as a guest lecturer.

2. Minutes of the previous years' faculty meetings, handbooks, school bulletins, and syllabi of all current courses are sent to new faculty.

3. At pre-service orientation conferences with the dean, an analysis is made of areas of felt needs of the new faculty member and plans are made for independent study.

4. The new faculty members submits to the dean or to a senior member bibliographies and outlines for courses he will be teaching.

To maximize the availability of the pre-service period for these activities, a few schools report that the new member is appointed four

119

to six weeks before the beginning of the school year and the advent of the student body. In addition, four schools report formal orientation sessions. New faculty are frequently invited to attend the orientation sessions for new *students*.

Activities specifically addressed to orientation to the school of social work setting and program include:

1. Conferences with the dean or senior faculty, reported as informal or "as needed" in eight schools, and formal or regular in two.

2. Faculty meetings and content area meetings, as well as faculty seminars, annual retreats, etc., are reported frequently as devices by which new faculty are quickly immersed in the ongoing life of the whole group.

3. Two schools report a variety of group meetings with field instruction agencies.

4. At one school, new faculty who had not had an adequate orientation experience undertook to plan the orientation to the school of those who would be coming the following year.

Since our questions did not differentiate between orientation to the school and to the university, there are very little data to indicate to what extent there is orientation to the latter. One dean reports the practice of assigning each faculty member responsibility for establishing a continuing working relationship with another faculty member outside the school of social work. Most of the practices described, however, appear to be cast toward the school of social work. However, support for new faculty to attend the Annual Program Meeting of the CSWE is widely used as a means of hastening orientation and acculturation to the educational scene as a whole; some schools make it a point that it be possible for *all* new faculty to attend during their first year.

New faculty had identified their need for role clarification, but administrators had not, and consequently it is not surprising that there is little record of current practices to indicate how this problem is being approached.

Many activities serve purposes both of orientation and of teaching. Six schools report the use of group meetings—faculty seminars, regularly scheduled colloquia, ad hoc discussion groups of scholarly articles, and workshops—in varying timing patterns as devices for introducing pertinent learning theory for all faculty, while also serving orientation purposes for new faculty. In six schools, new faculty audit courses, either in the school of social work or in other schools within the university, on a voluntary or required basis. Assignments to functional and curricular committees are specifically listed by seven schools. One school has been building a special dean's library of resource materials on educational and learning theory and pedagogy. Various arrangements of team teaching are described, such as, the new faculty member shares responsibility for a course, or teaches a section of a multi-section course with senior colleagues, in which he is involved in the setting of course objectives, selecting and planning learning experiences, and evaluation tools. New schools describe the intensive period of curriculum construction before accreditation as a major faculty development experience. "Most of our faculty commented frequently that nothing could do more for faculty development than working together in curriculum construction."

The approach to the concept of line authority as suggested by the team supervision is interestingly reflected in the variety of terms used: seventeen schools report some form of formal "supervision," "consultation," "tutorship," "preceptorship," and "mentorship." An additional ten schools use the term "advisor" to describe the designation of a senior faculty member to be available, usually on an informal basis, for helping new faculty. At several schools, new faculty meet regularly throughout their first year with the Assistant Dean for Curriculum, where the emphasis on "course planning, teaching methods, relating to the rest of the curriculum, and the particular interests and concerns of faculty." One dean reports that he "has reserved the right for visitation of classes in order to gain some knowledge of the effectiveness of teaching to better enable (him) to discharge his responsibility for the evaluation. . . . . This is in accord with the first priority . . . in which excellence of teaching is our stated first objective."

In a few schools faculty who start as field instructors gradually move into classroom responsibilities, at first on a short-term basis. In some instances, they first audit courses they will teach. The group structures for orientation as well as for the curricular and teaching components are used frequently for field instructors; in fact, the suggestion was made by new classroom faculty at their workshop that they would have benefitted from meetings of the kind that had been used for field instruction faculty.

Only ten of the responding schools report that they are able to lighten the load of the new classroom or field instruction faculty during their first year. "It has always been our intention to help newly appointed staff . . . by having them appointed as assistants to a senior faculty member. . . . However, we have had to invest some of our junior staff with rather heavy responsibilities. . . ."

DESIRED ARRANGEMENTS

Both new faculty and deans were asked to project into the future. New faculty were asked for suggestions that they thought might help their successors, and administrators were asked to "day dream."

In the faculty group, those who felt the least need for help did not recommend any changes. With one exception, no one suggested less than he found available. Those who had minimal help during their transition period and who had problems suggested a variety of structures and planned experiences. Those who found their help fortuitously were grateful to their individual colleagues, but generally urged more structure, and those who had the benefit of planned experiences and administrative structures generally urged continuation of these, or their intensification.

One dean did not feel that anything more than individualized help where needed is appropriate and another stated that "teachers vary so much that it is hard to specify any one program." However, these were minority viewpoints.

An interesting observation which emerges from the many thoughtful responses to this question is that what is already a practice in one school is still a day dream in another. The inventory of the suggestions from some schools matches the inventory of current practices in the other schools.

There are a few suggestions which are new, however; an innovation, the one most frequently mentioned (by nine schools), is the suggestion for the provision of central or regional "workshop" institutes, seminars, annually for new faculty, under the auspices of the CSWE or regional groupings, either prior to the Fall semester or during the year. Several suggestions deal with a gradualized induction, such as part time teaching before undertaking full time responsibility, or arrival at the school one semester before given a teaching assignment. "Under optimum circumstances, it would be well to have the new faculty person on the campus earlier—during the Spring semester: (1) to participate in faculty meetings which concentrate on an evaluation of the academic year just concluding; (2) to assist in plans for the Fall session; (3) to become acquainted with the climate of the school while the students are on campus."

It may be well to note at this point that mutual class visitation by teachers, i.e., auditing or visitation by senior or administrative faculty is listed several times as desirable. One dean suggests the periodic use of process recording of class teaching. A distinct impression is gained that many of the schools which do not now use some mentor arrangement would be willing to introduce it if economically feasible. One dean writes: "If we ever get a complete complement of staff, I would like to assign one senior faculty member the responsibility to plan a careful program. . . ." Budgetary limitations as well as faculty shortages are listed several times as the primary causes for the fact that many of these ideas are not realized. Choices frequently have to be made from among several desiderata.

Summary

Many new faculty and administrators believe that the problems of induction require attention. The needs identified by the larger number fall into three categories, namely, socialization—to the school itself, to the university, and to the larger educational field—role clarification, and the development of teaching skill.

There is considerable recognition and response to these problems, and current practices are varied and imaginative. Probably all schools attack one or another of the categories of needs and probably none has a design for covering all three with equal thrust and with equally satisfactory results. Much of the effort is fragmentized. Variations arise from the differences in size and history of the schools. Typical practices focus upon familiarization with immediate curricular activities; some with role identification, and a few with socialization to the school and to social work education. There is less evidence of provision for socialization to the university. A substantial number of schools use some form of mentorship for new faculty which deliberately avoids the essence of the supervisory model, although there are few exceptions.

What is an established practice in one school is a day dream in another, i.e., something considered highly desirable but for which the means has not yet been developed. The overall mood, however, is characterized by a desire to strengthen induction practices by means of a planned design consistent with university mores and climate to hasten the productivity and security of new faculty. Before turning to proposals for the induction phase, we shall consider problems of continuing development in the next chapter.

STRENGTHENING THE INDUCTION PHASE

The induction period indeed has its special characteristics and needs. Induction practices, however, are generally subtle, and with some exceptions are perhaps more appropriately called customs or styles. It may be useful, to keep in mind that proposals for the induction of new faculty in a school will have an impact on "old" faculty, and induction programs must be seen within the context of the climate and style for continuing learning of the total faculty, which will be discussed in the next chapter. In a comprehensive program for in service development each phase will reinforce the other. The proposals which follow aim to strenghten what already exists, rather than to substitute for formats and programs which have proven themselves.

Faculty Development as a Function

There is near universal agreement that the colleagueal tradition of university life be retained and strengthened. In this system one is free to turn to any colleague guided by inclination and the kind of "ear" or counsel or stimulation which he seeks. However, this informality is not strengthened just because needs are not recognized officially. It is also agreed that informality is not inconsistent with the fulfillment of administrative and academic responsibility. There can be no quarrel with consciously developed faculty norms for induction and continuing development within each school. It is proposed that faculty development be identified as a discreet and explicit administrative responsibility, assigned to an individual in the same formal manner in which other responsibilities are assigned.

It may be noted at this point that names of individuals from only twenty-nine different schools appear on a listing maintained by the CSWE as responsible for Faculty Development or Improvement of Teaching Methodology and Instruction." A reasonable explanation for the fact that more than half the schools do not specify such an individual, and that almost half of those specified are deans may be that faculty development is typically seen as a residual responsibility of the dean. It is an assigned function in about one quarter of the schools. Inspection of the listing does not suggest that this difference is associated with size or newness of school.

Although the faculty development function is analogous to that of staff development in any agency, it should be remembered that the idea faces some of the same psychological hurdles that staff development as a function encountered before it became widely accepted. As Diekhoff noted:

> Whatever the sponsorship, faculty opposition to formal programs for the improvement of instruction is likely to be strong. Proposals for such programs are regarded by many as explicit or implicit adverse criticisms of their work. Perhaps rightly, for no one would

propose a program for the improvement of the perfect. . . . By some curious twist of logic, freedom from supervision seems sometimes to be regarded as an aspect of "academic freedom."

This tradition of the classroom sovereignty of the professor is so strong that it may be impracticable to apply programs for the evaluation and improvement of instruction to the current generations of older college teachers. But senior faculty members are less likely to object to the training of their juniors. . . .[11]

But this attitude is also not absolute. In many quarters of high prestige, such as in medical schools, it is standard procedure that when new courses are introduced members of the faculty attend each others' lectures; sometimes the chairman of the department sits in on the lectures. On the basis of data obtained from deans at 1,110 colleges and universities, supervision of *new* college teachers by a designated member of the faculty is used as a method of assessing teaching effectiveness in 10 per cent of arts and science colleges, 25 per cent in liberal arts colleges, and in 50 per cent of schools of engineering and business.[12]

Without an adequate orientation to the requirements of a specific teaching job and its relation to the programs of the college and to the overall aims and objectives of the institution, an individual faculty member cannot satisfactorily fulfill his proper role.[13]

The person who accepts this responsibility, whether it be the dean or another faculty member, must be abreast of the best thinking in continuing education, be committed to the process, and have the specialized skills for giving leadership to an active program which embraces the whole faculty, junior and senior. Whether the faculty development chairman should be the dean or other administrative official or should be one selected from faculty not identified with administration is open to debate.

The faculty development chairman may appropriately be the educational mentor of a new faculty member during his induction period, coordinate the career teacher internships (though not necessarily be the only mentor for the school) and be responsible for planning a comprehensive in-service program.

---

[11] Diekhoff, *Domain of the Faculty, op. cit.*, p. 63.

[12] Alexander W. Astin, Calvin B. T. Lee, "Current Practices in the Evaluation of Training of College Teachers," *Improving College Teaching, loc. cit.*, pp. 296-311.

[13] Clarence H. Thompson, "Faculty Development in Evening Colleges," *Adult Leadership,* 16:1 (May, 1967), p. 16.

Provision for "Tooling Up" and Reduced Assignment During First Year

A standard procedure for making appointments to start early enough so that the necessary orientation process can begin before the onset of all the pressures associated with the beginning of a new semester is indicated. Assuming that the new teacher is fully prepared with the requisite knowledge and teaching ability, he will nevertheless need time to think through how he wants to proceed, now with more responsibility *and* pressure than when he was in his career teacher year. If he does not have time to relate what he brings to *this* assignment, he must necessarily fall back on other people's outlines and assignments, based on planning which was not his. If he has not had specific experience as a teacher, the danger is greater.

It seems unnecessary to argue the case for the lighter load for all new faculty. Yet, when a school is short staffed, the protection of the first year assignment yields too readily to "necessity." Although other studies[14] analogous to the present one specify by percentage or proportion of released time equivalencies, this proposal urges instead a conscientious investment by each school according to its situation and resources, with provision for evaluation of this practice after there has been enough experience with it.

If a protected load during the first school year and the initial summer appointment cannot be managed for financial or other reasons, at least one of them should be considered indispensable. If it is to be a summer appointment only, then it is important that a mentor also be available. Although a person who has attained faculty status can be expected to operate with considerable independence and self generating direction, he also needs administrative sanction that this activity is indeed part of his initial assignment.

Socialization and Role Clarification

Since our view of the basic induction period is that it is universal and not merely remedial, and since current practices are largely addressed to immediate curricular responsibilities, suggestions are included for a sharpened focus on the other two needs, namely socialization and role clarification. These have both informational and psychological dimensions.

---

14 See, for example, Dexter Perkins and John L. Snell, and Committee on Graduate Education of the American Historical Association, *The Education of Historians in the United States* (New York: McGraw Hill, 1962).

The means for socialization to the school of social work are readily available and used in most instances. In the relatively few schools where a new faculty member feels isolated, administrative awareness brought on by this reminder seems all that is necessary. However, socialization to the university appears to be generally neglected and is not accomplished by formal introductions to university officials or receptions by the president of the university. Since we are dealing here not only with factual information about who is who and what is where, but with attitude formation and reinforcement, peer interchange can be useful. A means which has intriguing promise because it can be a long-term investment in interdisciplinary contact is to join forces with other departments and schools within the university for orientation of all new faculty. On the other hand, clarification of roles and concerns which are unique to social work are best considered within the school itself. Two group structures therefore suggest themselves, one an interdisciplinary one, with the school of social work taking the initiative if necessary, and the second within the faculty of the school of social work.

Socialization to the Field

Optimally, the transition may be consummated in interschool contacts by new faculty with the social work *educational* enterprise. Many schools deliberately send *new* faculty to the Annual Program Meeting of the CSWE for this purpose. However, at these meetings, which are new for them, they are on their own and may feel isolated, or depend on their own school colleagues whom they can just as readily meet back home. Having "known their way around" at other professional meetings, their naivete to the educational scene is emphasized. Although the workshop for new faculty conducted for the purposes of the present project had as its primary objective securing data from participants, many said they found the meeting with their peers from other schools useful.

A special workshop for new faculty, scheduled at the Annual Program Meeting of the CSWE in January, coming as it does at the end of the first semester of teaching, can be addressed to their specific needs and provide a perspective for the issues before the forum.

An estimate of what these proposals will cost is not feasible at this time. They call for a financial commitment, but relatively a modest one. The induction of new staff into any setting always costs money, but often the costs are not itemized. These proposals make explicit that financial resources should be allocated for these purposes. The investment, moreover, cannot be seen as a luxury or an option. If the ends are important, effective means are ultimately not too expensive.

Summary of Proposals

Proposals have been outlined for strengthening both the interest in the needs of faculty during their induction and the intent of programmatic efforts to deal with these needs. Recognition, in the schools, of faculty development as a specific function assigned to one who is qualified for, and interested in, the leadership tasks involved is urged. The importance of provision for "tooling up" and reduced assignment during the first year, attention to the needs for role clarification, for socialization to the university and to the field of social work education, are also proposed.

CHAPTER 8

The In-Service Period: Continuing Development

Our sights and efforts are directed to scholarship in social work education, to the teacher-scholar and the research-scholar. We are remiss if we imply in any definition of these terms that the attributes of scholarship or of scholars are absolute rather than developmental. Faculty development is appropriately seen as a process which surely does not terminate at the end of an induction period. Rather, individual creativity *and* the collective strength of a faculty body can be expected to flourish only by continuing investment in building upon the strengths which the individuals bring.

> The need for constant interaction of inquiring minds does not stop with the attainment of the Ph.D. University faculties, to be productive, must provide a climate and process of mutual interaction to assist each member in his lifelong career of analysis and accumulation.[1]

Knowledge, practice wisdom, and research in social work will be changing at an exponential rate in the immediate future and the best prepared, experienced, and scholarly faculty will do well not to fall behind, let alone give leadership to these developments. The traditional view of faculty growth has been of the growth of the individual faculty member whose achievements redound to his and to his school's credit and for the benefit of his students. Because he is a scholar he is self-generating in energy and in the use of resources. He and the members of his *collegium* use each other reciprocally to their mutual benefit. Surely this informal medium of faculty growth is to be valued and supported.

---

[1] J. Douglas Brown, "The Development of the Creative Teacher-Scholar," *op. cit.,* p. 619.

However, the traditional view does not go far enough. While the individual interrelationships within the *collegium* must remain free and informal, the *sense of collegium* is amenable to strengthening, and the climate *within the collegium* can be affected constructively. Unquestionably, the dynamics of this group life have operated and been acted upon intuitively in the past. However, an example of some of the prevailing counterforces which operate within a faculty is reported by one dean: Having noted a flyer about a new book, he sent the flyer to a faculty member to whose area of the curriculum it seemed pertinent. He was completely unprepared, he reports, for the sense of threat which this action aroused, since he had intended it as a service with no other implication. The book was about a subject matter area.

With reference to the teaching component, the problem is at once more subtle yet persistent.

> One is struck by the lack of literature about college teaching. Several inferences seem possible. Professors may know all there is to know about teaching and hence there is no market for books about the art. Or, no one knows enough about teaching to fill more than a few books. Or, nobody really cares. In 1964, a reasonably typical year, only two books dealt primarily with this subject.[2]

This criticism should not be taken as absolute. The periodical literature about teaching in higher education is more abundant. The *Handbook of Research on Teaching*[3] has a chapter (XIII) on "Research in Teaching at the College and University Level." The interest in teaching in social work education, to which we shall shortly be turning, is indeed increasingly evident.

The issue is stated boldly and sharply by David:

> It may sound rude, even though it is not so intended, to suggest that some of the emphasis upon the better preparation of future teachers may be somewhat misplaced. Some of it might with profit be placed upon the urgent need to improve the quality of present teaching personnel.[4]

---

[2] Lewis B. Mayhew, "The Literature of Higher Education," *Educational Record*, 46:1, (Winter, 1965), p. 40. Incidentally, the two books to which Mayhew refers are: Earl V. Pullias, Aileene Lockhard *et al.*, *Toward Excellence in College Teaching* (Dubuque, Iowa: William C. Brown Co., 1964), and Herman A. Estram and Deler M. Goode, *College and University Teaching*, by the same publisher, 1964.

[3] Norman L. Gage, ed., Chicago: American Educational Research Association, Rand McNally, 1963.

[4] Henry David, *op. cit.*, p. 182.

The Advisory Committee of the Project noted that as new, better prepared faculty become available, with more advanced education, with greater sophistication and skill in teaching and research as well as specific social work content, they may constitute a threat to their more traditionally prepared seniors, even the very good ones. No content area is static, and continuing education in all components is a pertinent need for all faculty. It is therefore appropriate to include continuing faculty development of the whole collegium as an essential phase in the process.

CURRENT CONTINUING DEVELOPMENT PRACTICES

Eleven schools responded to the survey questionnaire sent to twenty-nine individuals identified by their schools as responsible for "Faculty Development or Improvement of Teaching Methodology and Instruction." The following questions were posed:

What is the scope and what are the objectives of this assignment? What have been the activities and what structures have been employed? Do you have any "pet ideas" that may be helpful?

The responses to the question about scope and objectives, (including analogous data from the earlier survey questionnaire sent to all deans) fall into two categories: one is the in-service growth of the members of the faculty and the second is curriculum development, i.e., evaluation, planning, coordination. In one sense, of course, the two categories are closely related, since participation in curriculum building inevitably results in both individual and collective growth. It is not surprising therefore that several schools assign the scope of these responsibilities to the "coordinator of educational programs" and the "director of curriculum."

The activities and structures are essentially similar to those listed in the earlier chapter on induction: various groupings and subgroupings of faculty which meet and work together on a regular or periodic basis; annual seminars and faculty retreats, the latter in several instances lasting for a three-day period away from the campus; the use of consultation; and invited authorities from social work and from other disciplines, e.g., from education, introduce new content and teaching methodologies. One school noted that their two-year experience of preparing for a ten year reaccreditation visit had ben an "exhausting but eminently worthwhile effort because it sparked changes and openness to new ideas; improvements in teaching method, content, structure, and organization of the curriculum resulted." A few schools sent examples of plans for institutes on which they are currently or have recently been working.[5]

In this connection, it should be noted that there has been an increasing number of requests made to CSWE staff for consultation and help in conducting faculty workshops on teaching and learning. Schools and individual faculty have reached out eagerly for the publications, e.g., the *Source Book of Readings on Teaching in Social Work*, and the *Teacher's Compendium*. Active use is made of the library in this area at the offices of the CSWE. There is lively interest in the increasing number of sessions and workshops (many of which are frequently oversubscribed) at the Annual Program Meetings of CSWE that deal with teaching and learning.

Here, as in the instance of the induction phase, the impression one gathers—our survey was not rigorous enough to make it appropriate to draw conclusions—is that there is recognition both of a range of need for continuing development and of a degree of administrative responsibility for enhancing it. Action on this responsibility, however, is based less upon long-term design than it is upon imaginative thrusts, the seizing of fortuitous moments, or the response to a pressing concern. Again, what is at the level of idea and dream at one school is an established modus operandi at another.

ADDITIONAL CONCERNS

There are three additional concerns which have been noted from sources other than the surveys and workshops conducted for this Project, concerns which appear to fall most appropriately within the continuing development phase.

The first is the need for research in social work *education*. It is not necessary here to review the volume of useful educational research which is currently being done in many quarters whose findings have applicability for social work education. Referring to the generic field of teacher education, Hermanowicz describes the "uncertainty of knowledge and curriculum most pertinent to teacher education" and notes "newer developments in the systematic study of teaching" in the past decade.

> Such systematic studies represent points on a continuum starting with purely descriptive studies of teaching but advancing to controlled investigations which yield broad generalizations about the

[5] See, for example, Victoria Olds, "Activities To Improve the Quality of Instruction at a School of Social Work," *Social Work Education Reporter*, XIV: 3 (Sept., 1966), pp. 37 ff.

phenomenon. A proposal for utilizing present descriptive studies of teaching for improving teacher education merits attention. Essentially the proposal suggests that teacher candidates emulate the mode of inquiry of the researchers in a clinical approach to direct study of ongoing teaching.[6]

The need for increased research into the effectiveness of teaching in the social work curriculum on an organized and comprehensive basis is also evident. Current effort appears to be accounted for essentially in occasional dissertations by the small number of doctoral candidates in social work. Perhaps the following observation about the "vagueness of educational aims . . . of contemporary American education" is too harsh to apply to social work education, but it cannot be completely discounted:

> Statements of the purposes of universities and colleges found in their catalogues are often cast in the most general terms. Course descriptions, on the other hand, are often precise, but the precision is in describing what is done, but not the outcomes hoped for or the relation of these to the general purpose. This lack of precision in defining aims presents a criterion problem for the experimenter. If one does not know what he is aiming at, how can he tell whether one method or another achieves it more economically?[7]

A promising response to this problem in professional education is to be found in the emergence of centers for the study of medical education, which grew out of short institutes for medical educators in the 1950's. At the present time nine centers are active in research in medical education and a rapid rate of growth is anticipated.[8]

---

[6] Henry J. Hermanowicz, "Studies of Teaching and Their Impact on Future Developments in Teacher Education," paper prepared for the Conference Honoring Florence B. Stratemeyer, French Lick, Indiana, June 10-12, 1965.

[7] *Better Utilization of College Teaching Resources*, A Summary Report (New York: The Fund for the Advancement of Educaiton, 1959) p. 56. See also, Samuel Baskin, "Innovations in College Teaching," with commentaries, and W. J. Mc-Keachie, "Research in Teaching: The Gap Between Theory and Practice," with commentaries, in *Improving College Teaching, op. cit.,* pp. 181-251.

[8] Interview with Dr. George E. Miller, Director of the Center for the Study of Medical Education, University of Illinois, College of Medicine, May 31, 1966. In order to meet the needs of medical faculty currently holding responsible positions in universities and hospitals, a 40 day medical teacher training program is offered. Independent study with close tutorial support is the primary format and highly individualized activities predominate. Attention is given to: (1) planning for learning —how to make the best use in the medical setting of what is known about learning; (2) how to select the most useful instructional materials and methods for different learning objectives; (3) the evaluation of students and programs—how to measure the results of instruction, documenting student progress, and determining suit-

Schools of social work situated in sparsely populated areas have a special problem. These schools are faced with what has been referred to as "geographical incest," namely, many of the faculty personnel they recruit have had contact only with that school: first they were students at the school, they then remained in the same area as practitioners and supervisors after graduation, and subsequently they returned to the school as faculty. Even though the schools deliberately recruit for "outsiders," they face the likelihood of the development of an inbred faculty with a sense of isolation from the mainstream of the field.

A third area of concern stems from what appears to be the uneven use of opportunities for individual continuing education, such as postdoctoral research and study through planned leaves of absence. In some schools there is supportive policy and effective use. In general, however, social work schools and faculty appear to have been underrepresented in the use of grants for which they are eligible, such as the postdoctoral research fellowships of the Public Health Service and the Office of Education.

Social work faculty are probably uniquely close to developments in the field and in practice. They often serve as consultants in the development of new programs. Their mature students, who come to school for their professional education, have field placements in new programs and in agencies where innovation is constant. All these serve to prevent obsolescence of the teacher. However, it may be helpful to note that in a program of the psychology section of the NIMH Training Branch, special efforts are made to provide opportunities for *senior* faculty to renew direct contact—through direct service—with new developments.

The outstanding characteristic of current practice is that it grows out of the immediate tasks of curriculum building and evaluation, and only incidentally provides for both individual and collective growth. Long-term overall designs for continuing development within the school is the exception.

---

ability and effectiveness of the teaching program; (4) educational research—how to add new knowledge to understanding of the educational process; and (5) educational leadership—how to recognize the importance of group activities in forming policies, making decisions, and implementing change in educational institutions.

In addition to the heavy research emphasis in the postgraduate program described above, the Center provides fellowships for those medical teachers desiring to make a stronger commitment to education through independent study, utilizing the resources and staff of the Center for one year periods. Also graduate degree programs are designed to help meet the need for competent researchers, teachers, and leaders in medical education to provide an integrated program of basic course work, independent study, and individual research in medical education.

STRENGTHENING THE CONTINUING
DEVELOPMENT PRACTICES

As in the proposals for the induction phase, the intent is to build upon the interest, activities, and structures that are now current. The programs will be intensified, however, to the extent that their objectives are precisely formulated and their scope broadened to include updating in the areas of educational and research theory as well as to developments on the frontiers of knowledge. Social work educators may be more sophisticated than some of their colleagues in the academic world with respect to educational methods; literature on education as such well reflects that sophistication. But they dare not be smug on this score. Similarly, faculty who never had an opportunity to develop research sophistication—some are the pioneers of social work education—may well want to add this dimension to their professional lives. A thoughtful in-service design can achieve these goals.

The rationale for the identification of faculty development as an established function in each school with explicit assignment of this function has been presented in the previous chapter. This responsibility will not be an incidental one, if its scope is conceived as including not only the induction of new faculty, but also coordination of career teacher internships and the planning of comprehensive in-service programs for all faculty. A productive climate for continuing development and for *valuing* creative and innovative teaching is not happenstance! Also, day-to-day responsibilities can be skillfully designed and utilized to be growth-producing (or they may fail to be so).

The ingredients for a program of continuing faculty development are succinctly enumerate by Tschudin:

1. A philosophy of continuing faculty education that recognizes the responsibility of both the individual faculty member and the administrator for its accomplishment.

2. A school climate that is conducive to faculty self-direction, individual freedom of thought and action, and a sense of personal responsibility for that action.

3. School policies and practices that support the concept of continuing faculty education together with a corresponding system of rewards and recognition.

4. A willingness on the part of the administrator to develop

long-range goals and to seek vigorously the means, financial and other, of achieving these goals.[9]

The responsibility of administration and responsibility of individuals for their *self-development* are not mutually exclusive:

> Since 90 percent of all learning is self-learning, then it goes without saying that the most effective and the most meaningful development is self-development. Many of us need some external stimulus. . . . This role can best be filled by our colleagues, the department chairman, the supervisor of instruction, the dean, or a combination of these professional associates.[10]

A major thrust in this direction is to be found in a proposal being developed by the CSWE Committee on Teaching Methodology and Materials. A two-week seminar is to be offered that will bring together faculty development personnel from all the schools, outstanding experts in learning and instructional theory, and carefully selected educators from other professions. Careful preparation by the participants in advance of the seminar will be followed by a year of operational experience, and a closing two-week seminar period, with documentation of the seminar proceedings and the interim year. The participants, in turn, will bring impetus to their schools for influencing the climate for continuing faculty development.

RESEARCH IN SOCIAL WORK EDUCATION

The focus in all the proposals thus far has been on the faculty member, his preparation, and development. In the following proposal the focus shifts to the systematic collection and increase of data about the educational enterprise *per se* and about the teaching-learning process—the content base for faculty development.

There are several alternatives and combinations by which increased research in social work education may be effected. Sustained and possibly increased activity by the CSWE as sponsor of projects about the educational enterprise as a whole is indicated. It is important that

---

[9] Mary Tschudin, "The Administrator's Responsibility for Continuing Education of Nurse Faculty Members," in *Nursing Education—Creative, Continuing, Experimental,* papers presented at the Twentieth Conference of the Council of Member Agencies of the Department of Baccalaurate and Higher Degree Programs, New York: National League for Nursing, 1966, p. 43.

[10] Thompson, *op. cit.,* p. 38.

there be continuing updating of data about sources of faculty, their preparation, their assignments, practices developed by schools for induction and continuing development, and evaluation of these practices. In short, recent or current projects such as the Survey of Graduate Faculty and the present Project are preliminary, and their value will be minimal unless they are used as bases for more intensive study. Many of the proposals listed earlier depend upon continuing central research.

With reference to building greater sophistication in the methodologies used by social work education, including patterns of field instruction, advising, classroom teaching, etc., two alternate or supplemental patterns suggest themselves. One fruitful approach may lie in cooperative projects stimulated by the needs of this field, to be undertaken in existing centers of educational research. Exploratory steps in this direction have already been undertaken by CSWE staff. A second approach may be found in the development of a center for research in social work education by one of the schools that is interested in making social work education one of its specializations, analogous to other centers which specialize in social welfare policy, or practice research may be encouraged. Powers sees research in medical *education* as one ingredient in knowledge building in medicine itself.[11] There is reason to believe that one of the schools which has a traditional or campus-wide enthusiasm for educational research may well bid to make its distinctive contribution in this area of specialization.

The objectives of an educational research program, at either of the two types of centers, will include both the profession-wide upgrading of teaching, and the expansion of knowledge about the educational process for social work education, hopefully for other professional education as well. In addition, activities to achieve these ends will include: seminars for faculty development chairmen, conducted on a continuing basis, provision of fellowship opportunities for specialized studies in the educational process, and encouragement of evaluative and experimental research in education. It is reasonable to encourage an increase in the number of doctoral dissertations dealing with social work education. Finally, research in higher education, in education for other professions, as well as in social work education, may usefully be collected, summarized, and reported centrally, in media such as the CSWE's *Journal of Education for Social Work* and *Social Work Education Reporter*.

---

[11] Interview with Lee Powers, M.D., Association of American Medical Schools, June 3, 1966.

EXCHANGES OF FACULTY AND
LEAVES OF ABSENCE

Several practices, indigenous to higher education, have special pertinence to our present concern. Schools that are small or are geographi-
cally isolated (not necessarily the new ones) may well benefit from
exchanges of individual faculty members with those from other schools.
(Of course, as more faculty become available who have completed
advanced study, and as even the remotely located schools participate in
career-teacher internship arrangements, part of this problem will be
diminished.) It is not suggested that the exchanges of faculty be made
on the basis of "lend-lease" which implies "help to the underdeveloped,"
which is the tone of some of the exchange-of-faculty programs reported recently. The intent is clear that the exchanges should be mutually stimulating.

No specific attention was directed in the study to the extent of the
use of leaves of absence and sabbaticals as ingredients in faculty development programs. To urge these arrangements is probably gra-
tuitous, since their rationale is well known. It may be helpful, however, to note a specific device encouraged by the NIMH Training
Branch, Psychology Section. In this program, special efforts are made
to provide opportunities for senior faculty to renew direct contact with
new developments in the field of practice for relatively short periods
of time.

Social work faculty are probably uniquely close to developments in
the field, as has been noted earlier. It may be appropriate, however,
to urge formulation of policy which would encourage full leaves of
absence by senior faculty for short periods of time for the benefit
of the individual, the agency, and the school. It would also serve an
additional purpose: it could help "short circuit the cultural lag" between teaching and practice in the field,[12] which presents a constant
problem in all professional education.

Summary of Proposals

The importance and the problems of continuing faculty development have been briefly reviewed. Current practices have been described. Here, as in the discussion of the induction phase, the desirability for identification of faculty development as an explicit func-

---

[12] Term suggested by Dr. Forrest Tyler, Training Branch, NIMH.

tion with responsibility for comprehensive in-service programming is apparent. In addition, increased activity in research in social work education is urged and suggestions are considered for assuring the increase. Exchanges of faculty and leaves of absence for continuing renewal, both of the individual and the collectivity, are also suggested.

Proposals have been outlined in these chapters for increasing the quantity and use of sources of potential faculty and for insuring the quality of their preparation and in-service development. In the next chapter, these proposals are recast as recommendations to the CSWE and its appropriate committees for evaluation, as "agenda items" for consideration by the faculties of the several schools, and as implications for the social agencies. All of these have a stake in faculty development in professional education for social work, and in the "habitual vision of greatness" which Whitehead has called the essential quality of any great faculty.

CHAPTER 9

Activating the Proposals

The proposals in the preceding chapters have been formulated and discussed at the level of concept and principle. The discussion has aimed to explicate intent, rationale, and direction. Before intent can become reality, the proposals must be further tested by all the sectors of the educational enterprise. In this chapter, therefore, the proposals are recast as policy recommendations to the Council on Social Work Education in the attempt to give impetus to the long process ahead.[1]

Each recommendation will need to be evaluated and developed into a program by appropriate staff and committees within the Council, by the individual schools of social work, and by the constituent national agencies of the Council. The recommendations, therefore, become "agenda items" to be selected according to institutional priorities. Specific programming suggestions are provided as examples, but are not intended to be definitive or restrictive. It is to be expected that alternatives will emerge from intensive discussion which will insure achievement of the essential purposes of the present Project.

THE PRE-SERVICE PHASE

A major thrust behind several of the proposals for the long view is to be found in the emphasis upon the need to identify components of educational preparation rather than to argue for specific formal degree or experience requirements. Personal and charismatic qualifications are, of course, important. Identification with the values of the professions of social work and of education has not been included, because these are *outcomes* of appropriate preparation.

---

[1] The recommendations included in this chapter were accepted in principle by the Board of Directors of the Council on Social Work Education on March 30, 1967.

Of the four components of preparation that have been identified, substantive mastery of an area of content and ability to teach that content seem to be beyond debate: they are essential components of preparation and serve as basic criteria for any teaching faculty member. On the other hand, there are at least two levels that are fruitfully identified in each of the practice and research components: a basic level of sophistication and a high level of aptitude and skill. As components of preparation for teaching in a graduate professional school, a high level of skill either in practice or research with basic knowledge and "valuing" of the other are desirable, and may eventually come to be considered essential for all social work faculty.

1. *Profiles*—The balance of these components in the profile of a faculty will reflect the unique mission and emphases of each school. The availability of profiles will make possible a more deliberate and increased use of points of entry within the professional route as well as of the academic and acculturation routes. They may also provide more concrete points of reference for giving direction to potential faculty.

It is therefore recommended that the Council on Social Work Education

a) offer consultation and assist in the development of guidelines for faculty profiling by schools of social work, and

b) maintain an up-to-date inventory of faculty profiles which will show the kinds and numbers of positions for which potential faculty may prepare.

Concurrently, each of the schools of social work is urged to identify the balance of special competencies desired, and to develop faculty profiles which reflect that school's character and emphasis. As a consequence of the profiling activity, schools may find opportunities for a planned increase in the use of the heretofore relatively neglected points of entry and routes.

2. *Advanced Education*—The second major thrust of this report is directed to the need for advanced education beyond the master's level as the means for securing the desired preparation in each of the components. The formats currently available for advanced educational programs may need to be revised or new formats developed; all, however, must reflect a rational articulation with, and response to, the balance of components specified by the profiles which emerge.

It is therefore recommended that the CSWE undertake responsibility to

141

a) establish advanced education as a major means for faculty qualification in the requisite components, and

b) increase opportunities for advanced study.

Activities suggested by this recommendation include: the offering of consultation to schools which have advanced certificate and doctoral programs with teacher preparation objectives in a review of the curricular offerings designed to achieve them; a continuing review of the programs' objectives against the inventory of faculty profiles to identify where new programs are needed; assistance in achieving for the field as a whole a balance between available specializations and the priorities indicated by the inventory of profiles; development of guidelines, in consultation with appropriate representatives of advanced education in social work, for responsible expansion of programs of advanced education; and maintenance of an up-to-date inventory of available resources for those who undertake advanced education, with reference both to specializations and to financing.

A major activity under this recommendation provides for continuing initiative by the CSWE in working for the expansion of financial resources for advanced study, and for any indicated adjustments in current criteria so that they are appropriate to the distinctive needs in social work education.

Leadership by the CSWE is also indicated for exploring with schools of social work their interest in working toward acceptance of a two-year doctorate (in addition to the two-year MSW) which will appropriately symbolize qualification for a *professional educator* in social work; and for considering proposals, or taking the initiative, if appropriate, for collective action in cooperation with other interests in higher education in gaining acceptance of a new doctoral degree for educators.

Finally, the recommendation covers the encouragement by the CSWE of increased short-term opportunities, by means of institutes, workshops, and short courses *at the advanced level* in the subject matter, research, and teaching components. A major contribution may be made by reviewing annually the availability of short-term educational opportunities. Schools that are equipped to do so may be encouraged to increase the regional availability of post-master's offerings and to participate in inter-school regional planning where appropriate. Coordination and publicizing of the availability of short-term or summer programs is indicated.

Each of these groupings of activities has concurrent counterparts as agenda items for consideration by the schools, to the end that they set

142

their own priorities among the alternative for advanced study either offered by them or whose use they encourage. For example: schools which offer advanced educational programs are urged to review their curricular offerings to assure that they provide appropriate opportunities for those preparing for educational careers to qualify in the subject matter, research, and teaching components. Many will conceivably need to introduce or strengthen the curricular offerings designed to improve teaching ability. Hopefully, it will also be possible to make adjustments *within the essential requirements* to provide opportunities for individuals at mid-career to fulfill residence requirements (possibly in two half-year periods) and to give appropriate recognition for the invaluable professional life experience which they bring.

All schools are urged to assess their capacity for introducing or increasing summer session and non-degree short term offerings at the advanced level, with a balance of the content, research, and teaching components.

They are also urged to seek opportunities consistent with their own faculty profiles to make increased use of the several points of entry as well as the academic and acculturation routes. Administrative adjustments such as leaves of absence will need to be made so that faculty not fully qualified in the basic components may participate in advanced educational programs and agency employment designed to provide practice experience.

Agencies are urged to evaluate their current experience in making available summer and part-time employment designed to provide practice experience for those who come by way of the academic and acculturation routes, and to assess their ability to increase the availability of such opportunities. Hopefully, agencies will consider administrative adjustments necessary so that their personnel on part-time teaching assignments in schools can exploit opportunities for the meaningful development of their teaching ability.

3. *Ability to Teach*—Ability to teach can best be improved through a combination of seminar and field experiences under skilled guidance. A considerable input will be required to achieve this goal. Curricular offerings as ingredients of advanced education have already been stipulated. The use of a career teacher internship has also been described. Alternatives for making the career teacher experience operational include: (1) availability of a career teacher internship associated with existing advanced certificate and doctoral requirements, (2) incorporation of career teacher programs within new doctoral programs which may be developed as a "way station" between the period of advanced study and a full-time teaching appointment (as in

143

the current NIMH-supported format), or (3) as a discrete year for prospective faculty.

> It is recommended that the CSWE take the initiative in emphasizing the importance of the teaching component, in exploring the alternatives for career teacher internships designed to insure ability to teach, and in expanding the acceptance and use of one of the alternatives.

The Council should plan and offer summer institutes dealing with the teaching component in regions where they are not available under individual school auspices. The CSWE sponsored institutes should be planned to provide for follow-up on their effectiveness and acceptance with a view to the ultimate development of format and content on a demonstration basis.

The Council's leadership role also envisions the developing of guidelines and in assisting interested schools—those which offer advanced programs and those which are available for making career teacher year appointments—enter into compacts for interschool cooperation. It may call a conference of interested schools to develop the mechanics for interschool cooperation, and for exploring with schools their interest in working toward acceptance of a doctorate which incorporates a career teacher internship to testify to qualification of professional educators for social work.

Each school is urged to assess the feasibility of developing its resources for serving as a locus of a qualitative career teacher internship, either in compact with an advanced educational program offered at another school, or as a "way station" for prospective faculty. All schools are also urged to give serious consideration to instituting some of the controls of an internship in the appointment and planning for their own new faculty who have not had previous preparation or who are not qualified in this component.

4. *Recruitment*—The several recommendations and activities included thus far must be supported by concurrent and continuing efforts to attract and to inform prospective faculty about career opportunities in social work education, about alternate routes and points of entry and their associated preparation, and about resources for planning new careers, as well as the rewards.

> It is recommended that the CSWE undertake responsibility for a major comprehensive and planned recruitment effort to inform, interest, and attract potential faculty.

144

Under this recommendation, the following activities are indicated: contact with key agencies, institutions, and individuals throughout the country to identify and reach social workers who have interest and potential for teaching; organizing special meetings and programs in large cities, and state, regional, and national conferences to inform individuals about career opportunities, and to follow up with those who express interest; the development, publication, and distribution of recruitment publications to provide information about opportunities and resources; the design of further research to study factors affecting recruitment of faculty; providing consultation to those who approach the CSWE, and publicizing the availability of this service; developing of placement procedures to help all individuals learn of faculty vacancies and help schools become aware of all interested individuals.

A concurrent task of all the schools for participating in the field-wide recruitment program includes identifying and encouraging as early as feasible among their own students, at the master's and advanced levels, and from among their contacts with agency personnel those who show potential for faculty careers. They can then be referred to resources, including the CSWE, for help in selecting programs by which they can qualify, and to resources for financial aid.

The constituent agencies are urged to review their planned participation in the total recruitment effort, including the identification and encouragement of potential faculty within their staffs, and to inform them of resources for help in planning for faculty careers.

THE INDUCTION PHASE

Many schools are employing a variety of practices which assist the new faculty member make the transition to full responsibility as an educator. Some of the practices are specifically designed for new faculty; much of the orientation to the day-to-day life of the school and the socialization to the *collegium* is informal. Established practices at some schools are desired projections for the future at others.

Two areas of need during the induction period that are least accounted for are: (1) socialization to the university and the establishing of working interdisciplinary relationships on the campus, and (2) orientation to the total educational enterprise which includes higher education and social work education.

It is recommended that the CSWE undertake responsibility for participating with the schools in programs designed to assist new faculty in their transition during the induction phase.

145

The Council can play a key role in strengthening transition practices through activities such as gathering information and assessing group and individual approaches to meeting the several transition needs, and offering consultation to the individuals in the schools responsible for the induction of new faculty. The Council also has a specialized responsibility for orientation of new faculty to the social work educational scene. For example, through specially scheduled sessions for new faculty at regional centers or at the Annual Program Meeting, a perspective can be provided for understanding the significance of the current issues before the field and specific concerns of new faculty can be discussed. Although in the long view the teaching component will be provided as preparation in the preservice period, the Council can meantime make a significant contribution for those who do not have adequate preparation in this component by offering special workshops on teaching at the Annual Program Meeting or on a regional basis.

Schools are urged to continue efforts towards enriching the transition period and to consider structural and programmatic innovations designed to that end. It is suggested, for example, that faculty development be identified as an explicit responsibility to be assigned to a member of the faculty for developing a comprehensive program both for the induction of new faculty and the continuing development of the whole faculty. An induction program may well include orientation and socialization to the university as well as to the ongoing curricular and other concerns of the school's faculty. Structural elements will ideally include provision for a "tooling up" period before the assumption of full teaching and other responsibilities, and a protected reduced assignment during the first year. Support and encouragement of new faculty to attend the Annual Program Meeting during the first year are also urged.

CONTINUING DEVELOPMENT

Continuing development is as crucial for a faculty of a school of social work as it is for a staff of an agency. Although all schools and their individual faculty members currently participate in a variety of activities which enhance their continuing development, much of it is on a fortuitous basis.

It is recommended that the CSWE undertake leadership responsibility in strengthening practices for the continuing development of social work faculty.

The Council can appropriately organize invitational seminars for enhancing the leadership within the schools charged with responsibility for the continuing development programs. This recommendation also includes the dissemination of information about practices and opportunities, such as leaves of absence, to make greater use of post-doctoral research fellowships and positions in agency practice and research. Schools may welcome assistance in arranging compacts for the exchange of faculty to accomplish cross school fertilization.

The designation of faculty development as an explicit administrative function has been suggested in the section on Induction. This function, analogous to the staff development function in agency administration, is inclusive both of the induction and continuing development phases. In addition, schools are urged to consider how they can give structural support to faculty so that they can make fuller use of leaves of absence for research career development fellowships, and for direct practice experiences, particularly in innovative practice settings. Faculty exchanges on a reciprocal basis among the schools should also be explored.

Concurrently, agencies will be looked to for cooperative arrangements by which short-term opportunities may be made available for faculty to participate in practice in the emerging programs.

Complementary to the responsibility for research in social welfare policy, programs, and practice, and as underpinning for the continuing improvement of teaching in social work, research in social work education must be strengthened.

It is recommended that the CSWE take leadership responsibility for increasing research in social work education.

The scope of the research will include continuing updating of information about current faculty as well as long-term designs for testing the efficacy and efficiency of the several methodologies with which the field is concerned.

This recommendation may be operationalized by alternate means, including the encouragement of the development of a center for research in social work education at one of the schools, and/or research with this focus at an existing educational research center, in addition to continuing and increased sponsorship of research by the Council itself. The Council has a role in the dissemination of research findings to the field.

147

CHAPTER 10

Epilogue

The discussion in these pages has been limited arbitrarily to a focus upon our stated purpose: increasing the quantity and improving the quality of faculty for social work education. Additional considerations related to the discussion might well have received attention, but did not find their place in the body of the text.

The tasks for the Faculty Development Project have been approached from the point of view of the social work educational enterprise as a whole—the partnership within the Council on Social Work Education of the graduate schools, the social agencies across the country, and individuals interested in its work. Parts of the report may also be found to be pertinent to the problems of undergraduate programs in social welfare. But faculty development must also be viewed from the perspective of the individual faculty member and the individual school. This postscript weaves together three essential themes which are too easily underplayed in a broad-based undertaking: autonomy, interdependence, and opportunity for the individual faculty member and for the individual school.

To the individual faculty member—more than five thousand are now so identified—and the even larger number expected in the coming years, a message so obvious that it may too easily be overlooked bears explicit repetition. The essential quality of scholarly activity is to be found in the actualization of autonomy in delicate balance with productive interdependence. Just as the ultimate test of the professional is the degree to which he has learned to take responsibility for his own growth, so is the responsibility for the pre-service and in-service development of a faculty member retained by the individual himself. At best, the "establishment" can help; it cannot insure.

The other side of the coin also bears repetition: in addition to the minutiae about career lines, needs, and problems in preparation, induction, and continuing development, there are rewards of teaching. Those who have taught know the rewards; those who may be considering a teaching career should not overlook the promise. Each successful teacher tries to communicate the quality of the satisfactions in his own words. Consider these, for example:

> . . . For it is the teachers who will make the [educational] pro-grams, and keep them fresh and thriving. Programs, no matter how well conceived, will wilt and die . . . with poor teachers. . . .

> But the prospective social work teacher has a responsibility too, one we should not and cannot take away from him. He may have to resist our efforts and blandishments to recruit him for teaching, unless teaching is right for him. His is the responsibility for look-ing beneath any surface reasons which may have attracted him to teaching initially, and beyond our importuning, as he asks himself whether he can truly find his best fulfillment through being the kind of teacher social work needs. Some of this he can discover only as he tries, with the planned devoted help of the individual school to which he comes. He will know with a deep inner cer-tainty, despite all the inevitable ups and downs along the way, whether it is worth it to him to undergo the discipline of continu-ous study and independent professional production in writing and research, to sustain the steady warm giving response to group after group of students. . . .

> If he is really a teacher he will give it up for no other calling on earth, for he will leave each class, weary certainly, but touched with new life too, having been a part of . . . many others becoming, not only social workers, surer of purpose and possessed of in-creased knowledge and skill for pursuing it, but *persons* of greater dimension.[1]

These themes apply also to the individual schools within their own larger configurations. Their autonomy carries with it both responsibility and opportunity. No master plan can be proposed as good as the real-ity which must emerge as each unit within the whole undertakes in good faith to achieve and to discover. These achievements and dis-coveries, freely polled, will constitute the enduring outcomes to which all are committed.

Autonomy, interdependence, and opportunity are also appropriately tested in the relationship of social work education, as an entity within the larger encompassing context of higher education. The Project was

---

[1] Ruth E. Smalley, "Career Opportunities in Social Work Education: Requirements, Preparation, and Rewards of Teaching," presented at National Conference on Social Welfare, Chicago, June 2, 1966.

generated by pressures within social work education, and its proposals are addressed primarily to this field. Here has been an expression of its autonomy. Perhaps, also, here may be found a modest outreach to other sectors within the world of higher education and education for the professions toward the building of a mutually productive interdependence.

The affairs of modern man are complex, and the view of his future is uncertain. The affairs of university life have a parallel complexity and uncertainty. The future in this arena, as in the whole world of man, desperately seeks talent and daring to exploit the purposefulness and modest "know-how" which are now available. The hard work ahead is at once a burden and a joy.

Bibliography

BOOKS

Abbott, Edith. *Social Welfare and Professional Education*. Chicago: University of Chicago Press, 1931.

American Association of Colleges for Teacher Education. *Proceeedings Eighteenth Yearbook (Action for Improvement of Teacher Education)*, 1965.

American Council on Education. *Studies: The Preparation of College Teachers*, Theodore C. Blegen and Russell M. Cooper, eds., 1950. *Graduate Study for Future College Teachers*, Joseph Axelrod, ed., 1959. *Toward Improving Ph.D. Programs*, Edward H. Hollis, ed., 1945. *Vital Issues in Education*, A. E. Traxler, ed., 1957. *Expanding Resources for College Teaching*, 1956. Washington, D. C.: American Council on Education.

American Medical Association. *Medical Education in the United States, 1964-65*. Reprinted from the *Education Number of the Journal of the American Medical Association*, 194:7 (November 15, 1965).

Association for Higher Education. *Current Issues in Higher Education*, G. Kerry Smith, ed., 1959 and 1960. Washington, D. C.: National Education Association.

Association of American Law Schools. *Anatomy of Modern Legal Education*. St. Paul: West Publishing Co., 1961. *Proceedings*, 1965.

Association of American Medical Colleges. *Lifetime Learning for Physicians: Principles, Practices, Proposals*. Report by Bernard Dryer, Study Director, Part 2, *Journal of Medical Education*, 37:6 (June, 1962).

Berelson, Bernard. *Graduate Education in the United States*. New York: McGraw-Hill, 1960.

Berson, Robert C. *Medical Schools in the U.S. at Mid-Century*. New York: McGraw-Hill, 1953.

Blauch, Lloyd E. *Education for the Professions*. Washington, D. C.: U.S. Government Printing Office, 1955.

Blaustein, Albert P. and Porter, Charles O. *The American Lawyer*. A Summary of the Survey of the Legal Profession. Chicago: University of Chicago Press, 1954.

151

Blessing, James H. *Graduate Education. An Annotated Bibliography.* Washington, D. C.: U.S. Government Printing Office, 1961.

Boehm, Werner W., ed. *Objectives of the Social Work Curriculum of the Future.* Vol. I, Curriculum Study. New York: Council on Social Work Education, 1959.

Borrowman, Merle I., ed. *Teacher Education in America: A Documentary History.* New York: Teachers College, Columbia University, 1965.

Bruner, Jerome S. *The Process of Education.* Cambridge: Harvard University Press, 1962.

Carmichael, Oliver. *Graduate Education.* New York: Harper and Brothers, 1961.

Carnegie Foundation for the Advancement of Teaching. *The Flight From Teaching.* New York: The Carnegie Foundation for the Advancement of Teaching, 1964.

Conant, James B. *The Education of American Teachers.* New York: McGraw-Hill, 1963.

Cottrell, Donald B., ed. *Teacher Education For a Free People.* Oneonta, New York: American Association of Colleges For Teacher Education, 1956.

Council on Graduate Schools in the United States. *Proceedings of Fifth Annual Meeting. Theme: The Graduate Student,* James N. Eshelman, ed., 1965.

Council on Social Work Education. *Contemporary Education for Social Work in the United States.* New York: Council on Social Work Education, 1966.

————. *Education for Social Work.* Proceedings of Annual Program Meetings. New York: Council on Social Work Education, 1953 through 1963.

————. *Field Instruction in Graduate Social Work Education—Old Problems and New Proposals.* New York: Council on Social Work Education, 1966.

————. *Social Work Education and Social Welfare Manpower: Present Realities and Future Imperatives.* New York: Council on Social Work Education, 1965.

————. *Statistics on Social Work Education, November 1, 1966 and Academic Year 1965-1966.* See also *Annual Statistics* for previous years.

Cutler, James E. and Davie, Maurice R. *A Study in Professional Education at Western Reserve University.* Cleveland: Western Reserve University Press, 1930.

Deitrick, John E. and Berson, Robert C. *Medical Schools in the United States.* New York: McGraw-Hill, 1953.

Diekhoff, John S. *The Domain of the Faculty.* New York: Harper and Brothers.

————. *Tomorrow's Professors.* New York: Fund for the Advancement of Education, n.d.

Elliot, Jo Eleanor. *Toward More Effective Teaching in WCHEN Schools. Report of a Course in New Training Techniques for Nurse Faculty.* Boulder, Colorado: Western Interstate Commission for Higher Education, 1964.

Estrin, Herman A. and Goode, Delmer M. *Improving College and University Teaching.* Dubuque, Iowa: C. Brown Co., 1964.

Frankel, Charles, ed. *Issues in University Education: Essays by Ten American Scholars.* New York: Harper and Brothers, 1959.

Freeman, Howard E. *et al.*, eds. *Handbook of Medical Sociology.* Englewood Cliffs, N. J.: Prentice-Hall, 1963.

Fund for the Advancement of Education. *Better Utilization of College Teaching Resources. A Summary Report.* New York: Fund for the Advancement of Education, 1959.

Furniss, Edgar S. *The Graduate School of Yale,* New Haven: Carl Purington Rollins, 1965.

Gage, Norman L., ed. *Handbook of Research on Teaching.* Chicago: American Educational Research Association, Rand McNally, 1963.

Gardner, John. *Self-Renewal: The Individual and the Innovative Society.* New York: Harper & Row, 1963.

Gray, William Scott, ed. *The Preparation and In-Service Training of College Teachers.* Chicago: University of Chicago Press, 1938.

————, ed. *The Training of College Teachers.* Chicago: University of Chicago Press, 1930.

Hamachek, Don E., ed. *The Self in Growth, Teaching and Learning.* Englewood Cliffs, N. J.: Prentice-Hall, 1965.

Harno, Albert J. *Legal Education in the U.S.* San Francisco: Bancroft-Whitney, 1953.

Higher Education and the Demand for Scientific Manpower in the United States. Paris, France: Organization for Economic Cooperation and Development, 1963.

Higher Education for American Democracy: A Report of the President's Commission on Higher Education. Vol. 4. *Staffing Higher Education.* New York: Harper and Brothers, 1947.

Hofstadter, Richard and Metzger, Walter P. *The Development of Academic Freedom in the United States.* New York: Columbia University Press, 1955.

Hollis, Ernest W. and Taylor, Alice. *Social Work Education in the United States.* New York: Columbia University Press, 1951.

Horowitz, Milton J. *Educating Tomorrow's Doctors.* New York: Appleton-Century-Crofts, 1964.

Ingham, R. J., ed. *Institutional Backgrounds of Adult Education.* Boston: Center for the Study of Liberal Education for Adults at Boston University, 1966.

Jones, Howard Mumford. *Education and World Tragedy.* Cambridge: Boston Technical Publishers, 1946.

Kaplan, M. Stephen. *The College Teacher Shortage: What You Can Do.* Boulder, Colorado: Western Interstate Commission for Higher Education, 1963.

Koen, Frank and Ericksen, Stanford C. *An Analysis of the Specific Features Which Characterize the More Successful Programs for the Recruitment and Training of College Teachers.* Ann Arbor, Michigan: Center for Research on Learning and Teaching, University of Michigan, 1967.

Lee, Calvin B. T., ed. *Improving College Teaching.* Washington, D. C.: American Council on Education, 1967.

McGlothlin, William J. *Patterns of Professional Education.* New York: G. P. Putnam's Sons, 1960.

————. *The Professional Schools.* New York: Center for Applied Research in Education, 1964.

McGrath, Earl J. *The Graduate School and the Decline of Liberal Education.* New York: Columbia University Press, 1959.

————. *Liberal Education in the Professions.* New York: Columbia University Press, 1959.

Merle, Sherman. *Undergraduate Social Welfare Education in the United States: A Survey of Programs, Faculty, Students.* New York: Council on Social Work Education, 1967.

National Association of Social Workers. *Encyclopedia of Social Work.* Harry L. Lurie, ed. New York: National Association of Social Workers, 1965. See "History of American Social Work," by John C. Kidneigh, pp. 3-19; and "Education for Social Work," by Rachel B. Marks, pp. 277-283.

National Commission on Teacher Education and Professional Standards. *Remaking the World of the Career Teacher.* Washington, D. C.: National Education Association, 1966.

National League for Nursing. *Nursing Education—Creative, Continuing, Experimental.* New York: National League for Nursing, 1966.

National Society for the Study of Education. *Education for the Professions.* 61st Yearbook, Part II, Nelson B. Henry, ed. Chicago: National Society for the Study of Education, 1962.

National Woodrow Wilson Fellowship Foundation. *Handbook of Fellowship Awards.* Princeton: National Woodrow Wilson Foundation, 1960.

Perkins, Dexter, Snell, John L., and Committee on Graduate Education of the American Historical Association. *The Education of Historians in the United States.* New York: McGraw Hill, 1962.

Perkins, James A. *The University in Transition.* Princeton: Princeton University Press, 1966.

Pins, Arnulf M. *Who Chooses Social Work, When and Why?* New York: Council on Social Work Education, 1963.

Pohek, Marguerite V., ed. *The Teacher's Compendium.* New York: Council on Social Work Education, 1963.

Pullias, Earl V., Lockhart, Aileene, *et al. Toward Excellence in College Teaching.* Dubuque, Iowa: William C. Brown Co., 1963.

Regensburg, Jeanette, ed. *Some Educational Patterns in Doctoral Programs in Schools of Social Work*. New York: Council on Social Work Education, 1966.

Reynolds, Bertha Capen. *Learning and Teaching in the Practice of Social Work*. New York: Rinehart & Co., 1942.

Sanford, Nevitt, ed. *The American College: A Psychological and Social Interpretation of the Higher Learning*. New York: John Wiley and Sons, 1962. See Chapter VII, "Changing Functions of the College Professor," by Robert Knapp, pp. 290-311.

Schwartz, Edward E., ed. *Manpower in Social Welfare: Research Perspectives*. New York: National Association of Social Workers, 1966.

Sourcebook of Readings on Teaching in Social Work. New York: Council on Social Work Education, 1965.

Towle, Charlotte. *The Case Method in Teaching Social Work*. New York: National Association of Social Workers, 1959.

————. *The Learner in Education for the Professions*. Chicago: University of Chicago Press, 1954.

United States Department of Health, Education, and Welfare. *Closing the Gap . . . in Social Work Manpower*. Report of the Departmental Task Force on Social Work Education and Manpower. Washington, D. C.: U. S. Department of Health, Education, and Welfare, 1965.

————. Office of Education. *Prospective Teacher Graduate Fellowships, Graduate Programs, 1966-67* and *National Defense Graduate Fellowships, Graduate Programs, 1966-67*. Washington, D. C.: U. S. Department of Health, Education, and Welfare.

Walters, Everett, ed. *Graduate Education Today*. Washington, D. C.: American Council on Education, 1965.

Wilson, Logan, ed. *Emerging Patterns in American Higher Education Today*. Washington, D. C.: American Council on Education, 1965.

ARTICLES AND PERIODICALS

Abrahamson, Stephen. "The Professional Educator and Medical Education," *Journal of Higher Education*, 31:1 (January, 1960), pp. 38-41.

Baker, Mary R. "Personnel in Social Work," in *Encyclopedia of Social Work*. Harry L. Lurie, ed. New York: National Assn. of Social Workers, 1965. pp. 532-540.

Beach, Mark. "Promoting Good Teaching in the Microversity," *Journal of Higher Education*, 37:6 (June, 1966).

Becker, Howard S. and Carper, James W. "The Development of Identification with an Occupation," *American Journal of Sociology*, 61:4 (January, 1956), pp. 289-298.

Benjamin, Harold R. W. "Ph.D.'s Preferred," *Journal of Higher Education*, 19:4 (April, 1948), pp. 189-193.

Bent, Henry E. "Professionalization of the Ph.D. Degree," *Journal of Higher Education*, 30:3 (March, 1959), pp. 140-145.

Blackey, Eileen. "Selection and Preparation of Faculty for Schools of Social Work," *Journal of Education for Social Work*, I:1 (Spring, 1965), pp. 5-12.

Blauch, Lloyd E. "Professional Education," in *Encyclopedia of Educational Research,* Chester W. H. Harris, ed., for the American Educational Research Association. New York: Macmillan Co., 1960. pp. 1056-63.

Blegen, Theodore C. "The Graduate Schools and the Education of College Teachers," *Educational Record,* 29 (January, 1948), pp. 12-25.

Brickman, William W. "Speed Up of the Ph.D. Degree," *School and Society,* 87:2146 (January 31, 1959), pp. 51-52.

Brogran, Albert P. "Restoring the Master's Degree," *Graduate Journal,* I:1 (Spring, 1958).

Broudy, Harry. "The Education of Teachers," *Journal of Teacher Education,* 13:3 (September, 1962), pp. 284-291.

"Career Instructors at University of Massachusetts," *School and Society,* 86:2132 (May, 1958), pp. 227-229.

Cox, Lanier. "The American Council on Educational Academic Administration Internship Program," *Educational Record,* 47:2 (Spring, 1966), pp. 163-172.

Coyle, Grace L. "The Role of the Teacher in the Creation of an Integrated Curriculum," *Social Work Journal,* 33:2 (April, 1952), p. 73ff.

Cutten, George B. "The College Professor as Teacher," *School and Society,* 86:3129 (October 25, 1958), pp. 372-75.

————. "The Professor and the Art of Teaching," *School and Society,* 87:2140 (January 31, 1959), pp. 36-50. Also, *Graduate Journal,* 2 (Fall, 1959), pp. 269-77.

Daedalus, 92:4 (Fall, 1963). Entire issue entitled *The Professions.* Bernard Barber, "Some Problems in the Sociology of the Professions," pp. 669-688; Paul A. Freund, "The Legal Profession," pp. 689-700; Everett C. Hughes, "Professions," pp. 655-668; James Harold Means, "Homo Medicus Americanus," pp. 701-723.

Daedalus, 93:4 (Fall, 1964). Entire issue entitled *The Contemporary University: U.S.A.*

Daedalus, 94:3 (Summer, 1965). Entire issue entitled *Creativity and Learning.* J. Douglas Brown, "The Development of Creative Teacher-Scholars," pp. 615-31; David Hawkins, "The Informed Vision," pp. 538-52; Jerome Kagan, "Personality and the Learning Process," pp. 553-563.

Dodd, Stuart C. "A Ph.D. Defined in Three Tenses," *Journal of Educational Sociology,* 30:9 (May, 1957), pp. 423-27.

Dunkel, Harold B. "Training College Teachers: A Progress Report from the University of Chicago," *Journal of Higher Education,* 39:1 (January, 1958), pp. 57-58.

Dykstra, John W. "The Ph.D. Fetish," *School and Society,* 86:2133 (May 24, 1958), pp. 237-39; and "Reply" by James M. Davis, 86:2144 (December 20, 1958), pp. 458-59.

Eckelberry, R. H. "A New Study of a Notable Graduate Program," *Journal of Higher Education,* 30:6 (June, 1959), pp. 341-43.

Eckert, Ruth E. "Some Neglected Aspects in the Preparation of College Teachers," *Journal of General Education,* 3:2 (January, 1949), pp. 137-44.

Elder, J. P. "Reviving the Master's Degree for the Prospective College Teacher," *Journal of Higher Education,* 30:3 (March, 1959), pp. 133-36.

Fahey, George and Masoner, Paul. "An Interdisciplinary Seminar in College Teaching," *Journal of Teacher Education,* 11:3, pp. 3-97.

Fischer, John. "Is There a Teacher on the Faculty?" *Harper's Magazine,* 230:1 (February, 1965), pp. 18-28.

"Foundation-Financed Activities Bearing Upon College Teaching," *Educational Record,* 37:2 (April, 1956), pp. 152-62.

Gardner, John W. "Remarks," at the Annual Program Meeting of the Council on Social Work Education, *Journal of Social Work Education,* 2:1 (Spring, 1966), pp. 5-9.

Goheen, Robert F. "The Teacher in the University," *School and Society,* 94:2276 (April 2, 1966), pp. 177-179.

"Graduate Training for College Teachers: A Panel Discussion," *American Association of University Professors Bulletin,* 46:3 (September, 1960), pp. 294-99.

Gusfield, Joseph and Reisman, David. "Faculty Culture and Academic Careers: Some Sources of Innovation in Higher Education," *Sociology of Education,* 37:4 (Summer, 1964), pp. 281-305.

Hartman, Gerhard and Levy, Samuel. "Doctoral Study in an Emerging Profession: Hospital Administration," *Journal of Medical Education,* 37:4 (April, 1962), pp. 299-303.

Hechinger, Fred M. "Reappraising the Ph. of the Ph.D.," *New York Times,* April 16, 1967.

————. "What Should a University Be?" *New York Times,* May 16, 1966.

Hunt, Erling M. "An Ed.D. for College Teachers," *Journal of Teacher Ed.,* 13:3 (September, 1962), pp. 279-283.

Jones, Charles W. "The Truman Report and the Graduate Schools," *Journal of Higher Education,* 20:7 (October, 1949), pp. 355-59.

Justman, Joseph. "What Makes a Good College Teacher?" *School and Society,* 70:1827 (December 4, 1949), pp. 417-21.

Kadushin, Alfred, "Two Problems of the Graduate Program: Level and Content," *Journal of Education for Social Work,* I:1 (Spring, 1965), pp. 33-46.

———— and Schenk, Quentin. "An Experiment in Teaching an Integrated Methods Course," *Social Casework,* 38:8 (October, 1957), pp. 417-22.

Kandel, I. L. "Some Educational Paradoxes," *Educational Forum,* 22:3 (March, 1958), pp. 261-72.

Kindelsperger, Walter L. "Responsible Entry in the Profession—Some Current Issues," *Journal of Education for Social Work,* 2:1 (Spring, 1966), pp. 41-51.

Kozacik, Patricia. "Future Professors, Coming Up!" *College and University,* 34:1 (Winter, 1959), pp. 205-207.

Leary, Lewis. "The Scholar as Teacher," *School and Society,* 87:2158 (September 26, 1959), pp. 362-363.

157

Little, J. Kenneth. "Graduate Education," in *Encyclopedia of Educational Research*, Chester W. H. Harris, ed. for the American Educational Research Association. New York: Macmillan Co., 1960, pp. 593-603.

Maslow, A. H. and Zimmerman, W. A. "College Teaching Ability, Scholarly Activity and Personality," *Journal of Educational Psychology*, 47:3 (March, 1956), pp. 185-189.

Maxwell, Jean M. "New Settings for Field Instruction," *Social Work Education Reporter*, 14:3 (September, 1966), p. 30ff.

Mayhew, Lewis B. "The Literature of Higher Education," *Educational Record*, 46:1 (Winter, 1965), pp. 5-32.

McGlothlin, William J. "The Aims of Professional Education," *Education for Social Work*. New York: Council on Social Work Education, 1958, pp. 20-31.

McCutcheon, Roger P. "The Preparation of College Teachers," *Graduate Journal*, 1:2 (Fall, 1958), pp. 139-43.

McGrath, Earl J. "The Goals of Higher Education," *Journal of Higher Education*, 20:4 (April, 1949), pp. 171-80.

Meier, Elizabeth G. "Preparation for Teaching Social Work," *Social Work Education Reporter*, 13:3 (September, 1965), p. 14ff.

Merrifield, Aleanor. "Changing Patterns and Programs in Field Instruction," *Social Service Review*, 37:3 (September, 1963), pp. 274-82.

Miller, George E. "An Inquiry into Medical Teaching," *Journal of Medical Education*, 37:3 (March, 1962), pp. 185-191.

————. "Continuing Education for What?" *Journal of Medical Education*, 42:4 (April, 1967), pp. 320-326.

Miller, John Perry. "The Teaching Assistantship: Chore or Challenge?" Reprint from *Ventures*, magazine of the Yale Graduate School, 4 (Fall, 1964).

Ness, Frederic W. "The Case of the Lingering Degree," *Saturday Review*, January 15, 1966, p. 64ff.

Ogletree, James R. and Edmonds, Fred. "Programming for In-Service Growth," *Educational Leadership*, 21:5 (February, 1964), pp. 288-91.

Olds, Victoria. "Activities to Improve the Quality of Instruction at a School of Social Work," *Social Work Education Reporter*, 14:3 (September, 1966), p. 37ff.

"Opportunities for Teacher Education," *American Education*, (April, 1966).

Pace, C. R. "The Preparation of College Teachers," *Review of Educational Research*, 19 (June, 1949), pp. 230-34.

Perlman, Helen Harris. ". . . And Gladly Teach," *Journal of Education for Social Work*, 3:1 (Spring, 1967).

Pfnister, Allan O. "The Preparation of College Teachers," *School and Society*, 88:2177 (October 8, 1960), pp. 348-50.

Phillips, Ellis L., Jr. "Toward More Effective Administration in Higher Education," *Educational Record*, 47:2 (Spring, 1966), pp. 148-162.

Pohek, Marguerite V. "Toward Methodology of Teaching," *Education for Social Work*. New York: Council on Social Work Education, 1964, 149-161.

"Proposed Curriculum with a Practice Emphasis on Doctoral Programs," *Social Work Education Reporter*, 14:3 (September, 1966), p. 33ff.

Riesman, David. "The Academic Career: Notes on Recruitment and Colleagueship," *Daedalus*, 88:1 (Winter, 1959), pp. 147-169.

Rosinski, Edwin F. and Miller, George E. "Seminars and Medical Teaching," *Journal of Medical Education*, 37:3 (March, 1962), pp. 177-184.

————. "A Study of Medical School Faculty Attitude," *Journal of Medical Education*, 37:2 (February, 1962), pp. 112-123.

Schwartz, William. "The Classroom Teaching of Social Work with Groups, Some Central Problems," in *A Conceptual Framework for the Teaching of the Social Group Work Method in the Classroom*. New York: Council on Social Work Education, 1964, pp. 3-10.

Smalley, Ruth E. "The Attributes of a Social Work Educator," *Social Work Education Reporter*, 13:2 (June, 1965), p. 10ff.

Somers, Mary Louise. "Toward the Improvement of Social Work Teaching Methods and Materials," *Social Work Education Reporter*, 14:4 (December, 1966), p. 28ff.

Stein, Herman D. "Cross Currents in Practice, Undergraduate and Graduate Education for Social Work," *Journal of Education for Social Work*, 1:1, pp. 56-67.

Thompson, Clarence H. "Faculty Development in Evening Colleges," *Adult Leadership*, 16:1 (May, 1967), p. 15ff.

Towle, Charlotte, "The Distinctive Attributes of Education for Social Work," *Social Work Journal*, 33:2 (April, 1952), p. 63ff.

Tyler, Ralph W. "Distinctive Attributes of Education for the Professions," *Social Work Journal*, 33:2 (April, 1952), p. 55ff.

Walters, Everett. "The Immutable Ph.D.," *Saturday Review* (January 15, 1966), p. 62ff.

————. "A New Degree for College Teachers," *Journal of Higher Education*, 31:5 (May, 1960), pp. 282-84.

————. "What Degree for College Teachers?" *Journal of Higher Education*, 31:2 (February, 1960), pp. 69-74.

Weintraub, Ruth G. and Diekhoff, John S. "A Program of Faculty In-Service Training," *Journal of Higher Education*, 26:7 (October, 1955), pp. 343-49.

Wellington, Jean and Wellington, C. Burleigh. "Method for College Teachers," *School and Society*, 87:2158, pp. 363-64.

Whaley, Gordon W. "American Academic Degrees," *Educational Record*, 47:4 (Fall, 1966), pp. 525-537.

Wilson, O. Meredith. "The Ph.D. Program as Preparation for College Teaching," *Association of American Colleges Bulletin*, 44:1 (March, 1958), pp. 55-59.

Wittman, Milton and McNabola, F. Marie. "Major Trends of Support for Social Work Education Under the National Institute of Mental Health Training Program," *Social Work Education*, 11:6 (December, 1963-January, 1964), pp. 1-4.

Woodring, Paul. "The Profession of College Teaching," *Journal of Higher Education,* 31:5 (May, 1960), pp. 280-282.

Unpublished Materials

Armacost, Peter H. and Howland, Diane. "Background Materials on Selected Topics for a Conference on Preparing the College Professor for Liberal Arts Teaching," Mimeographed. Association of American Colleges, 1965.

Association of American Colleges and Council of Graduate Schools in the United States. "Preparing the College Professor for Liberal Arts Teaching." Unpublished manuscript, 1965.

Berg, Renee. "Practices and Problems in the Selection and Development of Faculty as Viewed by an Inducted Faculty Member new to Full Time Teaching." Paper presented at the Annual Program Meeting, Council on Social Work Education, Toronto, Canada, January 30, 1964.

Burns, Mary E. "Advanced Curriculum and the Faculty Manpower Problem." Paper presented at the Annual Program Meeting, Council on Social Work Education, New York, January 26, 1966.

Corrigan, Dean. "The Personal Dimension in the Education of American Teachers." Paper prepared for the Conference Honoring Florence B. Stratemeyer, French Lick, Indiana, June 10-12, 1965. Mimeographed.

Council on Graduate Schools in the United States. Statement: "New Doctor of Philosophy Degree Programs."

Council on Social Work Education. "From Practitioner to Teacher." Institute Reports, 1957 and 1958.

Hermanowicz, Henry J. "Studies of Teaching and Their Impact on Future Developments in Teacher Education." Paper presented for the Conference honoring Florence B. Stratemeyer, French Lick, Indiana, June 10-12, 1965.

Jennings, Daniel. "Characteristics of Faculty Members of Graduate Professional Schools of Social Work in the United States and Canada." Unpublished doctoral dissertation, Catholic University, 1965. See also paper based on this dissertation, "Characteristics of Social Work Faculty Members," *Social Work Education Reporter,* 14:3 (September, 1966), p. 23ff.

Kendall, Katherine A. "The Choices Before Us." Paper presented at the National Conference on Social Welfare, Chicago, June 2, 1966.

Kindelsperger, Walter and Cassidy, Helen. "Social Work Training Centers: Tentative Analysis of the Structure and Learning Environment." Mimeographed.

Miller, John Perry. "The Master of Philosophy: A New Degree is Born." Announcement of the Graduate School, Yale University.

Regensburg, Jeanette. "Recruitment to Post-Master's Programs in Schools of Social Work." Paper presented at Annual Program Meeting, Council on Social Work Education, New York, January 26, 1966.

"Selected Statistical Highlights on Growth and Change of Social Work Education." Mimeographed. Council on Social Work Education, December 29, 1966, #66-26-18.

Smalley, Ruth E. "Career Opportunities in Social Work Education: Requirements, Preparation and Rewards of Teaching." Paper presented at National Conference on Social Welfare, Chicago, June 2, 1966. Mimeographed.

Soffen, Joseph. "Practices and Problems in the Selection and Development of Faculty as Viewed by an Inducted Faculty Member Changing His Teaching Area and Joining the Faculty of a School Other than the One in Which He has Been Teaching." Paper presented at the Annual Program Meeting, Council on Social Work Education, Toronto, Canada, January 30, 1964.

Summer Offerings Reported by the Graduate Schools of Social Work. Mimeographed. Council on Social Work Education, #67-5-4.

U. S. Department of Health, Education, and Welfare, Public Health Service. *Mental Health Trainee Stipends in Social Work, 1966-67; Research Career Program, National Institute of Mental Health; Predoctoral Research Fellowships; Special Research Fellowships; Information for Postdoctoral Research Fellows; Information for Predoctoral Research Fellows; Information for Special Research Fellows.*

Wessel, Rosa. "Practices and Problems in the Selection and Development of Faculty as Viewed by One Inducting School, University of Pennsylvania School of Social Work." Paper presented at the Annual Program Meeting, Council on Social Work Education, Toronto, Canada, January 30, 1964.

Wessel, Rosa. "Response," on receiving award on the occasion of her retirement, April 29, 1966. Mimeographed.

Younghusband, Dame Eileen L. "Developing the Faculty: The Opportunities and Demands of Teaching." Paper delivered at the Thirteenth International Congress of Schools of Social Work, Washington, D. C., August 31-September 3, 1966. Mimeographed.

Appendixes

Appendix I

ADVISORY COMMITTEE OF THE FACULTY DEVELOPMENT PROJECT

WILLIAM SCHWARTZ, *Chairman*
Associate Professor, School of Social Work
Columbia University

HERBERT H. APTEKAR
*Professor, The Florence Heller Graduate School for
    Advanced Studies in Social Welfare*
Brandeis University

LEONARD BLOKSBERG
Assistant Professor, School of Social Work
Boston University

MARY E. BURNS
Professor, School of Social Work
University of Michigan

MRS. ALICE TAYLOR DAVIS
Professorial Lecturer, School of Social Work
Howard University
(Chairman, CSWE Committee on Teaching Methodology and Material)

ANNE FURNESS
Associate Professor, School of Social Work
University of British Columbia

DAVID JENKINS
Chairman, Department of Educational Psychology
Temple University

WALTER KINDELSPERGER
Dean, School of Social Work
Tulane University

RALPH KOLODNY
Associate Professor, School of Social Work
Boston University

163

GERTRUDE LEYENDECKER
Senior Associate, Department of Family Services
Community Service Society of New York

HORACE W. LUNDBERG
Dean, Graduate School of Social Service Administration
Arizona State University

ELIZABETH G. MEIER*
Professor, School of Social Work
Western Reserve University
(Chairman, Subcommittee on Faculty
  CSWE Committee on Advanced Education)

JOHN J. O. MOORE
Professor, School of Social Work and Community Development
University of Missouri

ALEX ROSEN
Dean, Graduate School of Social Work
New York University

FLORENCE STRATEMEYER
Professor, School of Education
Eastern Kentucky State College

HILDA TEBOW
Regional Staff Development Specialist, Welfare Administration
Department of Health, Education, and Welfare, Region VI

CHARLOTTE TOWLE*
Professor, School of Social Service Administration
University of Chicago

FRED H. WEAVER
Vice-President for Administration
University of North Carolina

* deceased

Appendix II

SURVEY OF DEANS AND DIRECTORS OF
SCHOOLS OF SOCIAL WORK

COUNCIL ON SOCIAL WORK EDUCATION
345 East 46th Street   New York, New York 10017

February 21, 1966

TO: Deans and Directors of Schools of Social Work

FROM: Joseph Soffen

RE: Faculty Development Project

Your response to my earlier communication for setting up a Workshop on Faculty Development (#15B) at the Annual Program Meeting was very much appreciated. Many of you, or your representatives who participated in the Workshop, helped sharpen our understanding of problems inherent in any program of faculty development, e.g., identifying and securing potentially good faculty, and providing for their orientation, induction, and deployment. It was agreed that the design of the Project would be improved if we surveyed all the schools to insure more systematic responses than is possible at a workshop session.

I am therefore writing to ask your cooperation, once more, so that we can have as complete an inventory as possible of the current practices and points of view among the several schools. In responding to the two questions below please use any format which is most convenient for you:

A. Describe what your school is doing—what experiences are planned before or during their first year of full-time teaching to help new faculty as they move into social work education.

B. What experiences, administrative structures, or other resources would you consider to be appropriate or desirable under optimum circumstances? (This question legitimizes day dreaming.)

I know that this request adds to your burdens, but hope you will be willing to provide a response which will reflect the practices and points of view of your school, hopefully toward the ultimate benefit of social work education.

Replies to this questionnaire were received from the following institutions:

Adelphi University, Graduate School of Social Work
Arizona State University, Graduate School of Social Service Administration
University of California, School of Social Welfare
University of Chicago, School of Social Service Administration
University of Denver, The Graduate School of Social Work
Fresno State College, Department of Social Work
University of Georgia, School of Social Work
The University of Iowa, School of Social Work
University of Kansas, Graduate Department of Social Work
Louisiana State University, School of Social Welfare

University of Louisville, The Raymond A. Kent School of Social Work
Loyola University, School of Social Work
University of Maryland, School of Social Work
University of Michigan, School of Social Work
University of Missouri, School of Social Work and Community Development
University of Minnesota, School of Social Work
University of North Carolina, The School of Social Work
University of Oklahoma, School of Social Work
University of Ottawa, School of Social Welfare
Our Lady of the Lake College, The Worden School of Social Service
University of Pennsylvania, School of Social Work
Portland State College, School of Social Work
Richmond Professional Institute, School of Social Work
Saint Louis University, School of Social Service
San Diego State College, School of Social Work
Smith College, School of Social Work
University of Southern California, School of Social Work
University of Tennessee, School of Social Work
University of Texas, School of Social Work
Tulane University, School of Social Work
University of Utah, Graduate School of Social Work
Washington University, The George Warren Brown School of Social Work
Western Reserve University, School of Applied Social Sciences
University of Wisconsin—Milwaukee, School of Social Welfare
Yeshiva University, Wurzweiler School of Social Work

Appendix III

SURVEY OF INDIVIDUALS RESPONSIBLE FOR
FACULTY DEVELOPMENT

COUNCIL ON SOCIAL WORK EDUCATION
345 East 46th Street   New York, New York 10017

August 1966

Dear Colleague:

In my work on the Faculty Development Project I am including a section on continuing faculty development within the schools. I note the inclusion of your name on the 1965-66 listing in the Council on Social Work Education's document of "Social Work Faculty Assigned Major Responsibility for Faculty Development or Improvement of Teaching Methodology and Instruction." I am anxious to have the Project Report as complete and useful as possible, and am therefore turning to you.

May I have your responses to the following questions—but do not feel restricted by the outline:

1) What is the scope of these responsibilities at your School? What ongoing faculty development activities or programs have been carried out in recent years? What have been their specific objectives?

2) What structures have you used, and how extensively: e.g., faculty meetings, seminars, retreats, colloquia; committees; individual or group consultation?

3) What aspects of your program, or "pet" ideas you have, may be of particular interest and value to other schools?

I shall be doubly appreciative of your responses because I know that this request adds to your burdens at a busy time.

Very sincerely,

Joseph Soffen
Project Director
Faculty Development Project

Replies to this questionnaire were received from schools of social work in the following institutions:

Atlanta University
Boston College
Université Laval
Loyola University
University of Missouri

Université de Montréal
University of Nebraska
New York University
University of Oklahoma
Portland State College

Western Reserve University

167

Appendix IV

SURVEY OF NEW FACULTY

COUNCIL ON SOCIAL WORK EDUCATION
345 East 46th Street   New York, New York 10017

October 29, 1965

Dear Colleague:

You may have read in recent months that the Council on Social Work Education has initiated a Faculty Development Project. The primary objectives of this Project, made possible by a grant from the National Institute of Mental Health, include the exploration of a number of unresolved issues regarding the optimum means for helping faculty in schools of social work in their transition from the practitioner to the educator roles, a study of patterns now used by social work and other professions for the preparation of faculty and the projection of sound and realistic patterns for the future.

It seems to use that one extremely valuable source of data for helping us achieve these objectives is the new full-time faculty member (class or field instructor) who has recently made this transition himself. We have therefore selected the names of current faculty who began their teaching careers as full-time faculty in graduate social work education in 1963 or 1964 to solicit experiences and opinions. We assume that their memory is still fresh and they have had at least one year to develop their own perspective on this problem.

Because the procedure for identifying individuals for this survey could not be precise, we may have included your name inappropriately; should this be true in your case, please return the enclosed questionnaire indicating the error. If you have become a faculty member of a school of social work in the past two years, we invite your thoughtful contribution, using the enclosed questionnaire as a guide. We have economized on the number of items, and have left item 8 "open" so that you can respond as you see fit. Please feel free to offer whatever you think may be helpful. We are asking for your thinking on a matter which is now in the past for you, but on which you can make a contribution for the next generation of social work educators.

We will want to use your responses initially for a meeting of the Advisory Committee of the Project in mid-December, and are therefore asking for your returns by November 10, 1965, in the enclosed envelope.

Very sincerely,

Joseph Soffen, Project Director
Faculty Development Project

COUNCIL ON SOCIAL WORK EDUCATION
FACULTY DEVELOPMENT PROJECT

Your name _____

Name of School _____

1. Are you a full-time faculty member (class or field instructor)
   in the 1965-66 academic year?   ___Yes ___No

2. Did you begin teaching (class or field instruction) full-time in 1963 or
   1964? _____

3. Where is the key locus of your teaching? Class_____ Field_____
   If classroom, in what curriculum area or areas do you teach?
   ___1. administration
   ___2. casework
   ___3. community organization
   ___4. group work
   ___5. research
   ___6. human growth and social environment
   ___7. social welfare policy and services
   ___8. other (please specify) _____
   If field instruction, do you do any classroom teaching? Yes___ No___

4. Education:
   a) What was your undergraduate major? _____
   b) Was your master's degree in social work?   ___Yes ___No
       If yes, what was your method concentration? _____
       If not social work, in what field of study? _____
       In what year did you receive your master's degree? _____
   c) Do you have a doctorate? ___Yes ___No ___Working toward
       If Yes, year completed? _____ where?_____
           Degree: ___Ph.D. ___D.S.W. _____(other)
           Area of study? _____

5. In which of the following has your social work practice experience been?
   For how many years? (Primary areas only)
   No. of years in—
   _____1. administration
   _____2. casework
   _____3. community organization
   _____4. group work
   _____5. research
   _____6. social welfare policy development
   _____7. other (please specify) _____

6. When did you decide on teaching in a school of social work as your
   career?
   ___1. Before beginning graduate professional study in social work
   ___2. During graduate professional study in social work at the master's
          degree level
   ___3. After completion of the master's degree work and during subse-
          quent practice
   ___4. During graduate study at the doctor's degree level
   ___5. After completion of the doctorate

_____6. Do not remember

_____7. Other (please specify) _____

7. Prior to your current full-time appointment to a faculty of a graduate professional school of social work, did you teach social work? ____Yes ____No

    _____1. part-time undergraduate

    _____2. part-time graduate

    _____3. full-time undergraduate

    _____4. full-time graduate on a faculty other than social work

    _____5. other (please specify) _____

8. Please respond to the following questions, organizing your content in whatever manner is appropriate for you.

    a) What experiences were available to you before or during your first year of full-time teaching in schools of social work to help you in the transition to social work educator? Were they: formal or informal, planned or fortuitous? Courses? Administrative structures? etc.?

    b) What were the major problems (if any) associated with this transition?

    c) What experiences, administrative structures, or other resources would you have liked to have had provided, or would you recommend for the next generation? Would you be interested or willing to pursue this question further? (e.g., at a workshop, if it can be arranged?)

Completed responses to this questionnaire were received from the following individuals:

Naomi Abramowitz	L. Daniel Carter	Joann G. Gannon
Jacques Alary	Robert L. Castagnola	Leon H. Ginsberg
Howard R. Ancell	C. Arthur Choate	Ruth L. Goldberg
Ralph E. Anderson	Barbara H. Cleaveland	Irwin Golden
Harold Bardonille, Jr.	Thomas L. Coffey	Elmer L. Good
Ellen Bateman	Wanda Collins	Harold G. Goodwin
V. Edward Bates	Ronda S. Connaway	Norman N. Goroff
Kay Belanger	Philip W. Cooke	Palma Festa Greenwood
Geneva Beller	Fred M. Cox	Marah Grist
John Bendekovic	Sister Mary of	Philip A. Hampton
Edward Berkowitz	Mercy Cunningham	Roberta Miller Hampton
Sydney E. Bernard	H. Otto Dahlke	Eleaner M. Hannon
Rosalyn S. Bernstein	Ruth S. Dahlke	Laura M. Hardy
Andrew Billingsley	Augustus D'Aloise	Josephine Harris
Suzanne Blais-Grenier	Rosalina Rosado	Carl Hartman
Leonard Bloksberg	de Kamarauskas	Elizabeth C. Harvey
Marvin Bloom	Nathalie Drews	Helen R. Henderson
William A. Bourke	Elizabeth Dubansky	Dolph Hess
James Breedlove	Elizabeth N. Easton	Imogene Smith Higbie
Dawn I. Brett	Philippa H. Eggleston	Elizabeth F. Johnson
Kathryn Brisbane	Arthur Faber	Gladys Johnson
Edna Earl Brooks	O. William Farley	E. Ann Jones
Larry L. Brown	Rosa Felsenburg	Jean Boyd Jones
Edmund M. Burke	Calvin Fenton	James D. Jorgensen
Mary F. Carswell	Hans F. Fink	Marion Kahn

170

Edna-Ann Katz
Hazel Grover Keenan
Robert W. Kessel
Stanley Kim
Margaret Kime
Marjorie H. Kirkland
Ralph M. Kramer
Alvin Landy
Norma C. Lang
Joseph E. Laycock
Esther Lentschner
Edith G. Levi
Herman Levin
Baruch Levine
Ruby Little
Arthur W. Lockner
Alfred A. Lucco
Mary M. MacLean
Robert Carey Mahoney
Betty Mandell
Frank Maple
Olga M. Mattes
Faye McCandless
P. Ross McClelland
Frank J. McGilly
Willette Pierce McNary
Erma C. Metz
Mary K. Miles
Jacqueline Mirkin
Jules Mondschein
Anne M. Montague
Joan Ward Mullaney
Martha Copeland Munk
Robert L. Neubauer

William M. Nicholls
Helen L. Olander
Marilyn Lee Olds
Carolyn L. Otey
Ronald H. Ozaki
Fred E. Parsons
Dorothy M. Pearson
Morton S. Perlmutter
Margaret S. Perrin
Richard D. Pickering
Gérard Poirier
Marian A. Powell
Florence E. Ray
Ronald Berry Rea
Helen Reinherz
Nolan Rindfleisch
S. Jerome Roach
Blanca N. Rosenberg
Sheldon Rotter
Gerald K. Rubin
Carmine J. Salerno
Don E. Savage
Leonard Schneiderman
Marjorie Schultz
Mary M. Seguin
Bradford W. Sheafor
Joanna M. Sherman
Edward J. Shiner
Rita M. Silvestro
Norris L. Smith
Louise C. Spence
Jacqueline Stackhouse
Harvey Stalwick
Samuel D. Stellman

Max Stern
Richard Sterne
Annalee Stewart
Manuel W. Strauss
Eugene J. Sullivan
Forrest L. Swall
Elaine Switzer
Mary Y. Tatlock
DeEtta S. Taylor
Patricia Theimer
Joseph Victor Thompson
Myra Tieder
Ignacia Torres
John Tretton
Albert C. Tricomi
Francis J. Turner
Barbara Underwood
Mollie Utkoff
Mary W. Van Allen
Alice M. Varela
Allan M. Velicer
Catherine Wallace
Lois R. Webb
Mildred Webb
Olive R. Wertz
Harold R. White
Warren White
John M. Whitelaw
Ruth Wickney
Preston R. Wilcox
Lorain C. Will
Margaret Yeakel
Alexander G. Zaphiris
Gerald A. Zoutherland

Appendix V

CORRESPONDENCE, INTERVIEWS, AND WORKSHOP

Grateful acknowledgment is herewith made to the individuals and institutions listed below.

Extensive interviews were granted by the following individuals:

U. S. OFFICE OF EDUCATION

John W. Ashton, Director, Division of Graduate Programs, Bureau of Higher Education

James Blessing, Chief, Graduate Academic Programs Branch, Division of Graduate Programs, Bureau of Higher Education

PUBLIC HEALTH SERVICE, NATIONAL INSTITUTE OF MENTAL HEALTH

Bert Boothe (Research Career Development)

Esther Garrison (Nursing)

Edgar A. Perretz (Social Work)

Forrest Tyler (Psychology)

Reber Van Matre (Psychiatry)

HIGHER EDUCATION AND PROFESSIONAL EDUCATION

Peter H. Armacost, Program Director, Association of American Colleges

James N. Ashelman, Assistant to the President, Council of Graduate Schools in the United States

Gaylord Harnwell, President, University of Pennsylvania

George E. Miller, Director, Office of Research in Medical Education, University of Illinois

Lee Powers, Director, Association of American Medical Schools

George E. Ruff, Associate Professor of Psychiatry, University of Pennsylvania

Edward Joseph Shoben, American Council on Education

SOCIAL WORK EDUCATION

Milton Chernin, Dean, School of Social Welfare, University of California, Berkeley

Katherine Lower, Dean, Carola Woerishoffer Graduate Department of Social Work and Social Research, Bryn Mawr College

Mary MacDonald, Professor, School of Social Service Administration, University of Chicago

Helen Harris Perlman, Professor, School of Social Service Administration, University of Chicago

Alex Rosen, Dean, Graduate School of Social Work, New York University

Ruth E. Smalley, Dean, School of Social Work, University of Pennsylvania

Malcolm B. Stinson, Dean, School of Social Work, University of Southern California

Substantive correspondence and institutional materials were received from the following:

Roger Axford, Professor, Southern Illinois University

Waldo Beach, Director of Graduate Studies in Religion, Duke University

Philip Bernstein, Executive Director, Council of Jewish Federations and Welfare Funds, Inc.

Eileen Blackey, Dean, School of Social Welfare, University of California, Los Angeles

Michael H. Cardozo, Executive Director, Association of American Law Schools

Stanford C. Ericksen, Director, Center for Research on Learning and Teaching, University of Michigan

_____, Department of History, Washington University

Victor I. Howery, Professor, University Extension Division, Department of Social Work, University of Wisconsin

Morris Keeton, Academic Vice President, Antioch College

R. E. Kelley, Field Work Instructor, Tulsa Oklahoma

John Perry Miller, Dean, Graduate School, Yale University

Merrill D. Peterson, Chairman, Corcoran Department of History, University of Virginia

Frances Rein, Administrative Assistant, Department of Baccalaureate and Higher Degree Programs, National League for Nursing, Inc.

Paul J. Sanazaro, Director, Association of American Medical Colleges

S. Frederick Seymour, Research Associate, Center for the Advanced Study of Educational Administration, University of Oregon

Cecil G. Sheps, General Director, Beth Israel Medical Center

Peter Siegle, Staff Associate, Center for the Study of Liberal Education for Adults

Clifford L. Winters, Dean, University College, Syracuse University

WORKSHOP FOR NEW FACULTY

The following faculty members participated in the workshop for new faculty, held in New York City on January 26, 1966.

Name	University
Naomi Abramowitz	Yeshiva University—Wurzweiler
Sarah Austin	Howard University
Ellen Bateman	University of British Columbia
Leonard Bloksberg	Boston University
Dawn Brett	University of British Columbia
C. Arthur Choate	University of Missouri
Barbara Cleaveland	University of North Carolina
E. Ann Jones	University of Toronto
Marion Kahn	Richmond Professional Institute
Alvin Landy	State University of New York—Buffalo
Esther Lentschner	Yeshiva University
Robert L. Neubauer	University of Wisconsin—Milwaukee
Marilyn Lee Olds	Wayne State University
Morton S. Perlmutter	University of Wisconsin
Margaret S. Perrin	George Warren Brown School of Social Work
Richard D. Pickering	Florida State University
Sheldon Rotter	Rutgers University
Jacqueline Stackhouse	Richmond Professional Institute
Samuel Stellman	Ohio State University
Max Stern	University of Iowa
Manuel W. Strauss	University of Connecticut

173

Eugene Sullivan	Catholic University
Patricia Theimer	University of Nebraska
Mollie Utkoff	University of Pennsylvania
Mary Van Allen	State University of New York at Buffalo
Alice M. Varela	University of California Berkeley
Lorain C. Will	Indiana University
Gerald A. Zoutherland	University of North Carolina

Appendix VI

COLLEGE TEACHER PREPARATION PROGRAMS

The following questions were sent to 39 institutions listed by the Ford Foundation as participating in its grant program for experimental designs to improve the preparation of college teachers:

1. Operations: When the program was instituted; number of candidates involved thus far.
2. Provision for the "teaching" component: supervisor, mentor or preceptor; seminars; educational theory.
3. Acceptance: within the department or school; within the University.
4. Evaluation of Program: outcomes for candidates; outcomes for the profession; the future of such programs as you see it now.

Descriptive and evaluative responses were received from the following institutions:

University of Arizona
Brown University
University of California, Santa Barbara
University of Colorado
University of Denver
Emory University
University of Florida
Florida State University
University of Georgia
Goucher College
Indiana University
University of Nebraska
University of New Hampshire
University of New Mexico
New York University
University of North Carolina
Saint Louis University
Southern Methodist University
Stetson University
Tulane University
University of Utah
University of Virginia
University of Washington
Washington University

Appendix VII

ABSTRACT AND EXCERPTS OF GROUP
INTERVIEW WITH STUDENTS

On May 24, 1966, Dr. William Schwartz, chairman of the Project's Advisory Committee conducted a group interview with eleven students at the Columbia University School of Social Work. The students had completed all requirements of the master's curriculum and were shortly to be awarded the Master of Social Work degree. Participation was by invitation, but clearly voluntary. The announced focus for the group interview was: "Teaching— Through the Eyes of the Student."

In addition to Dr. Schwartz and the Project Director, the participants were: Toye Brown, Diane Dorke, Mary Cummings, Gary Goldberg, David Heymann, Sandy Katz, Eve Lowery, Toba Schwaber, Geraldine Wallman, Ilene Waxler and Rose Zweig. All three methods specializations, i.e., casework, group work, and community organization, were represented by these participants.

Following is an abstract with excerpts from the tape-script of the three-hour interview. Because it is one-dimensional, it cannot capture the quality of hard thinking and of the involvement of the participants throughout the interview.

After a short explanation of the purposes of the Faculty Development Project and the place of the group interview within the Project, the interviewer established the climate for sessions by stating that the participants' own perceptions were the ones being sought—not what they thought were the "right" ones, and by requiring that no names of instructors be used at any time. No fixed agenda was proposed and the interviewer urged freedom to approach his opening question in any way which seemed easiest. He began by asking:

> What is a good teacher? If that doesn't make a good first question, then ask your own first question.

The quotations which follow were some of the responses of the participants.

> Maybe it would begin the answering of the question by thinking for a moment on what *isn't* a good teacher.

> A good teacher has got to be *sensitive* to the class. I have two different teachers in mind. One is very good, and one, I thought, very bad. The one who I thought was good had a little trouble, took a couple of weeks to get the class started, even though there was no doubt in the world that she knew her subject. And at one point she just stopped and said, 'Now look, what's going on here? You have not done the readings, that's one thing. Tell me what it is. I'll be relieved if it's just the readings, because then you can go out and do them.' Well, this just changed the whole *atmosphere* of the class for the whole semester. The class sort of got *cohesive* after that. The teacher that I thought was bad *underestimated* us tremendously. And what happened was that he asked a

175

very simple question that no one would answer because it was so simple, and since the question wasn't answered he thought he would make it one step simpler. Then he didn't know where to go from there. All of us in the class thought, well, not that we knew more than he did, but that we were somehow 'wiser' than he was, because we were one step ahead of him the whole time.

Did this feel like condescension or was it lack of skill in asking questions?

I don't think he was condescending; he underestimated the class. He was sincere, he tried very hard, but I think he *underestimated* what *we had learned in the year and a half,* or what kind of experiences we were having in the field or our level of understanding.

Then it wasn't essentially a problem of attitude which he brought to the class, but rather a lack of skill . . . he didn't know . . . was that it?

I think it's almost a 'position' that a teacher takes toward the class. Some teachers put themselves into the class and need the response of the class in order to be able to teach. . . .

Are you putting a judgment on that?

I'm saying it's good, because the farther the teacher removes himself from the class the farther away he gets.

I think you can go overboard on that too. If you shut out the teacher it's a one way street. Something has to come from the head of the class also.

I find that I need a more direct kind of instructor. I recall I was quite upset at one point when a certain instructor did not do this. Yet the experience was one that I'll always remember—the anxiety I felt in class to the point where it immobilized me at first, until I went to speak to him and I was told that I had to produce, I had to give. It worked out successfully in the end for me, because I learned, but I felt that the teacher had so much to give and was not giving it to the class.

I guess I must have been involved in that also. But there was a lesson in that: it wasn't complete passivity either. There was method to his madness, because the class did come around. Everybody was being bugged by something and we really didn't know what for a while. And the superficial discussion that was going on in the class—

From what you're all saying it sounds as though the teacher walked out on his responsibility—

No, he didn't really.

At this point the interviewer urged the participants to pursue the question of "directedness versus passivity."

Looking back, I see it differently, but at that time I thought it was a complete waste of time. I wanted to shake the instructor and say "Let's get on with it, stop with this relationship thing." I remember being frustrated.

You could answer that the other way too. Many of us sat through classes where there's a dead spot and then the instructor comes in with some kind of knowledge and he's putting it across and everybody falls asleep, because you just don't want to hear it—

But that wasn't the kind of class I'm talking about. We would have liked the instructor to step in.

The focus shifted to anxiety and freedom of the student and the skill of the teacher in using discussion.

There were a lot of things going on between the instructor and the class. It was a new class with an old teacher—half the class had had him before—and there were all kinds of conflicting feelings and sibling rivalries and people were afraid to talk. Half the people were afraid to talk and the other half were afraid that the people who were afraid were going to talk and take the subject away from them.

I think there are two extremes that ought to be avoided. One is the personalized relationship where the student is reluctant to talk because he's always on the line, so to speak, by this person he admires. That over-personalization is to be avoided. And at the same time, the "lecturer is unresponsive to the class" is to be avoided. The first year I felt that I wanted more directedness. . . . The class was expected to offer an awful lot and we had nothing to say; we had no experience. But now this year I feel I have a lot to say and what I want to hear about is what the other students have to say. I'm impressed with what they're doing. . . . And when a teacher cuts this off . . . it's frustrating. So I say the teacher has to know how to deal with both these situations.

In pursuit of the balance between teacher-input of "knowledge" and student discussion, the responses to the proposition that the teacher lectures for the first hour, then has feed-back, for the second were:

But we also have something to offer. . . . For specific subject matter—this is why we are here—the instructor is there to direct the discussion so we do stay on the subject matter and at the same time he should be receptive to what the students have to offer, to the experiences we have in the field, because this is social work. All this has to be integrated.

I've had classes where the instructor did have a great deal of knowledge in the field but she attempted to let the class discuss it and I felt that I was missing a lot of what she had to say. She knew so much and we really knew so little and she should have told us a great deal more. People brought in a lot of irrelevant experience. You're not learning a process in that case.

When I say ask questions I don't mean questions like "What did this writer say?" but questions such as "What are you getting from this?" "What's happening to you in this classroom?" Also, before that, to find out what you think is going to happen in the course, what you want to happen, to press a little about what could happen. I think that has to come first.

First of all, listen to what the students are saying. Also, see, look, feel the atmosphere of the class; all these are skills that I think some teachers don't have.

177

To pick up things that might not be on the agenda and somehow work them in. Because one way you know that a teacher is not listening is when someone asks a question that is a little bit irrelevant to what the teacher was planning to do and the teacher says, "Later" or "That's for three sessions from now" or "We don't intend to cover that here." I guess this goes back to his fear—

A participant returned to this theme later when she pointed out to the interviewer:

I notice what you did after lunch to get back to what you said we were going to talk about. Although we got a little off, you were able to integrate where we were and where you wanted to head for, so that you weren't cutting anyone off.

The following challenge was presented by the interviewer:

I'll give you a model. . . . He knows his subject, he's brilliant, he is charming, he is known on campus as a popular teacher!

I'm not saying that lecturing is bad in all cases. In some cases it's good.

What makes it good?

I had two teachers in a course. One of them could have been a tape recorder. The other one was really involved and wanted us to understand his material.

What's the quality? . . .

Involvement.

Involvement with the student or the subject matter?

With the subject matter; also, being able to sense where the class is and that's where a tape recorder wouldn't do.

Another participant who felt that she didn't learn unless she was "involved in some way—not afterwards, but in class" recalled:

Having what someone here was describing as actors and it was magnificent. But two weeks later I didn't remember what they said. The way I really learned was . . . in a seminar type situation. But I think we can get into trouble trying to draw that same conclusion in other courses that *can* be lectures. This year I have a course. . . . The teacher came into the class very prepared. He had something to offer. Perhaps the word I have in mind is honesty.

What's that? Let's stay with that for a while.

Well, he was a real straight shooter. And I think that this is part of why I got involved in the class, even though he presented a lot of theoretical material and expected us to read it. *And we did.* But at the same time, he talked about his experiences in class and had us talk about them. I think it was his presentation that got me involved, because he was very honest about what he was aiming to do and what social work failed to do and so on. Somehow that broke down a kind of barrier or facade or whatever it is that can prevent learning.

Honesty is a rare commodity, is that what you're saying? What are some of the forms dishonesty takes?

178

I think a lot of what you're calling dishonesty is really defensiveness on the part of the teacher. We had teachers who talked about conflict and all these things; then you disagree and suddenly you're cut off. And they say things like "this isn't political science," or "we don't discuss ideas in class."

When someone is being honest with you he respects you.

They're not afraid of you.

The first teacher I mentioned was one of these people that cut you off all the time. He claimed we had to stick to the point, but always he cut out any kind of—well, we always felt he was afraid. He never relaxed for a minute.

What do you think he was afraid of?

I think he was afraid of not being able to handle what would come up.

You know what I found among social work professors? They feel they need to be liked in a way that I never found when I was an undergraduate. They are sensitive to the class in the sense that they want the class to like them, to react positively to what they say; so they see disagreement as a threat.

What about the dishonesty when you have a class discussion and the instructor pulls from the students—"let's hear what you all have to say" —and he goes through this round table thing for 15 minutes—and then he says "But—it's this way." Isn't that dishonesty in a certain sense? Because he's honestly trying to involve the students but then he says: "no" and doesn't pick up on it. Now, there might be a way of doing it without being authoritarian. A good instructor will say perhaps "that's a possibility."

That perhaps investment and risking by the student was needed was introduced:

Now, I was going to give up at the beginning but for some reason I struggled through it. Now I say it was worth it for me. It was worth it but maybe it could have been less painful—

I don't know that learning has to be painful. I really don't think it does. It's an individual thing.

Maybe the choice of the word pain wasn't too good. I don't know how to get closer to it. Struggle? I don't mean getting beat over the head; or somebody forcing you to learn; that's not what I mean at all. I think I can get closer to it by saying that through any process of change there has to be an element of struggle.

Why can't it be exciting, what happens sometimes?

Well, what is that exciting thing. That's what we're trying to find out.

Somehow, we have pointed out to us our weaknesses, and that's the painful part. . . . And I really do prefer the emphasis on one's strength.

Isn't that demandingness? One can be demanding and still concentrate on one's strength. I don't think that's a contradiction.

And that will produce no pain?

179

It's a struggle, but it's not the painful, excruciating kind of thing and it is the exciting kind of thing, where it's a challenge but it's positive.

You have to look at your weaknesses but at the same time you do have the strength to keep on going.

The attitude of the faculty is that we're all weak, we come in here as little weaklings and they have to build us up.

The interviewer suggested they consider the teacher who underestimates, who makes no demands, in contrast to the one who makes many demands.

But the teacher can say, "look, there's things you don't know yet, but I know you can do it; I'm here to help you"—but not "I'm going to tear you apart."

When the teacher says, "No, I don't agree with you; convince me," does that leave you feeling stranded?

The way you just said it, I would feel as though I *could* do it, or at least I could make a good enough argument so that you'd respect it.

Then are you getting this support when I say "No, that doesn't come through." At that moment, are you feeling on the chopping block?

I think there's something supportive about it. Because when the teacher says, 'I disagree,' or takes it one step forward, at least you can see there's an interest, that he cares.

After considerable exchange about whether *what* is learned and *how* it is learned are intertwined or can be separated, the group returned to the theme of involvement for learning:

This is where the use of the other students is important. And it comes back to the original question of whether the individual student is being supported, about the receptivity of the professor when he asks you a question. Does he turn the other students against you so that you feel you can't open up your mouth and say something you know he is going to disagree with?

So that there's not just a dialogue between the student and the professor, and if he agrees you're right and good, and if he disagrees then you're bad and wrong. He must be receptive to what the rest of the class feels.

For a really good class group there has to be a kind of community; some of this has to come from the teacher, but the people in the class have to learn from each other.

People are at such different levels when they come into the school, that it's hard for the class to move or to be integrated at all. Some people come with four years of background and some with none. And I think when there's this kind of situation, the obstacles are almost insurmountable.

Where there's a willingness of the people in the class to help each other these obstacles can be removed. A classic example is my seminar this semester where some people were being very dissatisfied with the whole social work profession, that their illusions had been shattered

180

and all that. Other people were just sitting there very comfortably saying, "I don't have that feeling," instead of saying "I don't have that feeling, tell me more about yours, so I can tell you where I get my gratification."

There's a certain protection in not shairing with the other members of the class and this also can become an obstacle. To exchange ideas with each other and with the professor also means sometimes exposure of feelings, of inadequacies, and many of us, maybe all of us are afraid of this kind of thing. So it could be far safer for people to sit like dummies and listen to the guy up there and go through the illusion that there's some learning going on.

Besides giving up your A. If you know more, you're ahead; if you share it, everybody catches up with you. If you know more in that class, it puts you in a superior position. The same thing is true of the teacher. A good teacher is one who isn't afraid to share things, who will ask questions even when he doesn't know the answer.

What you're saying is, "I'm ahead, because I know how to learn; I know what to put myself through." Not everybody has been trained in how to study and how to learn. One of the implications here is that it is one of the responsibilities of the teacher to teach students how to work. We haven't said that. Just as a case worker, for example, has to teach a client how to be a client.

In some classes, for example, you'd be stoned if you questioned the whole concept of democratic group leadership or how far can clients go, and so on. So you shut up about these things because the teacher is going to turn the students against you—

The interviewer noted that in such instances one had to pay too great a price for responding to the invitation to participate. The invitation to participate is not enough, but it's the support that goes with that invitation.

I think that's what we meant before when we said it didn't have to be painful. That's an unnecessary sort of pain; it's not even growing, really.

But can the risk be made close to zero, can you minimize the risk to the point where there is almost no risk involved?

There's always some risk in expressing your ideas, but if you feel that they're going to be listened to without any *personal* judgment of yourself, and, if the class is also going to be involved in it in a positive way—

Apparently a quality of learning took place in the following sequence:

I get the feeling here that you think you don't learn from a person who lectures. And this bothers me because I don't feel the same way. Maybe we're talking about different learning. I had nothing but lecture courses and I learned a great deal.

How do you know?

Well, from the fact that I came here knowing something, first of all—

Oh, that doesn't mean you learned it from them!

I can remember classes with two-three hundred people where I still felt involved in the learning process. For example: history. I learned it from the teacher.

How? How did you learn it from the teacher? Describe the process.

He described what happened in certain periods in Germany and how it affected political systems in Europe—

That's good. Let's take it one step at a time. You've established the fact that the teacher knew certain facts about the history of Germany. Through his saying those facts, you learned them.

How is that different from reading? Doesn't one learn from reading?

No, you're leaving out a step.

Why? Is there a difference between teaching and learning?

I see what you're getting at: learning takes place with something *you* bring to it.

Later, whether or not one can learn from hearing was asked.

I was thinking about a class where you sit there and are very seldom called on—maybe twice in a semester—most of it is hearing what the professor has to say. But the only way you're going to get anything out of it is if you have an investment in what went on, then you go out—

And conduct your own seminar.

But you've got to open yourself up. You can't just have an investment in the idea. . . . That's what I'm saying—I made an investment of thoughts of my own.

There are other classes where you can thrash it out in the cafeteria, but there are other times where the stuff is so far from you, so far removed, that you shut yourself off.

Experiences in different courses were recalled with reference to what the student brings to the course, and the concept of motivation was introduced.

Isn't it possible that this idea happened to hit you at a time when you needed it. Two things came together. If this idea had been thrown out at a different time it might not have been as exciting.

It's such a tragedy when a course boils down to that. It's like fertilizing a fish-egg, all that stuff floating around and one happens to it—

Good analysis!

If he just happens to say the word that sparks you—but God knows what it was!

That's where the relationships comes in, so it's less of an accident.

Finally, one participant added: "And it's not only between you and the teacher but between you and the class; the class is also important." Later, a participant asked another whether he had experienced good learning in large classes. This question led to the following exchange:

182

No. Not for the kind of experience that we have got to go through in order to become good social workers. A lot of it has to come from our own participation which you can't do in a large class.

I don't think that is so important.

I don't either. I had a large class, it was an excellent class, and I was sorry it was so large—

What was good about it?

The professor, he was interesting—

Interesting. Fascinating. Going back to your earlier definition of learning—you could connect up with where he was—

Yes.

If he knows what you do and how you feel, he can throw out stuff that some of the people will pick up.

He did a beautiful job.

He personalized even though it was a large class.

I just wanted to say that last year we had some of the same professors in small classes whom we had had in large classes and we got exactly the same thing. The class size was not the important variable.

But the method is much more difficult in a large class.

One participant offered the following summary:

You know what I think every teacher has to be taught to do—to sense not what the subject matter is but what he wants the students to learn about the subject matter. This is what happened in my . . . course. I had the feeling that the professor came in wanting us to know not social work administration, but knowing that there were certain things we would have to know out in the field. He formulated these things; he thought up these issues. And at the beginning of the class he gave us an outline of what he wanted to tell us. He pin-pointed everything and said, "I have some ideas on every one of these things. And I want to know what you think about them. And is there anything else you want to add. And what were you expecting from this course?" And each week we took these things—he assigned some really rough reading—and he was always able to integrate the theory.

The interviewer summarized this phase of the discussion by noting: "You're describing a process in which there's a very close engagement in which demands are being made back and forth, in which demands are not only between student and teacher but between student and student. There's a lot of demand in it; there's a lot of affect in it; there's a lot of work in it."

The discussion turned to learning for practice and a participant suggested that "you have to see your teacher as a good model," and the discussion turned to whether one had to be a good social worker to be a good teacher. In turn this led to the difference between skill for one-to-one relationship and classroom skill—fear of the classroom.

Is that how you learn practice, from watching your teacher?

183

The good teacher is the good human being.

Human being? No skills involved at all?

Haven't you ever had a teacher who was an awfully nice guy, but you didn't feel you had learned from this?

I would distinguish between the awfully nice guy and the person who's a real person. I don't think good teachers are necessarily good role models or vice versa. One of the people I would take as a role model actually happens to be a fairly poor classroom teacher.

You must explain that, because that's antithetical to what we've been saying here. A person who is a good role model for a worker but is a lousy teacher? What is it that he can do as a worker that provides him as a good role model and yet he's a lousy teacher?

He's a very real human being, and very honest, and very direct and forthright, spells out a good contact for you, and unfortunately in the classroom some of this gets lost.

Does the contact get lost?

The contact doesn't begin.

How can he be a good social worker if the contact doesn't begin?

I don't know why, but maybe in a one-to-one relationship he's not afraid. He can say, "I'm here to do this, you're here to do that, what do you think?" In the class, he writes on the board, because what are all these people going to do to him?

That's it. You've had to have contact with him outside the classroom to know he's a good role model.

Returning to the question of honesty in the teacher and responsibility of the student, one participant recalled an unholy situation:

Cynicism? Is that what you're getting at?

No, it wasn't cynicism. . . . He wasn't even reacting to the class; he was so caught up in this great thing he had done that he—

It was Madison Avenue slickness. It had nothing to do with the process of the class. I haven't heard a thing since that lecture, incidentally. That's when I turned it off. And if you look at the faces of the rest of the class you'll find the same thing.

But students have a responsibility in that case to the teacher—

(Everybody talking at once)

People react in two different ways. They turn themselves off, and some of them strike out.

Actually what happened: it was a kind of informal thing set up in the classroom. When the formal communication was cut off, a very interesting informal thing went on in the classroom. I think most of us sort of needled pomposity. There was a great deal of needling. The "body English" of that class would have told you a great deal—chairs turned, groupings pulled together, smoking was banned but you should have seen the cigarettes that were lit over and over again—so there was quite a bit of warfare going on in that classroom, don't you think so? And there were many, many flat edicts about . . . "you don't accept it now, but I'm telling you and this is the way it is and if you don't believe it you aren't ready to go out into the world" and that sort of thing.

One of the problems I think is the professor's inability to get the feedback of what's actually happening. It's just like in an agency, if the Head doesn't have good informal channels, formally he is going to hear what he wants to hear.

One participant gave an example of the skillful use of feedback by a fourth grade teacher whom he knew:

It suddenly occurred to her that nothing was happening in the class. So she very honestly said that she didn't know what was wrong and she asked the class. One of the kids took the risk and said "This class is terribly boring." She said she knew it was boring, because it was boring to her too, and she asked, "Maybe you have some ideas as to what to do about this." One kid started: "Maybe we could. . . . " Then— she told me—it became a fascinating class project, something the kids could be related to.

What was the skill?

She listened.

She was responsive; she recognized the tone.

She accepted it.

She trusted it.

She wasn't afraid of what might come out of it.

Later, the need of students for help in integrating for themselves the course and field experiences and the development of a perspective about their field of practice and the profession as a whole was considered.

I think on this issue another skill is demanded of the instructor—the ability to change, because there are a lot of pressures on change, particularly in the field. And you have caseworkers or group workers that don't want to listen to anything that's being said in the other disciplines. A number of instructors are using the same lecture that they gave ten or fifteen years ago, and there's so much that has happened in the field since. . . . The implication here is that the teacher should be helped, in a way, to represent within himself the integrative aspects of the profession. Not so much to obliterate all differences but at least to be able to tolerate and merge differences into a kind of theory that incorporates difference and that faces the differences frankly. That's a hard demand, but I can see where it would be important.

But it *can* be integrated. I had a class in Social Policy where it *was*. The fact that it could be integrated around social policy made it important. The professor never said, "caseworkers have nothing to do with planning or with policy." The roles were spelled out, and the similarities were spelled out and discussed by the whole class. And then it was related in terms of what *you* can do in social policy.

They also have to integrate the present with the future.

I want to test out something that you said that I think is a lot deeper. You're saying that in a social policy course, which is by caricature a content course as against a process course, one of the attributes that you want of the teacher is that he also knows the three processes as it were.

Yes, and what's interesting is that the professor is not a social worker, but an economist, and yet is very closely identified with the field. And maybe this is why she was able to say, "everything has something to offer." She didn't come in with this bias, "I'm a caseworker and now we'll find out how case work is related to social policy."

I don't want only someone who's terribly competent in his field. I want it to be related also to what I'm going to be doing. What we're doing is applying things. I don't want to have to do all the work by myself.

Just like we're asking that all the teachers have the same kind of method in teaching the different content, I wonder if even the three methods come down to the same method with different content.

Which is?

Which is dealing with a group of people or individuals.

So you want your field instructors to be intellectuals too, to have a conceptual grasp of their subject—

They have to.

The interviewer asked whether "These demands you're making on the teacher . . ." are realistic? "Are you asking for a paragon of virtue?"

A human being who's not afraid. I think it boils down to not being afraid. I really do.

The students will be better students because these teachers will be looking for things from the students too. They will demand more and the students will give more. They won't shut them off.

Instead of arguing about the different entities that social workers have invented, people can start talking about common problems.

More nearly match education with the world outside.

I wonder if the social work professor should also have to be a practitioner at the same time.

I'm assuming that the teacher has a nice knowledge of what he's teaching, but we're asking for something over and above that—

It's pretty hard to "community organize" a class—

Didn't you mean by 'practice' that he be concurrently in the field?

Yes.

We have to have a teacher who is a role model, so whatever he does has to go on in the class too, because social work and teaching are so related. And he should be practicing outside the school, not only teaching, because when you put yourself into an ivory tower you forget—

186

You're contradicting yourself. You said teaching is so close to social work and then you say there's an ivory tower in the classroom.

There's a difference, because you're dealing with problems on a different level. The content is different, although the method is the same. You have to help clients with something different than you do students—

The contact is different but the method is the same.

And to teach somebody how to teach a client, how to get into a housing project, after you've been in a classroom just telling, and not helping to get clients into a housing project, you sometimes forget some of the difficulties.

In teaching skills, they have to be *like* social workers.

No, I'm saying not exactly, but there *is* something different.

What is the difference? Now, we've talked about what is the same; let's talk about what is different.

We said the contact was different.

The interviewer closed the session with the following summary:

What interests me in this very difficult business that you're being trained in is that in the course of the engagement both sides are making demands on each other to do things that they can't do themselves. The teacher is in a sense saying to the student, "Do certain things," or "be certain things" that you wish he were, and vice versa: which I suppose is in the nature of the fact that this is a very difficult business. . . . I think the field has a long way to go to recognize how difficult are the challenge and the demand.